PENGUIN BOOKS
DOWNSIZE YOUR DEBT

An award-winning freelance writer, Andrew Feinberg is a regular contrib-
utor to *The New York Times*, *Money*, and *Worth*. Over the last fifteen years,
his articles on business and personal finance have appeared in *The Wall
Street Journal*, *Barron's*, *Playboy*, *GQ*, *The New York Times Magazine*, *Self*,
Working Woman, *Lear's*, and *SmartMoney*. He holds degrees from the University of Pennsylvania and Stanford University. He lives in New York City.

DOWNSIZE
YOUR DEBT

HOW TO TAKE CONTROL OF YOUR
PERSONAL FINANCES

$

ANDREW FEINBERG

PENGUIN BOOKS

PENGUIN BOOKS
Published by the Penguin Group
Penguin Books USA Inc., 375 Hudson Street, New York, New York 10014, U.S.A.
Penguin Books Ltd, 27 Wrights Lane, London W8 5TZ, England
Penguin Books Australia Ltd, Ringwood, Victoria, Australia
Penguin Books Canada Ltd, 10 Alcorn Avenue,
Toronto, Ontario, Canada M4V 3B2
Penguin Books (N.Z.) Ltd, 182–190 Wairau Road,
Auckland 10, New Zealand

Penguin Books Ltd, Registered Offices:
Harmondsworth, Middlesex, England

First published in Penguin Books 1993

1   3   5   7   9   10   8   6   4   2

PUBLISHER'S NOTE
This publication is designed to provide accurate and authoritative information in regard to
the subject matter covered. It is sold with the understanding that the publisher is not
engaged in rendering accounting, legal, or other professional services. If expert assistance
is required, the service of a competent professional person should be sought.

Portions of this book first appeared in somewhat different form in *New Woman*,
SmartMoney, *Working Mother*, and *Working Woman*.

LIBRARY OF CONGRESS CATALOGING IN PUBLICATION DATA
Feinberg, Andrew.
Downsize your debt: how to take control of your personal finances
/Andrew Feinberg.
p.   cm.
Includes index.
ISBN 0 14 01.3428 X
1. Finance, Personal—United States—Handbooks, manuals, etc.
2. Consumer credit—United States—Handbooks, manuals, etc.
3. Debt—United States—Handbooks, manuals, etc.   I. Title.
HG179.F39   1993
332.024'00973—dc20   92–31809

Printed in the United States of America
Set in Plantin
Designed by Ann Gold

TO CAROLINE
AND TO MY PARENTS

ACKNOWLEDGMENTS

The time has come to address *my* personal debts, which, appropriately enough, are considerable. I've incurred so many over the past three years that I'll never be able to repay all of them.

Throughout the country, hundreds of people surprised me with their graciousness and generosity—and with their willingness to spill the beans when it really mattered. Borrowers and lenders alike shared their stories, strategies, insights, experiences, and even their nightmares. If you find this book helpful and interesting, they deserve much of the credit.

Special thanks go to the experts who provided advice and feedback at crucial stages of the project: Norman Dawidowicz of Personal Capital Management, Marc Eisenson of The Banker's Secret and Good Advice Press, Paul Havemann of HSH Associates, Robert McKinley of RAM Research, Glenn Pape of the Ayco Corporation, Ross Richardson of Houston Asset Management, and the trio from Bankcard Holders of America: Elgie Holstein, Gerri Detweiler, and Mary Beth Butler.

I'm grateful to all the financial planners and authorities on taxes and the law, some of whom occasionally said, "What I'm about to tell you may be more than you or any human being wants to know about this subject." So thanks to: Alexandra Armstrong, George E. L. Barbee, Irwin Doben, Richard Friedman, Alan Goldfarb, Bradley King, Robert Klein, Lawrence Krause, Louis Lonetto, Kathy Muldoon, Bruce Ritter, Steven Sanders, Jerry Schneider, Peter Voisin, and Phyllis Wordhouse.

And thanks, too, to those who extend credit for a living: Brad

Champlin, Ted Colucci, Lynne Cornett, David Davitch, S. A. Ibrahim, Sidney Lenz, Bob Prinzi, Jeff Slawsky, Lowell Swanson, Gail Wasserman, and John Williams—and to many other merchants of debt who chose to remain anonymous but shared some of their secrets.

I'm grateful for the candor and good sense of the people who offer financial and psychological counsel to consumers with debt problems: Judy Barber, Luther Gatling, Jeanne Hogarth, Tom Hufford, Patricia Leonard, Richard Levin, Annette Lieberman, Karen McCall, Jerry Mason, Olivia Mellan, Paul Richard, Gary Stroth, Fred Waddell, and Flora Williams.

Thanks to Bill Hampel, Jerry Karbon, Larry Blanchard, and Paul Thompson of the Credit Union National Association; to David Robertson of the *Nilson Report*; to James Grant and Andrew Tobias; and to Lewis Mandell, whose fine history of the credit-card industry was so helpful.

And to Donald Auriemma, Robin Bell, Bruce Brittain, Robert Brooker, William Bryan, Monica Calhoun, Walter Cathie, Frank Claus, Susan Egan, Michael Edleson, Fritz Elmendorf, Stephen Gardner, David Ginsburg, Keith Gumbinger, John Hartman, Tahira Hira, Mariah Hunt, Jeff Johnson, Kathleen Keest, Peter Kochenburger, Peter Lessem, Gordon Levine, Bruce Liebman, Charles Luckett, Norman Magnuson, Ed Mierzwinski, Bob Miller, Peggy Miller, Dave Mooney, Susan Murdy, Patricia Neale, Jean Noonan, David Olson, Hugo Ottolenghi, Kurt Peters, Randy Petersen, Don Roberts, Ken Scott, Steve Sesit, Sandra Shaber, Allen Sinai, Jim Spencer, Dick Strauss, Greg Sullivan, Lou Valentino, David Watson, and R. T. Whitman.

I'm grateful to the magazine editors who helped shape, support, and encourage the project: Nancy Marx Better, Catherine Fredman, Deborah Harkins, Marci McNaghten, Lucy Schulte, and Deborah Wilburn.

And to friends and family, who for years put up with my extreme case of tunnel vision and occasionally obnoxious and invasive questions about their personal borrowing habits: Roberta Brackman, Jeff Burstein, Justin Clifford, Kim Constantine, David Elis, Paul Elis, Warren Elis, Doug and Meryl Freeman, Henry Mazel, Eileen Spinner, Cheryl and Fred Trenk, Robert Tucker, and my brother Ken and my sister-in-law Rikki.

I especially appreciate the cooperation of the many consumers who told me their credit stories: Kathie Anderson, Sharon and James Conti, Mary Davis, Marta Foth, Dave and Juliette Heim, Nanette and Phil Leonard, and Eran Rosenthal, as well as all those who shared their sometimes harrowing or embarrassing experiences without revealing their names.

Finally, thanks go to my agent, Mike Cohn, who had the original idea; to my patient editor at Viking Penguin, Lori Lipsky, whose keen suggestions and judgment made this a much better book; to her extremely helpful assistant, Nicole Guisto; and to Eva Resnikova and Theodora Rosenbaum for their copyediting.

Thank you, one and all. I'm forever in your debt.

Andrew Feinberg
New York City

CONTENTS

INTRODUCTION

$There's a secret about money. The easiest way to make it is to become smarter about your debt.

If you're a typical consumer, better borrowing could save you more than $100,000 in interest over the years—even if you don't change any of your spending habits. (Change just a few, and you can probably save much more.) Whether you're well-off, just barely getting by, or desperately in hock, the odds are there's a lot about savvy borrowing that you should know but don't.

Join the club. Americans are prodigious borrowers—personal debt now tops $3.5 trillion—but no one should confuse quantity with quality. Every year, we shell out hundreds of billions of dollars for interest payments, late fees, prepayment penalties, annual fees, origination fees, overdraft fees, cash-advance fees, credit counseling, closing costs, points, credit-repair clinics, biweekly mortgage contracts, private mortgage insurance, credit life insurance, credit disability insurance, credit unemployment insurance, dubious financial-planning advice, attorney's fees, mysterious and inexplicable processing charges, and reprocessing charges. Much of that money—tens of billions of dollars —is needlessly and utterly wasted.

That's *your* money.

It's time for us to learn how to borrow more intelligently and more confidently. Above all, it's time to reclaim some of that cash.

—

Mastering the ins and outs of borrowing, and the mechanics of debt planning, has never been more important—or more rewarding—than it is today. There are two primary reasons.

First, the federal government no longer subsidizes most of our borrowing mistakes. The deductibility of all consumer interest once papered over a lot of borrowing sins. But most deductions for consumer interest disappeared after 1990. Some economists predicted that consumer-borrowing behavior would, in turn, change dramatically to reflect the new realities of the tax code, but—what a shock—the economists were wrong. Most people haven't made any adjustments.

Yes, there has been an explosion in tax-deductible home-equity borrowing. While extremely significant, that trend is something of a red herring. Certainly, anyone who looks at the growth of home-equity loans and credit lines and concludes that Americans have suddenly become extraordinarily shrewd about debt is missing the bigger picture. (Millions of people who have home-equity loans aren't using them very shrewdly at all.) Even consumers who are well informed about some aspects of personal finance—equity investing, retirement planning, car insurance, or whatever—may know remarkably little about the best ways to borrow.

The second reason this is an ideal time for American consumers to get smarter about their debt is because they have so much debt to get smarter about. Consumer credit grew at a faster rate in the eighties than during any other period in American history. Credit-card debt more than quadrupled from 1980 to 1991, surpassing $230 billion.

From 1983 to 1991, the percentage of consumers' disposable income swallowed up by debt service jumped from 14.2 percent to 18.2 percent—an alarming rise. During the same period, the national household savings rate fell sharply—which is hardly a coincidence. Having too much debt imperils a family's ability to save for the future, and when the situation is left unremedied, it can constitute a kind of anti-retirement plan. For some people, too much debt will translate into a life of perpetual work. Perhaps two jobs today and maybe at least one job forever.

Many of us are headed for trouble. For most people, but not all, mastering the art of owing will mean owing less. At the very least, it means paying a lower interest rate on the amount you do owe.

—

These days, we all know people with good jobs who are—let's face it—insolvent. If they were stocks, you would short them. If they were S&Ls, they would be seized by federal regulators.

Exactly like S&Ls, however, people can get by for years without confronting financial reality. There's almost always another way to borrow money—until, finally, there isn't. The music stops.

Obviously, some people are still acting as if they were living in the late seventies or early eighties (when runaway inflation rewarded all borrowers because debts were eventually repaid with inflation-cheapened dollars) or the mid-to-late eighties (when debt was chic, a lack of leverage was considered pathetic, extraordinary price appreciation was assumed, and Donald Trump was considered smart).

Everything's different now.

"The whole world is in debt some way or another," said Rosalie, the title character of the 1990 movie *Rosalie Goes Shopping*, arguably the funniest film ever made about credit-card debt. The fact that Rosalie, a hyperactive consumer with thirty-seven credit cards, turned to crime to solve her financial problems is, for our purposes, slightly beside the point. What matters is that she correctly understood that owing money is an inevitable part of the human condition.

We're a nation of borrowers, and *Downsize Your Debt* is designed to help anyone who borrows any amount of money at any time. It will help you if you have thirty-seven credit cards (if so, please turn to chapter 8 *immediately*) or if you're struggling to acquire your first (in that case, see chapter 7). This book is intended to aid financial novices and sophisticates alike.

This book should be especially beneficial if you:

- aren't sure that you always get the best deal when you borrow
- find borrowing intimidating
- don't realize that the terms of almost every loan are negotiable
- owe any money on credit cards
- think your debts may be starting to get out of control (or know that they reached this state long ago)
- don't belong to a credit union
- have never seen your credit report
- don't know how to turn your credit report into a valuable tool that can save you thousands of dollars in borrowing costs

- are thinking of borrowing money from, or lending money to, a family member or friend
- don't know how to make hundreds of dollars a year by borrowing money with a credit card (honestly and legally, with absolutely no catch and no restrictions)
- own a home
- are considering a home-equity loan
- are thinking of getting an Elvis credit card, a National Wildlife Federation credit card, or a SPEBSQSA (Society for the Preservation and Encouragement of Barber Shop Quartet Singing in America) credit card

This book also includes detailed information about where to find the best loans, how to compare competing loan offers, how to determine a safe level of debt, which bills you can avoid paying temporarily, how to establish credit, how to re-establish credit, how to negotiate your best deal, how bankers think, whether bankers think, how credit-scoring systems work, and what debt scams are lurking out there waiting to snare you.

Downsize Your Debt will give you hundreds of specific ideas for saving money when you borrow. It also points out the most common—and most costly—mistakes borrowers make. I've made a few myself, and I'll share some of the humiliating details.

I'll also relate the stories of many other consumers who were kind enough to share their experiences with me. (Some of them, understandably, did not want their names divulged, so when you meet them in these pages you'll see an asterisk next to their fictitious names.)

Readers expecting a puritanical broadside about the virtues of thrift and the evils of indebtedness will come away disappointed, however. Debt is essentially a neutral thing. It can easily be used in both wonderful and horrible ways.

"Debt is a kind of household tool," says James Grant, editor of *Grant's Interest Rate Observer* and author of *Money of the Mind: Borrowing and Lending in America from the Civil War to Michael Milken.* "It's like a rope. You can use it for lifting or many other tasks. Or you can use it to hang yourself."

Unfortunately, the world is full of lenders who think their job is to build gallows for their customers. I can't eliminate all the people who will help you do harm to yourself. I *can* tell you how to spot them and how to take evasive action.

Some borrowers who think they're on top of things frequently focus on the wrong variables. For example, surveys reveal that credit-card holders are very aware of the annual fees they pay for their cards. Many people hate those annual fees and will pick one card over another to save five, ten, or twenty dollars.

But these people often don't know the interest rates charged by the cards they carry. Furthermore, they show little inclination to shop for bargain rates. This is not merely a statistical curiosity; it's a multibillion-dollar issue, because 71 percent of active credit-card holders carry balances from month to month (the average amount per household is $2,500). The upshot? The typical "smart" shopper in these surveys saves a few dollars on the annual fee and loses $120 to $200 a year, every year, by not seeking out a card with a lower interest rate. (Many consumers also allow their prejudices against "points" and adjustable-rate mortgages to cost them serious money when they borrow.)

One of my favorite cautionary borrowing tales was told to me by Andrew Tobias, the fine financial writer and software mogul. It concerns a man who was shopping for a $9,000 car but found that the dealer with the lowest price would offer only a 2-year loan on that vehicle. The buyer couldn't afford those payments.

So he continued shopping. Ultimately, he bought a $15,000 car, which he *really* couldn't afford, yet he was ecstatic because he received a 5-year loan, which meant that his monthly payments were about $90 less than if he had been "stuck" with the 2-year loan. (Over the full term of the loan, that $90-a-month bargain would cost him more than $9,600—an amount greater than the cash price of the first car.)

Now, this isn't some guy Alice met at the Mad Hatter's tea party. He's *real*. He's somebody's neighbor, somebody's friend, somebody's brother. And all he did was take two extraordinarily common borrowing mistakes to extremes. Like many other borrowers, he was more concerned with the monthly payment than the total cost of the loan, and too impatient to get the deal that approximated what he really wanted.

—

For the vast majority of Americans, taking control of debt is more important than learning how to invest. Besides, over time, reducing debt *becomes* an investment strategy. Saving $1,000 on a car loan is just the same as making $1,000 on a hot stock.

Actually, that's not true. The $1,000 you save is much *better*, because your "savings" are in after-tax dollars (unless you bought the car with a home-equity loan). The $1,000 stock profit may net you less than $600 after all taxes are paid.

What happens in real life, though, is that people often forget about dollars and cents when they're thinking about money. A person who'll take hours and hours to research and agonize over a fairly small equity investment might spend only a very short time trying to get the best deal on a loan involving a sum twenty times as large.

Why? First, because the act of investing captures the imagination. It has grandeur, romance, the stuff that dreams are made of.

It presents the possibility of making a lot of money for very little work (the real American dream, according to some). And a lot of money *could* change your life. Never mind that it probably won't happen; it *could*.

Making a killing has a lot more sex appeal than saving a bundle on a financial transaction. That's unfortunate, since both are perfectly marvelous activities, and it's far easier to achieve the latter than the former.

There's another basic reason humans don't borrow as well as they might. We tend to focus almost all our energy on what we're buying and what it costs. How we'll finance the purchase is often little more than an afterthought.

This is a pretty expensive way to do business.

Downsize Your Debt also addresses the big picture. No, this will not involve an interminable slog through macroeconomic theory. The big picture I'm referring to concerns the role debt should and shouldn't play in your life, how you should *think* about it, and the intense psychological impact it can have.

The big picture also includes your personal debt plan—some kind of blueprint for future borrowing. You have to take control of the borrowing process rather than letting debt just *happen* to you. This can occur only if you're willing to think about debt.

If you're a normal American, you're going to borrow hundreds of thousands of dollars over your lifetime, whether you think about it or not. Unlike, say, news from Sri Lanka, it's not a subject you can avoid even if you want to. By looking the problem straight in the eye, you'll have a much better chance of realizing your financial dreams.

If you use credit wisely and reduce your borrowing costs whenever possible—if you take charge of every borrowing transaction—I guarantee that you'll have a lot more money left over to spend on everything you value and enjoy.

PART I
MONEY-SAVING STRATEGIES

$

1

THE MOST COMMON BORROWING MISTAKES— AND THEIR TERRIFYING COST

$ Borrowing costs money—but it doesn't have to cost *that* much.

This short chapter is designed to give you an overview of the many ways you can slash your borrowing costs. All examples will be discussed in more detail later, but I want you to take a quick look at what a remarkably powerful tool smart borrowing can be.

After each error, I estimate the potential cost per year and approximate the devastating consequences such a mistake could have over a 40-year borrowing career.

Among the most common and costly borrowing mistakes are:

Not getting the best mortgage.
   Potential annual cost: $100 to $3,000-plus
   Potential lifetime cost: $4,000 to $120,000-plus

Not doing enough research when shopping for a loan, and therefore accepting a higher rate than you should.
   Potential annual cost: $50 to $1,000
   Potential lifetime cost: $2,000 to $40,000

Overpaying for plastic (carrying too many credit cards and paying too much in interest).
  Potential annual cost: $50 to $500
  Potential lifetime cost: $2,000 to $20,000

Carrying the American Express card (if you don't need it).
  Potential annual cost: $55
  Potential lifetime cost: $2,200

Buying credit insurance.
  Potential annual cost: $30 to $300
  Potential lifetime cost: $1,200 to $12,000

Failing to negotiate loan terms.
  Potential annual cost: $50 to $500
  Potential lifetime cost: $2,000 to $20,000

Not demanding that credit-card issuers reduce the annual fees they charge.
  Potential annual cost: $20 to $75
  Potential lifetime cost: $800 to $3,000

Ignoring cheaper sources of credit.
  Potential annual cost: $50 to $1,000
  Potential lifetime cost: $2,000 to $40,000

Concentrating only on the monthly payment.
  Potential annual cost: $300 to $1,000
  Potential lifetime cost: $12,000 to $40,000

Getting scammed.
  Potential annual cost: Thank goodness there's no "annual" cost
    here. But the per-scam cost could range from $99 to the loss of
    your home.

Not cleaning up your credit history.
  Potential annual cost: $50 to $1,000-plus
  Potential lifetime cost: $2,000 to $40,000-plus

Living with perma-debt (the condition of never getting out from behind the eight ball).
  Potential annual cost: $50 to $2,000
  Potential lifetime cost: $2,000 to $80,000

Ignoring the fine print.
   Potential annual cost: $10 to $300, plus the potential for catastrophe
   Potential lifetime cost: $400 to $12,000—much more if the catastrophe occurs

Using a home-equity line of credit unwisely.
   Potential annual cost: $50 to $500
   Potential lifetime cost: $2,000 to $20,000

Not knowing your borrowing rights.
   Potential lifetime cost: $100 to $5,000-plus

And that's just the short list. Obviously, you can deprive yourself of tens or hundreds of thousands of dollars with a lifetime of ineffective, underresearched borrowing.

If you follow the strategies in *Downsize Your Debt*, however, you'll save a small fortune—perhaps several small fortunes—by avoiding such credit traps.

If that prospect appeals to you, read on.

2

HOW WE THINK WHEN
WE THINK ABOUT DEBT, OR
WHY BAD LOANS
HAPPEN TO GOOD PEOPLE

$ Few of us always borrow as effectively as we should. One of the key reasons is that borrowed money somehow doesn't seem as real as cash.

Studies show that people who shop with credit cards spend more than those who pay cash. Anyone who has ever tried going without plastic for a week or more probably knows how strange and disorienting such abstinence can be. You find yourself stopping at ATMs a lot— that is, experiencing withdrawal symptoms.

Leaving home without plastic can give you a new, and not altogether pleasant, sense of clarity about your consuming habits. You're much more aware of what you're actually spending. Making a purchase is suddenly serious business. (Inevitably, you think: Was I really so casual about it before?)

Our payment methods and assorted cultural pressures encourage us to carry more debt than we should. Unsolicited credit offers arrive in the mail almost every week. Somewhat perversely, the higher a consumer's credit-card balances, the more unsolicited offers of new credit he or she receives. TV and radio commercials, magazine and newspaper ads, billboards, and classified ads encourage us to spend what we don't yet have.

EXPECTING TO LOSE

There's no longer much of a stigma attached to being overextended. Many people with respectable incomes have become accustomed to seeing their friends living on the edge—or going over it. Many wonder if *they're* next.

It seems that the majority of consumers don't expect to be winners in the debt game. They feel they are at the mercy of the system. They abandon control. Some feel so guilty or ashamed about being in debt that they tend not to look too closely at the type of debt they are carrying, its cost, and its terms.

Debt *is* a tool, but many people see it instead as a sinister or overwhelming outside force. Debt happens. Some people do themselves a disservice by assuming that everybody gets hurt by debt—that no one they know is handling it particularly well.

When he was interviewed by financial planner Lawrence Krause on a San Francisco TV show called "It$ Only Money," the artist Bill Stoneham described the borrowing life-style of the middle class, circa 1991: "You're semi-successful, you've got a steady income, it's okay for you to be overextended. It's perfectly acceptable. Everybody else you know is."

Such fatalism is common, and it's never good for your personal bottom line. This attitude is the best friend the credit-card industry has.

The main reason, researchers say, that consumers don't switch to cheaper credit cards is that they expect to be gouged when they borrow with plastic. Paradoxically, that's why they get so incensed over those annual fees. Being ripped off is one thing, but having to *pay* for the privilege? "That seems un-American, like being charged a membership fee so you can take advantage of those low, low prices at 7-Eleven," says Robert McKinley, president of RAM Research, a credit-card monitoring firm.

A DIFFERENT VIEW

One of the premises of this book is that such fatalism is both costly and unwarranted. In fact, even if a borrowing mistake has already been made, there's usually time to rectify it. Such errors are seldom irrevocable. One of the nice things about borrowing is that you almost always get a second chance. *There are always choices.*

But too often, borrowers are passive. They let inertia take over. Having obtained a bad loan or an overly expensive credit card, they rarely take advantage of opportunities to refinance. (You don't need to own a home to refinance; you just need to own a loan.) And, as I'll explain in many different contexts, refinancing can, on an hourly basis, be the most profitable legal act many humans are capable of performing.

If you already owe money, downsizing your debt can be a wonderfully profitable strategy. You can, in effect, *invest* in your debt.

This means you have the opportunity to earn an extremely high, risk-free return on your money by lowering your debt burden. You can earn—or, more precisely, save—24 percent, 21.6 percent, 19.8 percent, 18.9 percent, 15 percent, 13 percent, or 9 percent, guaranteed.

This is the essential logic underlying the various prepayment strategies discussed in chapter 16. If you owe Bloomingdale's $1,000 at 21.6 percent, you can save $21.60 over the next 12 months simply by adding an extra $100 to the minimum payment indicated on your next statement. Keep the money in a savings account, on the other hand, and you might make $4—before taxes. Buy a blouse or some power tools instead, and you won't save anything.

THE LONGER VIEW

There are many ways to feel better about borrowing. You can do it smarter. You can do it cheaper. You can do it for the right reasons. You can feel better about the debts you have—because you've purchased something of value with the money you've borrowed.

3

THE ART OF DEBT
PLANNING

$ Most of us live life on the install-
ment plan. (Do you know a lot
of people who buy their homes for cash?) But do we really know what
our particular plan costs?

Consider Jack, a 28-year-old, single marketing executive in New
York City who lives somewhat beyond his means and finances his
excesses with 19.8-percent credit cards. Jack is really paying almost a
20-percent premium per year for what he considers the good life.

But he doesn't see it that way. Jack is fixated on the monthly
payments—the minimum monthly payments. If he can meet those,
things will be okay. For another month, at least.

Jack doesn't realize that if he puts $2,000 worth of clothes on his
Visa card and makes only the minimum payments, he'll actually be
paying $4,254.01 for the duds, and he'll be paying them off for more
than 12 years.

Jack understands what 20 percent means—most of the time. He
just doesn't understand the problem with 20-percent debt.

Someone who pays 20 percent a year too much, year after year, for
basic consumer goods is ultimately going to have *less* of what he or she
wants, not *more*. Less for her children. Less for his retirement. Less
for traveling when there's finally enough time to travel extensively.

And there's an unfortunate ripple effect as well. The rich *do* get

9

richer, and people in debt *do* get poorer with every borrowing transaction. When you're perpetually out of cash, the cost of your funds is always higher than it would be if you were flush.

Let's take a moment to look at the potential added costs that Jack, a typical solvent but somewhat overextended borrower, might encounter.

- When Jack buys a car, he doesn't have money for a down payment, so he pays an interest rate that may be about 1 percent higher. He takes the longest term he can get—60 months—and that may cost .5 percent more than a 36-month loan, plus additional interest because he's paying off the loan for two extra years. The difference in finance charges between a 5-year, $15,000 loan at 10 percent and a 3-year, $13,500 loan at 8.5 percent is $2,280.53.

- When Jack buys a home, he can't afford a 20-percent down payment, so he has to pay for mortgage insurance (either FHA or private mortgage insurance). The cost: thousands of dollars on a $100,000 mortgage.

- Actually, it's possible that Jack may keep renting, because he can never afford to buy a home. Sometimes too much debt can lead to missed opportunities.

- Jack can't get the lowest-rate credit cards because his debts are too high. So he pays 2 percent, 3 percent, or 5 percent more in interest than necessary every month, which adds up to several hundred dollars a year.

- Jack frequently has to get cash advances—each time paying a fee of $5 to $20—to make ends meet.

- And what if Jack has any problems on his credit report? Then the rates he pays to borrow will be even higher.

It would be terrific if Jack could get ahead of the game for a change—or, at least, pull himself even—and I'll try to show him, and you, how. But even if you can't do that yet—and tens of millions of Americans can't—there are still more profitable ways of handling your debt. You can learn to look calmly at the future and assess your approximate borrowing needs for the next six months, the next year, perhaps the next five years. And then act accordingly.

PERMA-DEBT

Most people I know are used to carrying at least some nonmortgage, nonvehicle debt on a permanent or semipermanent basis. I call this perma-debt.

It seems to accumulate in good times and bad. My friends still have it after they've received a surprisingly large bonus; they most certainly have it after an emergency expense. Rain or shine, they're several thousand dollars—usually $5,000, $6,000, or more—in the hole.

Let's assume that the interest rate on this particular perma-debt is an after-tax equivalent of 13 percent. (Some people will pay 19.8 percent and not be able to deduct any of the interest; others will find a 7.75-percent home-equity line of credit and get to deduct all the interest.) That means the annual interest on $6,000 is $780. If you didn't have that debt, you'd automatically have an additional $780 a year. With that money, you could have $780 worth of fun (it would buy 260 games at my local bowling palace), or you could invest it at 8 percent and after 10 years you'd have $11,891.

If you were paying 19.8 percent on the $6,000, you could have $1,188 worth of fun per year (bowling and beer, too) or have $18,112 after 10 years, given the same assumptions.

Perma-debt is a truly insidious thing, and it's remarkable how many people have it. A 1990 survey by Phoenix-Hecht/Gallup Consumer Financial Services Monitor revealed that 48 percent of households with annual incomes of $75,000 to $100,000 carry Visa and MasterCard balances of $1,500 or more. In households with incomes over $100,000, the figure is 44 percent. This is not savvy money management. But it's understandable. In the last 10 years, credit-card issuers have actively *encouraged* perma-debt by reducing the average minimum monthly payment from about 5 percent of the outstanding balance to between 2 and 3 percent.

Nonetheless, there are many different ways you can fight perma-debt.

Seemingly trivial sums can help in the assault. Consider a recent behavioral change by Glenn Pape, a planner who heads the Money in Motion financial education program at the Ayco Corporation in Albany, New York.

Glenn's vice was diet soda.

Every workday, Glenn would buy four cans from a vending machine at 60 cents apiece. One day, after popping open his fourth soda, Glenn figured out how much this nickel-and-dime habit was costing him per year.

The answer was $576.

Then he took out his financial calculator and plugged in some assumptions. If the price of soda were to rise 5 percent a year and he could earn an 8-percent return on his $576 annual investment before taxes, what would he have after 30 years of abstaining from diet soda while at work? The total: $115,000.

Glenn almost spilled his soda. An impressive amount, obviously, but what would the money really be worth after 30 years of 5-percent inflation? What could you get—a few pieces of lawn furniture? The money would be worth a cool $25,000 in today's dollars.

Glenn began putting the savings into his Diet Soda Fund (DSF) the next day.

That $25,000 is just a number unless you're able to translate it into something you value. It could be a very nice new car, purchased for cash. For Glenn it was easy. "Four years at the University of Illinois, in my home state, now costs $25,000," he says. "My daughters may go there someday."

But what if, for you, a day without diet soda is just not worth living? Well, then, drink up. Think of cutting back on something else to build your DSF. List things you consume regularly. What gives you the least pleasure? It could be a snack, a beverage, dining out with your husband, cigarettes, newspapers, magazines, overpriced wines, a little-watched premium cable service. Chapter 20 contains many more ideas about relatively painless, yet ultimately powerful, changes you can make.

Life isn't always about trade-offs, but it is about priorities. Some people who don't want to give up anything—certainly not four cans of soda—find that they have to work overtime or moonlight to fund their needs. Then they get tired and cranky. They borrow too much and worry about their debts. They complain about not seeing their kids enough. (And, truth is, they don't.)

Actually, to build your own personal DSF you may not have to give up anything besides some overly expensive borrowing habits. Use the money this book saves you to start the fund. Call it the Debt Savings Fund. Whenever a strategy saves you money—and, I promise, many of them will—put a portion of the savings into the fund. Then put that money to work by using it to pay down your debt. Or put the money to play. Spend it on something you love. Spend it passionately. Have a diet-soda blowout.

WHAT SHOULD YOU BORROW FOR?

Ideally, debt should fund investment, not consumption. It is noble and theoretically correct to borrow for a house, an education, a business, or a car (especially if it takes you to work rather than to the mall).

It's fine to borrow to buy a second home; in fact, you can buy it by borrowing against your first home. One of the great things about building up equity is that you are able to borrow against it—cheaply.

What about borrowing to invest in other real estate, stocks, or mutual funds? Be careful. If you can generate a guaranteed higher after-tax return than your after-tax borrowing costs, wonderful. Most deals don't offer that.

Short-term, it's fine to borrow to fund an IRA or Keogh if you happen to be cash-poor as the deadline approaches. If you don't pay back the loan, however, this move will almost always be a loser.

It's smarter to purchase something lasting rather than ephemeral. A sofa beats a vacation, for example.

If you can't afford to pay for the vacation you want this year, then maybe you can't *take* the vacation you want. If you borrow to pay for it, and then borrow to pay for next year's expedition without having made a plan to pay off last year's adventure, you're setting yourself up for unpleasantness, if not outright disaster.

HOW MUCH SHOULD YOU BORROW?

Unless you're pretty affluent, no more than 20 percent of your take-home pay should go to debt service. For this calculation, debt payments do not include first mortgages or home-equity loans, but they include all other borrowed money: vehicle loans, credit-card debt, installment loans, personal loans, student loans, and so on. (Debt payments do not include rent, food, and utilities.)

Personally, I think it's often a mistake to *exclude* home-equity debt just because many alleged experts say you can. Be very careful here. If the home-equity debt is being used for investment (and home improvement and your own education should be counted as investments, just as surely as stocks or real estate), you can justify excluding the payments. But if you've tapped your equity to consolidate debts, to buy a car or boat, or even to pay medical expenses, include the monthly payments in your calculation.

To find your ratio, add up all your monthly payments and then divide the total by your monthly net income. If it's over 20 percent, you may be asking for trouble. Many of you will have ratios well over 20 percent. This is normal—potentially dangerous, but very normal. It may take some time before you're under 20 percent, but you can get there.

And if you're there already?

Don't be overjoyed just because the figure is lower. A family spending 17 percent to 19 percent on debt service may not find its solvency in jeopardy, but its ability to save and invest may certainly be diminished.

WHAT YOU CAN HANDLE

• The type of person who is most able to tolerate a 20-percent level of debt is single, middle-aged (hence unlikely to incur huge new debts), and makes a healthy living.

• If you and your spouse both work and you net $50,000 a year after taxes, 20 percent might be doable—but not if you have a child. With kids, knock the ratio down to 15 percent.

• If you're retired and living on a fixed income, your ratio should probably stay under 10 percent.

• If you earn less than $20,000, it's going to be tough for you to cover anything more than student-loan payments.

HOW SHOULD YOU BORROW?

With forethought.

• Don't have a credit-card mentality, which you can possess even if you don't use a credit card. With the credit-card mind-set, borrowing is usually casual and unplanned. It's totally ad hoc. You just reach for the nearest loan—plastic, overdraft checking, and so on. Generally, this is the worst financing you can choose.

It doesn't take a lot of work to change this habit. It does take some knowledge—you have to know what's available, how to get it, and what the likely cost will be. Sometimes it will pay to have the financing in place and ready to go before you need it. Chapters 13 and 15 explain when this is appropriate and how to do it.

• Always consider the total cost of the loan rather than the monthly payments. The great fallacy of living month to month is that you can scrape by for decades and end up with next to nothing. Getting the short end of the stick for 40 years adds up—or, more accurately, it subtracts. It takes away from your life.

You can pay $15,000, $16,426, $17,203, $18,003, or $18,902 for the same car, for example, depending on whether you pay cash or finance for two, three, four, or five years.

You can pay a total of $187,920 and $316,080 for the same house (15-year versus 30-year financing).

You can pay $50 or $106.35 for the same shirt (cash versus credit-card minimum-payment plan).

Some people don't realize that compound interest works *against* them when they owe money—they're paying interest on the interest. That's why extended-payment cycles and permanent debt are so expensive, and why prepayment strategies (see chapter 16) yield such wonderful returns.

DEBT-PLANNING TECHNIQUES

DEBT SHIFTING One of the best ways to be a better debtor is to avoid complacency about credit-card debt. If you owe money on credit cards, or anticipate that you soon will, look for a cheaper source of funds. It's practically inevitable that you'll be able to find one—and this book is filled with ideas about where to look.

The source might be home equity (either a credit line, a loan, or refinancing), a retirement plan, a life-insurance policy, a margin account, a credit union, a bank, or a much cheaper credit card. The source might even be a car loan.

A car loan? Sometimes a loan that might be undesirable in another context becomes a great idea because it fits into your overall debt strategy. Remember that 5-year no-down-payment car loan I was knocking? You could use part of the car loan to buy furniture and save hundreds of dollars in the process.

Here's how. If you don't have access to home-equity money or have a very cheap credit card, new-car loan debt is one of the best credit deals around. Instead of charging $3,500 worth of furniture on a credit card or financing it through Levitz at 21.6 percent, borrow more money for the car than you ordinarily would. If you can swing it, don't make a down payment. Then use the money earmarked for the down payment to fund the furniture purchase instead. The car financing might cost you 10 percent—less than half the cost of credit at the furniture store. (The strategy also works if you're buying a used car, even though the financing is somewhat more expensive.)

And, yes, pick a longer term for the car—maybe even the longest term possible—and use the monthly savings to pay down any remaining furniture debt. (If you don't apply the savings to the furniture, however, then you lose both ways.)

DEBT SHIFTING WITH STUDENT LOANS Many people carrying student loans have a unique opportunity to reduce their overall borrowing costs. Former students or parents with at least $7,500 in PLUS loans can consolidate debts with a SMART Loan from Sallie Mae (800 524-9100; Sallie Mae, SMART Loan Origination Center, P. O. Box 1304, Merrifield, VA 22116), a CONNECT loan from Nellie Mae (800 338-5626; Nellie Mae, Loan Consolidation Department, 50 Braintree Hill Park, Braintree, MA 02184-8756), or a similar deal from other lenders. (If your lender won't consolidate, apply to Sallie Mae or Nellie Mae.)

You shouldn't do this just because you *can*. Stretching out repayment terms is almost always a bad idea unless it's done strategically or under duress. Lengthening the payback period increases the total finance charges and encourages perma-debt.

But consolidation is smart in three specific situations: when making ends meet is a constant struggle, when you're already paying a much higher interest rate on credit cards or any other type of debt, or when you're anticipating borrowing money at a higher interest rate.

Refinancing student loans can reduce monthly payments by as much as 40 percent. You're eligible if you want to consolidate more than $7,500 in Stafford Loans (previously called Guaranteed Student

Loans), Perkins Loans (formerly National Direct Student Loans), Health Professions Student Loans (HPSL) and Supplemental Loans to Students (SLS—once known as Auxiliary Loans to Assist Students or Student PLUS), and Federally Insured Student Loans (FISL). To apply, you must be in your grace period or already in repayment.

Stafford, Perkins, and HPSL loans can be consolidated at a 9-percent rate. Add SLS and FISL to the mix and the rate will be the weighted average of all your loans (with a minimum of 9 percent and a maximum, under the SMART Loan program, of 12 percent).

Notice anything wrong? With these plans, you can repay a Perkins Loan, which carries a 3-percent, 4-percent, or 5-percent interest rate, at a new rate of at least 9 percent. Try to avoid this dubious maneuver. Perkins financing is just about the cheapest money anyone can find without a gun. It's not smart to swap it for anything.

The rest of the deal is more reasonable, especially for Stafford Loans. Since the rate for most Stafford loans starts at 8 percent and jumps to 10 percent after four years of repayment, switching to a 9-percent rate can actually save you a little bit of interest, if you don't extend the repayment period. (The new variable rate, though, is 6.94 percent, with a cap of 9 percent.)

Of course, most people *do* stretch out repayment. Instead of paying what you owe in 5 to 10 years, you can extend payments over 10 to 30 years. Sallie Mae's "Max-2" option requires interest-only payments for the first two years of the loan, followed by fixed payments for the rest of the term. With "Max-4," it's interest-only for the first four years, then gradually increasing payments for the remainder. (Nellie Mae offers interest-only plans for one to four years.)

What's the potential cost of consolidating? A 10-year, $15,000 Stafford Loan (the 8-percent/10-percent variety) would cost an average of $187.67 a month: total repayment, including interest, $22,520.64. Consolidate for 15 years with two years of interest-only payments and the monthly bill drops to $112 for the first two years and $163 thereafter. The additional interest cost: $5,677.36. Make interest-only payments for four years and the total tab rises another $1,367 to $7.044.36.

Think of student-loan consolidation as a cheap line of credit if you need it—and a bad idea if you don't.

THE SAVINGS PLOY Another way—admittedly a controversial one—to cut borrowing costs is to tap some of your savings or your emergency fund to get rid of costly perma-debt. A cash cushion equal to three to six months of living expenses is a terrific thing—financial planners swear by it, and some people can't get to sleep at night or enjoy life without it—but this is a very expensive form of security for anyone who is carrying high-interest debt.

Earning 4 percent on savings while paying 18 percent on debt is a good way to diminish your long-term ability to save. Applying that unfortunate interest-rate spread to $6,000 in savings and $6,000 in nondeductible debt would result in an annual loss of $907 after taxes, year after year. That's not my idea of a savings plan; it's my idea of a very bad debt plan. (The pros and cons of using savings or emergency funds to pay down debt are discussed in more detail in chapter 20.)

THE PERPETUAL 30 When you refinance a mortgage, don't automatically replace a loan that has 27, 25, 24, or 20 years remaining on its term with another 30-year mortgage. Consider a 15-year or 20-year mortgage instead, so you can someday own a home free and clear.

THE HOME-EQUITY DELUSION If you're smart enough to have a home-equity line of credit, don't undermine your intelligent move by being lackadaisical about repaying what you borrowed. Make a plan. These days, sloppy home-equity borrowing is the savvy consumer's preferred, and socially acceptable, form of perma-debt. There's a better way, as discussed in chapter 15.

CONCLUSION

Don't just let debt happen to you. Look at its true cost—and at all the financial alternatives—every time you borrow.

A SHORT HISTORY OF DEBT PLANNING

One of the great trends in twentieth-century America, says credit historian James Grant, has been the democratization of credit. In 1900, it was very hard for a regular working person to get any kind of conventional loan. Consumers were simply not in the credit mainstream. The first personal-loan department at a commercial bank was not established until 1924.

Citibank (then called National City Bank) didn't discover consumer lending until 1928—and even then it entered the business only because the New York State attorney general begged banks to lend to small borrowers, to provide them with an alternative to pawnshops and loan sharks.

As consumer credit exploded, notes Grant, two clear borrowing trends emerged: ever smaller down payments and consistently longer repayment terms. In the twenties, the normal term for a home mortgage from an insurance company was 6 years. If you bought a car, you paid it off in a year.

In 1939, the federal government allowed mortgage maturities of 25 years. By 1957, 44 percent of new-car loans had maturities greater than two and a half years. Just eight years later, that figure was 86 percent.

Both trends showed no signs of slowing until the late eighties, when the rubber band snapped for a lot of borrowers. New-car loan maturities have declined slightly since 1988.

4

DO IT RIGHT THE
FIRST TIME

$As the title *Downsize Your Debt* suggests, much of this book is about reducing and refinancing debt you already have. But new debt is crucial as well. If you handle each new debt wisely, you may never have to resort to refinancing at all (though you may want to, if interest rates fall sharply).

Techniques exist to get the best deal the first time around, no matter what type of loan you seek. Although I won't be spending much time covering first mortgages and automobile financing—good books exist on both subjects—this chapter may be particularly helpful to people shopping for a mortgage or a vehicle.

NEGOTIATING

In the borrowing world, negotiating will almost always get you a cheaper loan. But the overwhelming majority of consumers never try to negotiate. They assume it's not possible.

"Yes, we can negotiate," says Sidney Lenz, executive vice-president at Countrywide Funding, the nation's largest independent mortgage banker, "but not many people who do business with us try. The interest rate isn't negotiable, but we can certainly give someone a quarter-point break on the points. And sometimes we can lower the attorney's fees."

On a $100,000 mortgage, a quarter of a point equals $250. Add in another $50 or $150 or $250 for the break on the lawyer, and you're talking about an interesting amount of money—definitely enough to make raising the question worth your while.

And Countrywide's tough. Many lenders *are* willing to negotiate interest rates, especially if you make it clear that they won't be getting your business otherwise. Knock down the rate on a $15,000 4-year car loan from 9.5 percent to 9 percent and you save $171.43 over the life of the loan. Shave one-quarter of a percentage point off the rate on a $100,000, 30-year mortgage (from 8.25 percent to 8 percent) and you save $6,303.60. These days, with the rise of risk-based pricing formulas, consumers with excellent credit have more negotiating leverage than ever before.

So what's really negotiable? "With mortgages, almost every variety of closing cost is probably negotiable," says Paul Havemann of HSH Associates, "but most people either don't know that or don't make the effort."

You can't negotiate in a vacuum, however.

• Shop carefully, so you know what you should be negotiating for. To get someone to match or beat the best deal around, you have to have a pretty good idea what that best deal is. Make a lot of calls and perhaps a few in-person visits (although you can certainly save money even from afar).

• You can bluff about your intentions—maybe you'll walk away from the deal, and maybe you won't—but you can't count on bluffing lenders about the competition. Lenders usually have a pretty good feel for the market.

• Recognize the three types of negotiating leverage you have.

—If you're already a customer, a lender will try very hard not to let you find out that the money may be greener on the other side of town.

—If you're likely to bring a lot of future business to a lender, you can drive a harder bargain.

—If you can convince a lender that you're the kind of tough, principled, rigid (but not *necessarily* obnoxious) customer who is willing to drive a half hour to save another fifty bucks, you're more likely to cut the best deal.

ESPECIALLY NEGOTIABLE POINTS

The lender's attorney's fees. Starting to disappear, thank goodness. Tell the lending institution you'd prefer not to pay for its lawyer. Mention that it's a conflict of interest. Talk about another lender who doesn't charge for the service. (Neglect to mention that *that* lender's rate is one and a half percentage points higher.)

Document-preparation fees. "We charge $125 but will go down to zero when we know we're really competing for the business," says David Davitch, executive vice president at American Financial Mortgage Corporation, a mortgage banking firm in King of Prussia, Pennsylvania.

Points. Sometimes lenders like Davitch will give you a choice— either one-quarter off on the points or one-eighth of a percentage point chopped off the rate—but many other lenders who seem horrified at the idea of playing games with the stated interest rate will perform all kinds of tricks with the points, if they think they have to.

The rate. Always make it clear to lenders that they're in a very tough fight for your business. Mention competitors by name. Let the lender know what terms he'll have to beat to win.

What do you do when a lender offers to match your best deal but not beat it? Indicate on the phone or in person that this is a pretty boring offer at this point. Heck, you already had *that* deal in the bag before you had this conversation. Request that a bone be thrown in your direction. You've come this far, and now he's going to let you walk for a few dollars? You can't predict what the lender will do in this situation; there are certain concessions he can't make. But you can sure try.

(Note: The terms you're least likely to get a break on include the application and credit-check fees.)

Before actually taking your business elsewhere, tell your current institutional financial partner precisely what terms you're about to accept. If your institution cares a lot about keeping you, you may be offered a very special deal. Even if its offer is a bit more expensive, the convenience factor may make you stay put.

HAVE LATE FEES WAIVED

Smart borrowers can often avoid late fees as well. A good customer who is late with a payment for any reason (neglect, emergencies, temporary cash-flow calamity) should call the lender and ask to have the late fee waived. This will often work—but only once or twice on each debt. Just don't count on it. Try not to make it chronic.

The approach can save $10 here, $15 there. Not a lot, but certainly a reasonable return on an investment of a few minutes. And it's more money for your DSF.

If you know ahead of time that you'll be a few weeks late, consider alerting the lender before the due date.

LEVERAGING YOUR CREDIT REPORT

Both negotiating and shopping are a lot easier if you have a blemish-free credit report. Increasingly, good credit risks are able to command better and better terms. Some credit-card issuers, such as Optima, have slashed rates for customers with perfect payment records while simultaneously raising rates for less dependable cardholders.

Many lenders divide borrowers into four groups—A,B,C, and D—based on creditworthiness. While a C may be a passing grade, in the world of credit it's often a very expensive one. Roughly speaking, here are the guidelines for each group according to lender consultant David Olson of Columbia, Maryland:

GROUP A. No late payments, and usually a back debt-to-income ratio no higher than 36 percent. A ratio of 36 percent to 40 percent might merit an A−. ("Back debt-to-income ratio" refers to the percentage of a person's income consumed by mortgage payments [or rent], property taxes, property insurance, car loans, credit-card payments, student loans, installment loans, and child support.)

GROUP B. Perhaps a few 30-day late payments. Debt ratio could approach 44 percent.

GROUP C. Several 60-day late payments, or perhaps at least one 90-day delinquency. Debt ratio could reach 50 percent.

GROUP D. Real bad news. Credit file contains at least one default, repossession, bankruptcy, or judgment, and probably many other late payments as well.

With tiered rates becoming more common among lenders, you can realize enormous savings by improving your credit rating. Ford Motor Credit, for instance, ranks customers on a five-tier scale. Level-0 borrowers will pay about five and a half percentage points less than those who occupy Level 4. On a 4-year, $15,000 loan, the difference between a 9 percent rate and a 14.5 percent rate is $1,938.90.

MORTGAGE-SHOPPING STRATEGIES

Don't trust a realtor to guide you to the best rates in town. She or he is not necessarily your ally.

Seek out newspapers, such as *The Washington Post*, that publish complete rate lists. Consider buying current and complete information from any of the following:

• HSH Associates of Butler, New Jersey (800 873-2837), has rate lists for 36 metropolitan areas, either in hard copy or on disk, for $20.

• Gary S. Meyers & Associates of Chicago (800 472-6463) covers Boston, Chicago, Cincinnati, Denver, Detroit, Fort Lauderdale, Houston, Kansas City, Los Angeles, Milwaukee, New York, Norwich (Connecticut), St. Louis, and Washington, D.C., for $22.

• *National Mortgage Weekly* (216 273-6605; 800 669-0133 in Ohio and Michigan) surveys Cleveland, Columbus, and Detroit for $4 an issue.

SHOP FOR THE RIGHT MORTGAGE Too many people take 30-year mortgages, as opposed to 15-year or 20-year deals. A $100,000 mortgage at 8 percent for 15 years has a monthly payment of $955.65. For 30 years, it's $733.76. But if you took the 15 instead of the 30, you'd save $92,138 in interest, before taxes. And you'd own your home outright in half the time.

Actually, the savings will be $5,155 greater, because interest rates on a 15 are, on average, 50 basis points (or .5 percent) lower than they are for a 30. So by paying 30 percent more per month, you'd eliminate 59 percent of the total interest charges. And the higher the prevailing interest rate, the more dramatic the savings. If rates are 10 percent, you can cut the mortgage term in half by paying 22.4 percent more per month. When rates are 12 percent, you can accomplish the same goal by paying 16.7 percent more per month.

Selecting a shorter-term mortgage is one of the best ways of taking a huge bite out of your long-term debt load.

If you aren't sure you can afford a 15-year mortgage, don't get one. Get a 30 and try prepaying it as if it were a 15 (see chapter 16). If that's too tough, prepay a smaller amount. Maybe what you'll create is a 21.67-year mortgage—which may be perfect for you.

If you're getting an adjustable-rate mortgage (ARM) because you can't afford the house any other way, then you probably can't afford the house at all. Forget mortgage shopping; go back to house shopping.

Many people have such an intense philosophical aversion to ARMs that they cost themselves a lot of money. If you'll definitely be moving within a few years, getting an ARM may be the cheapest borrowing move you can make—no matter what happens to interest rates.

POINTS, GLORIOUS POINTS Points can be beautiful, but, oh, how people hate them! "People automatically get upset at anything over two points," says Countrywide Funding's Sidney Lenz.

"Automatically" is the operative word here. Borrowers' loathing of points is visceral; it's certainly not always based on rational financial analysis. It's also understandable. Points are a very visible additional out-of-pocket expense. They have the look of something extra, a perk for the lender. Nor does a definition of points, which usually represent prepaid interest on the loan, have the soothing quality one might wish. When you're about to drop a couple hundred grand in interest, you don't feel a burning need to prepay any of it.

But the loathing is often misplaced—pointless, if you will. Points can be your friend. They have at least three things to recommend them.

• If you pay for them separately up front, they're completely deductible in the year of the closing. (For a second home, the deduction must be spread out over the life of the mortgage.) Yes, you're paying more cash, but you're getting your tax break in one big chunk—and soon. (In fact, it can make sense to get a cash advance on your credit card to be able to pay the points up front—if you can pay off the credit-card debt in a few months.)

• If you're going to stay in a home for a long time, you'll save money by taking the loan with the most points and lowest interest rate (the points let you "buy down" the rate).

• Points aren't nearly as mysterious or unfathomable as many people think. You can calculate precisely when you'll break even—how long you'd have to stay to make the lower rate with more points save you money over the higher rate with fewer points.

The stated APR (the annual percentage rate—the effective rate consumers pay), however, doesn't do this, because it assumes, as the APR always does, that you won't prepay the loan. That is, it assumes you will remain in the home for the full term of the mortgage. Since you probably won't, the APR is underestimating the impact of the points. (It may surprise you to learn that today's average mortgage has a life expectancy of only seven years.)

If you are going to own the home for the full 15- or 30-year term, consult the Points Discount Table on page 27.

Otherwise, there's a quick-and-dirty method for converting points into an APR for a mortgage of shorter duration—(see Calculating Effective Interest Rate on page 28. There's a formula that's even quicker, albeit much dirtier: a point equals approximately one-eighth of a percentage point on a 30-year loan and one-quarter of a percentage point on a considerably shorter loan.

PRIVATE MORTGAGE INSURANCE

One of the best arguments for making a 20-percent down payment on a home if it is at all possible is that you get to avoid private mortgage insurance (PMI) or FHA mortgage insurance. PMI, like other credit insurance products, protects the lender (or the institutional investor that has purchased your mortgage from the lender) rather than the borrower. Instead of purchasing peace of mind for you, this insurance merely burns a hole in your wallet.

How big a hole? PMI typically adds the equivalent of at least .3 percent to .66 percent to the interest rate on a 30-year fixed-rate mortgage. That could be $250 to $560 a year on a $100,000 mortgage—or

POINTS DISCOUNT TABLE
Question: "Which is better:
9.75% with 1 point, or 9.5% with 3 points?"

By reading down the interest rate column, and then across the points column under the proper loan term, you can determine which combination of interest rate and points may cost less over the *entire term of the loan*. This value—called the *effective interest rate*—is *not* the same as the APR, because it does not include other loan costs.

Interest Rate %	15-YEAR TERM number of points: 1	2	3	4	30-YEAR TERM number of points: 1	2	3	4
6.00	6.16	6.32	6.48	6.64	6.09	6.19	6.29	6.39
6.25	6.41	6.57	6.73	6.90	6.35	6.44	6.54	6.64
6.50	6.66	6.82	6.99	7.15	6.60	6.70	6.80	6.90
6.75	6.91	7.07	7.24	7.41	6.85	6.95	7.05	7.15
7.00	7.16	7.33	7.49	7.66	7.10	7.20	7.30	7.41
7.25	7.41	7.58	7.75	7.92	7.35	7.45	7.56	7.67
7.50	7.66	7.83	8.00	8.17	7.60	7.71	7.81	7.92
7.75	7.92	8.08	8.25	8.43	7.85	7.96	8.07	8.18
8.00	8.17	8.34	8.51	8.68	8.11	8.21	8.32	8.44
8.25	8.42	8.59	8.76	8.94	8.36	8.47	8.58	8.69
8.50	8.67	8.84	9.02	9.19	8.61	8.72	8.83	8.95
8.75	8.92	9.09	9.27	9.45	8.86	8.97	9.09	9.21
9.00	9.17	9.35	9.52	9.70	9.11	9.23	9.34	9.46
9.25	9.42	9.60	9.78	9.96	9.36	9.48	9.60	9.72
9.50	9.67	9.85	10.03	10.21	9.62	9.73	9.85	9.98
9.75	9.93	10.10	10.29	10.47	9.87	9.99	10.11	10.23
10.00	10.18	10.36	10.54	10.72	10.12	10.24	10.37	10.49
10.25	10.43	10.61	10.79	10.98	10.37	10.50	10.62	10.75
10.50	10.68	10.86	11.05	11.24	10.62	10.75	10.88	11.01
10.75	10.93	11.11	11.30	11.49	10.88	11.00	11.13	11.26
11.00	11.18	11.37	11.56	11.75	11.13	11.26	11.39	11.52
11.25	11.43	11.62	11.81	12.00	11.38	11.51	11.64	11.78
11.50	11.69	11.87	12.06	12.26	11.63	11.76	11.90	12.04
11.75	11.94	12.13	12.32	12.51	11.88	12.02	12.16	12.30
12.00	12.19	12.38	12.57	12.77	12.13	12.27	12.41	12.55
12.25	12.44	12.63	12.83	13.03	12.39	12.53	12.67	12.81
12.50	12.69	12.88	13.08	13.28	12.64	12.78	12.92	13.07
12.75	12.94	13.14	13.34	13.54	12.89	13.03	13.18	13.33

(Source: HSH Associates, Butler, New Jersey)

CALCULATING EFFECTIVE INTEREST RATE

While the worksheet below won't calculate your Annual Percentage Rate (which takes closing costs into account), it will give you an easy way to compare how Rate + Points help determine your Effective Mortgage Interest Rate.

	Sample Mortgage	Your Mortgage
A) Interest Rate	10%	_____ %
B) Number of years you will own the home	4	_____
C) Multiply line A by line B	40%	_____ %
D) Mortgage Points (Discount + Origination)	3	_____
E) Add lines C and D	43%	_____ %
F) Divide line E by line B to determine Effective Annual Interest Rate	10.75%	_____ %

(Source: HSH Associates, Butler, New Jersey)

$2,500 to $5,600 if the insurance were to stay in force for ten years.

Rather than paying the money annually, you can elect to make a single premium (lump-sum) payment at the closing in either of two ways. On a $100,000 mortgage with 10 percent down, you could pay about $2,950 up front (with the possibility of getting some money refunded if you sell your home before the mortgage term is up) or pay $2,200 with no refund possibility. (Either way, the single-premium payment can be financed as part of the mortgage loan.) With a 5-percent down payment, the single premium might be about $4,300 —and it cannot be financed.

If you make annual payments, you will usually keep paying for the insurance for the entire life of the mortgage, *unless* you take steps to get rid of it. The lender or investor won't ever remove the insurance voluntarily. Only in California will the lender even tell you at the closing that you may have the right to have the coverage terminated—and only because it's the law in that state.

So make it your business to know when your loan-to-value ratio (LTV) falls to 80 percent, at which point your equity will have hit 20 percent. It can do so through regular mortgage payments, prepayment, or appreciation of the property. If you try to have the PMI removed on the basis of property appreciation, you'll have to pay for the appraisal (usually $250 to $300).

In a soft housing market, a lender or investor might require that PMI remain in place until the LTV falls to 75 percent. (The lender or investor may also balk if you've been late with a mortgage payment in the last year.) In any market, no one will be eager for you to drop the PMI. There's nothing in it for the owner of the loan. While the lender or investor isn't required to drop it at all, it usually will. Threatening to take your business elsewhere or to complain to higher authorities might be helpful.

(Note: Mortgage life insurance is an utterly different product. Almost inevitably, it's a bad deal. The insurance pays off the mortgage if you die, which is nice for both the lender and your heirs. You can save money, though, by buying straight term life insurance not linked to the mortgage.)

AUTOMOBILE LOANS

Many people squander large sums of money every time they buy, and especially every time they *finance*, a vehicle. Here are some tips to minimize your financing costs.

• Don't ever tell a car dealer how much you can afford to pay per month. This is inviting him to take you for a ride. Equipped with that knowledge, a dealer may talk you into a longer loan at a higher interest rate on a car with unwanted options—not to mention unnecessary insurance and overpriced warranties. Remarkably, though, the cost of all this will be almost exactly what you can afford to pay each month.

• Credit unions typically offer the best rates on auto loans, averaging 1.3 percentage points less than deals from commercial banks and 1.6 percentage points less than those from S&Ls. (The Baxter Credit Union in Deerfield, Illinois, charges only 6.25 percent for a 24-month new car loan.) Credit unions are also most likely to offer no-down-payment financing. Dealers can sometimes match bank rates but will seldom beat them. The better your credit, the less likely it is you'll find your best rate at a dealer.

• Don't take out a 5-year car loan and then trade in the car for a new one in three years. Either take a 3-year loan or lease. (The 5-year-loan/3-year-trade-in strategy amounts to de facto leasing—and it's very expensive.)

• If you do lease, beware of a predictable consumer quirk: people haggle more when they buy rather than lease. This makes a little sense—they usually have more at stake, after all—but not much. Hang tough.

• Shortening the loan term is more important than lowering the interest rate. Besides, it often has the benefit of reducing the interest rate as well. To illustrate how dramatically finance charges increase over time, let's see what happens to total interest charges when we finance $18,293:

For 2 years at 8 percent: $1,563 in finance charges

For 3 years at 8.5 percent: $2,496 in finance charges

For 4 years at 9 percent: $3,558 in finance charges

For 5 years at 9.5 percent: $4,758 in finance charges

The rising rates make the situation worse. Still, the bulk of the damage is caused by the longer term. To prove that, here's what would happen if we assume the rate on all four loans to be 9 percent.

For 2 years at 9 percent: $1,764 in finance charges

For 3 years at 9 percent: $2,649 in finance charges

For 4 years at 9 percent: $3,558 in finance charges

For 5 years at 9 percent: $4,491 in finance charges

• When dealers offer you a choice between a below-market interest rate and a cash rebate, how do you decide? It's not hard if you use a chart created by William Bryan, director of the Bureau of Economic and Business Research at the University of Illinois at Urbana-Champaign (see page 31).

At the risk of ruining the suspense, it's usually best to take the rebate and get a loan from a credit union or bank. But not always.

First, determine the market rate you could get. Let's say it's 9 percent. The dealer is offering you a choice of 2.9-percent financing (we'll call it 3 percent) or a $1,500 rebate on a $15,000 car. We're going to put 20 percent down and take a 4-year loan no matter what.

What do you do? When market rates are at 9 percent, a 3-percent rate on a 4-year loan saves you $110.54 for every $1,000 financed. (Look under 4-year loans, find the dealer's rate of 3 percent, and read across to the market rate of 9 percent and you'll see the number $110.54.) Then multiply $110.54 by 12, because you'll be financing $12,000 of the $15,000 purchase price. That equals $1,326.48, so the rebate wins—at least in dollars and cents. The $173.52 you could save by taking the rebate and borrowing elsewhere may not be worth the extra effort. That's your call.

Rule of thumb: The value of a cheap loan increases with the

price of the car. If you were financing $15,000, the same discounted rate would save you $1,658.10—$158.10 more than the rebate.

THE CHEAP LOAN OR THE REBATE?

Saving per $1,000 of the Loan Amount

Dealer's Rate	7%	8%	9%	10%	11%	12%	13%	14%	15%
				5-YEAR LOAN					
3%	$92.55	$113.81	$134.39	$154.30	$173.57	$192.22	$210.27	$227.76	$244.69
4	69.93	91.73	112.81	133.22	152.97	172.08	190.59	208.51	225.87
5	46.97	69.30	90.91	111.82	132.05	151.64	170.61	188.97	206.76
6	23.65	46.54	68.67	90.09	110.83	130.89	150.32	169.13	187.35
7	—	23.44	46.11	68.05	89.28	109.84	129.74	149.00	167.66
8	—	—	23.22	45.68	67.43	88.47	108.85	128.58	147.69
9	—	—	—	23.00	45.26	66.81	87.67	107.87	127.43
				4-YEAR LOAN					
3%	$75.67	$93.34	$110.54	$127.28	$143.59	$159.47	$174.94	$190.00	$204.68
4	57.09	75.12	92.67	109.75	126.38	142.58	158.36	173.73	188.70
5	38.29	56.68	74.57	92.00	108.96	125.49	141.58	157.25	172.52
6	19.26	38.01	56.26	74.03	91.33	108.18	124.59	140.57	156.15
7	—	19.12	37.73	55.84	73.49	90.67	107.40	123.70	139.58
8	—	—	18.97	37.44	55.43	72.94	90.00	106.62	122.81
9	—	—	—	18.83	37.16	55.02	72.41	89.34	105.84
				3-YEAR LOAN					
3%	$58.16	$71.97	$85.49	$98.74	$111.72	$124.44	$136.90	$149.11	$161.09
4	43.82	57.84	71.56	85.01	98.19	111.11	123.76	136.16	148.31
5	29.35	43.57	57.51	71.16	84.54	97.65	110.50	123.08	135.42
6	14.74	29.18	43.33	57.19	70.77	84.07	97.11	109.89	122.41
7	—	14.66	29.01	43.08	56.86	70.37	83.60	96.57	109.28
8	—	—	14.57	28.85	42.83	56.54	69.97	83.13	96.03
9	—	—	—	14.49	28.68	42.59	56.22	69.57	82.66
				2-YEAR LOAN					
3%	$40.01	$49.66	$59.18	$68.56	$77.81	$86.93	$95.93	$104.80	$113.55
4	30.10	39.85	49.47	58.94	68.29	77.51	86.60	95.56	104.39
5	20.13	29.98	39.69	49.27	58.71	68.02	77.20	86.26	95.19
6	10.09	20.05	29.86	39.53	49.07	58.48	67.76	76.90	85.92
7	—	10.05	19.97	29.74	39.38	48.88	58.25	67.49	76.60
8	—	—	10.01	19.89	29.62	39.22	48.68	58.02	67.22
9	—	—	—	9.97	19.81	29.50	39.06	48.49	57.79

(Source: William R. Bryan, University of Illinois)

OTHER BORROWING STRATEGIES

• Many lenders will give you a substantial break on the interest rate—as much as one percentage point, and sometimes even up to two percentage points—if you arrange to have your monthly payments automatically debited from a checking or savings account.

• Trying hard to avoid excess debt is admirable, but don't overdo it. Buying a car for cash or putting an extra 5 percent down on a house is fine—as long as circumstances don't cause you to run up a $5,000 credit-card bill over the next year.

• Don't borrow in anticipation of receiving a bonus, especially in today's economy.

PART II
ESSENTIAL INFORMATION

$

5

THAT'S MY CREDIT REPORT?

$ One of the standing jokes in the credit industry is that the initials TRW stand for "The Report's Wrong."

For years, consumer advocates and industry researchers have tried to figure out how many of the nation's 450 million credit reports contain errors. In 1991, Consumers Union determined that 48 percent of the reports it analyzed were inaccurate. Three years earlier, a study by Consolidated Information Services—an independent *credit bureau*, not a consumer lobbying group—found an error rate of 42 percent to 47 percent.

A 1992 study sponsored by the Associated Credit Bureaus (ACB), the industry's trade association, focused solely on consumers who had been turned down for credit and found that fewer than 3 percent of those who requested to see their reports were denied credit because of erroneous information. That sounds comforting, but it shouldn't be.

Certainly, it does not translate into an error rate of 3 percent or less. It merely means that no more than 3 percent of the reports studied contained "fatal" errors that led to denials of credit. The reports might have contained errors that could result in a denial next time, or they might have harbored mistakes that caused borrowers to pay higher interest rates. (Intriguingly, the ACB acknowledges that of the 9 million consumers who saw their reports in 1989, 3 million—33 percent—demanded changes.)

Finally, there's my own study. When I looked at the three financial dossiers compiled on *me* by the three major credit reporting agencies

—TRW, Trans Union Corporation, and Equifax Credit Information Services—I found that all three were wrong. Chillingly, each was wrong in a different way. (For the record, I don't have charge accounts at Saks Fifth Avenue, Bonwit Teller, and Bloomingdale's, although, yes, I'm flattered that someone thought I did.) Still, my files were monuments to scientific precision compared with that of one of my close friends. Of the twenty-eight entries in her TRW report, fifteen were wrong.

For the moment, let's not quibble about whether there are 10 million inaccurate credit files or 150 million. Whatever the number, it's clear that every year hundreds of thousands of Americans are inconvenienced—or driven nearly mad—by these mistakes. (As we went to press, Congress was considering legislation that would improve, but by no means eliminate, the mess.)

The glitches can be costly, and a bad credit report is like a financial time bomb—especially these days, when files are scrutinized for almost any reason. (Thinking of signing up for a dating service? They may pull your credit report. If you have a lot to hide, I'd suggest running a personal ad instead.)

Errors can make it difficult, if not impossible, to get a loan or a credit card, an apartment, insurance, a preferred loan rate, or even a job. Employer screening has become one of the hot new markets for credit reports. When tight limits on lie detector testing went into effect in 1989, employers began gobbling up credit reports to gauge the character of job applicants.

A good credit report is like a driver's license or a passport: it is an essential tool to help get you where you want to go. In the 1990s, an excellent credit report will allow you to borrow money more cheaply, as a growing number of lenders institute tiered (multiple-rate) lending policies. If you have black marks on your report—they're called "dings," "derogs," or "blips" in the industry—you might still get the loan, but you'll have to pay a higher rate.

BETTER DAYS AHEAD

The situation is improving. A combination of negative publicity, consumer rage, and impending congressional action convinced the three leading credit bureaus to make some changes. On April 30, 1992, TRW began giving away free credit reports to consumers. (You're allowed one freebie per year; additional reports can cost no more than $7.50.) It also started installing new software designed to lower the atrocious error rates and developed more readable reports.

Equifax instituted a toll-free customer service number (800 685-1111), spent millions of dollars to enhance its responsiveness, and also created a more user-friendly report. In addition, it stopped selling personal financial information to direct marketers, a move that has pleased privacy advocates. (TRW and Trans Union still peddle the stuff.) Trans Union, for its part, says it is pursuing significant software upgrades.

UNFORTUNATELY, IT'S YOUR JOB

Don't let the promised improvements make you complacent. Under current law, it's still your job to police the accuracy of your credit file. Ridding your credit report of errors is absolutely vital, and I'll show you how to minimize the pain of the process. Don't let yourself be "discredited."

To profit from all the borrowing strategies discussed in this book, you need to present your credit history in the best possible light, and that means taking control of your credit information. Furthermore, you should understand exactly what kind of borrowing behavior will damage your credit status—and what you can get away with.

WHAT IS A CREDIT REPORT?

American businesses analyze well over 1.5 million credit reports every day—more than 400 million every year. Think of them as handicappers scrutinizing the *Daily Racing Form*. Your credit file is a report card tracking performance in both the distant and the recent past.

The purpose of the information is similar: to help someone make an intelligent decision, or guess, about how you'll perform the *next time* there's money on the line.

At best, however, a credit report is an incomplete portrait. Many people are surprised by what it *doesn't* contain. It is supposed to include your name, birth date, address, and social security number, as well as the name of your employer and your spouse. It will also usually include much, but not all, of your credit history; a list of "inquiries" by credit grantors for at least the last six months (indicating how desperately you've been seeking credit lately); and all credit-related public-record information, such as bankruptcies, foreclosures, judgments, and tax liens.

But the file may not mention your salary (TRW's never will), and may not list some of the financial obligations you think about most.

It's hard to predict which payment items will be recorded. At least three factors are relevant. First, does the creditor report to any credit bureaus? Does it report to the bureau that supplied you with your file? Has a mistake been made?

Nonetheless, certain reporting patterns are quite predictable. For example, the fact that you owe money to any of the following will not show up on your credit report unless a collection action has been launched against you:

- utilities (phone, gas and electric, cable TV)
- landlords
- doctors
- hospitals
- lawyers

Many other accounts are reported according to the whims of the institution. Most oil companies do not report on charge-card accounts (but Unocal will if you ask, and Mobil was considering adopting a similar policy as we went to press). Some travel-and-entertainment-card companies do not report (but American Express does). Credit unions often don't send data to credit bureaus. First-time credit report recipients are invariably surprised and disappointed when their mortgage—the quintessential credit obligation—is not listed at all. (In most cases, it will be reported only if you've been 90 days late.)

The following items are usually, but not always, reported:

- charge accounts at large and medium-sized department stores
- bank loans
- auto loans
- student loans paid to a bank (if you're 30 days late, you may be reported as delinquent; if you're 90 days late, you almost certainly will be)

So what, if anything, should always show up on your report?

- all major credit cards (Visa, MasterCard, Discover, Optima, etc.)
- American Express and Diners Club cards
- accounts at the major national retailers (Sears, JC Penney, Montgomery Ward, etc.)
- finance-company loans

Finally, if you're a child-support scofflaw, beware. Delinquencies are starting to appear on credit reports, marking a trend that will probably continue throughout the nineties.

KAFKA WOULD HAVE UNDERSTOOD

What can go wrong? Here are a few recent horror stories.

After his year-long ordeal to reclaim his own financial identity, Steven White* came to a simple conclusion: "I picked the wrong city to move to."

The 24-year-old native Bostonian's calamitous mistake was to move to San Francisco three years ago. Once there, he soon discovered that two other men with the same name, but different middle initials, didn't have a perfect grasp of the debt-repayment concept. The other Steven Whites had repeatedly stiffed credit-card issuers, merchants, and local doctors.

After some wrangling, our Steven convinced the manager of a company where he was applying for a job that his damning credit report wasn't really about him. It helped that the Diners Club charge-off had occurred when Steven was 12 and the uncompensated medical treatment in California while he was in high school 3,000 miles away. But Steven could not get credit, nor would a landlord allow him to put his name on a lease.

For Steven, the 10-month-long nightmare seemed endless. He estimates that he spent 100 hours trying to clear up the errors, often taking days off from work to visit credit bureau offices. The matter wasn't resolved until Steven's mother contacted her congressman and the U.S. Public Interest Research Group (PIRG).

Steven's case, however, refuses to die. In May 1991, he learned that a Connecticut S&L had filed a claim against him and sent a collection agency to extract $11,695.91. So, once again, Steven took off from work and headed to his local credit bureau office to attempt to wipe the slate clean.

Anyone reading this story might think: Don't credit bureau computers check social security numbers? Don't they consider addresses? Don't they sometimes pay attention to middle initials? Read on.

Financially speaking, Donna Singleton* knows all about original sin. The 19-year-old Colorado college student had a negative credit report before she ever had credit! The reason? A credit bureau concluded that she was married to her uncle, which was not true. Her uncle's credit report did, indeed, have a large blemish, a 1987 lien for insufficient payment of taxes. (Spouses are held responsible for shared credit obligations.)

Divorce may be commonplace today, but dissolving this fictitious union has not been easy for Donna. When three certified letters failed to get any action, Donna went to the Federal Trade Commission, the Colorado Attorney General, and the U.S. Public Interest Research Group, which are currently pursuing her case.

Mary Davis, a Plano, Texas, librarian, saw her credit decimated in 1990, when she was confused with three similarly named deadbeats who lived nearby.

Sears, which had considered Mary a valued customer for 30 years, suddenly revoked her credit. A bank denied her a new-car loan. A credit union turned her down for a credit card. And when she applied for a new Visa card, Citibank said, "No way."

Mary responded aggressively. "I wrote a letter to TRW and then sent letters buckshot all over the country to every consumer protection agency associated with the government," she says. It took months, but with the help of the Texas attorney general's office, her credit record once again became spotless.

But the story doesn't end there. In April 1992, Mary applied for a credit-union car loan and was turned down. The reason? Many of the erroneous entries that had once blighted her credit report reappeared. (Clearly, software inadequacies persist at credit bureaus.) "Of the thirty entires on my report, twelve have nothing to do with me," Mary says. Her struggle to clean up her report continues.

HOW TO PROTECT YOURSELF

Check your credit reports every 12 to 18 months. In addition, always look at reports before seeking a major loan or applying for a new job. The emotional toll of a credit denial or delay—not to mention a lost job—can be extraordinary. Since one such incident could cost you hundreds of hours of work and worry, it's worth the inconvenience, and the expense, of keeping on top of your credit report.

Credit-report errors seldom cause would-be home buyers to lose out on a house—after all, the home purchase process is so protracted there's almost always time to fix things—but prevailing *eventually* is not the sole point.

"There's tremendous emotional distress," says David Davitch of American Financial Mortgage Corporation. "People find their dream house, they negotiate an agreement, and then comes the delay. They think they'll lose their home."

Before going house hunting, couples should check credit files individually under their own names and social security numbers. It's also worth checking your report after you've paid off a judgment, had a lien removed (supposedly) from your property, or been involved in a dispute with a merchant.

Many intelligent consumers have never seen their credit reports. Having always received credit when they asked for it, they assume, often falsely, that no problems are lurking in their files. Even if the file is clean today, it might be contaminated tomorrow. Regularly checking your report is like being innoculated against an electronic virus.

WHERE DO ALL THE
CREDIT-REPORT ERRORS COME FROM?

To be fair, credit bureaus process 2 billion changes in financial information every month, so they're bound to make a mistake or two. The bureaus say the most frequent type of error occurs when a consumer applies for credit under a slightly different name (Dan Quayle instead of J. Danforth Quayle, or Samuel C. Jones rather than Samuel C. Jones, Jr.). The bureaus are half right. These mistakes are common

—so be very careful and consistent when you apply for credit—but they're not nearly as prevalent as the more basic cases of mistaken identity just described.

Other common types of errors include:

Inaccurate public record information. Every month, two million pieces of public information—bankruptcies, foreclosures, judgments, and so on—are added to credit files. The data-gathering techniques are primitive, and mistakes abound. Credit bureau employees, who are often paid the minimum wage, copy the items by hand at the courthouse or transcribe them over the phone.

Remember the famous 1991 Norwich, Vermont, case, in which all 1,400 of the town's taxpayers were declared deadbeats by TRW? That was simple human error by an apparently very simple human who failed to distinguish between the town hall's list of *taxpayers* and *tax delinquents*.

Credit-grantor mistakes. The creditors who feed monthly data via computer tape to credit bureaus sometimes get things wrong, too. A typical error: The creditor will fail to report that an account has been closed or a loan paid off. These slip-ups may seem benign, but they could cost you a loan. That's because more and more credit grantors are now totaling your *available* lines of credit and asking, "What if citizen Feinberg suddenly got in trouble—or went bonkers—and decided to max out all his credit cards and credit lines tomorrow?" So if you canceled that gold card with the $7,000 credit line, be sure it's listed that way on your report.

Fraud. Credit-card fraud is at least a $500 million business. Every year scoundrels victimize tens of thousands of innocent consumers, trashing their credit files in the process.

Hacker mischief. Computer hackers sometimes feed disinformation into credit files. It's a very effective way of getting revenge or wreaking random havoc. And according to young programmers, it's also surprisingly easy to do.

HOW TO GET YOUR CREDIT REPORT

Obtaining your credit report isn't a mysterious process. The three major credit bureaus are listed in the white or yellow pages, sometimes under "Credit Reporting Agencies."

Here's how to get in touch with the national offices of the big three (only Equifax will let you order reports by phone, and it discourages the practice):

TRW
P.O. Box 2350
Chatsworth, CA 91313-2350
800 392-1122

Trans Union
P.O. Box 7000
North Olmsted, OH 44070
312 408-1050; 313 689-3888
(Regional offices: P.O. Box 360, Philadelphia, PA 19105,
   215 569-4582; 222 South First St., Louisville, KY 40202,
   502 584-0121; and P.O. Box 3110, Fullerton, CA 92634,
   714 738-3800.)

Equifax
P.O. Box 740241
Atlanta, GA 30374-0241
800 685-1111

But it's quite possible that one report won't be sufficient. Remember, my three reports were wrong in different ways. Edmund Mierzwinski of the U.S. Public Interest Research Group (PIRG) recommends that every adult look at reports from two or three credit bureaus. If you choose to look at only two, how do you know which other credit bureau to call?

Begin with your TRW report, because it's free. Then ask your bank or a targeted creditor which other bureau it generally uses. Call the bureau, and it will tell you where to send a written request and a check. (When requesting a report from Trans Union or Equifax, California residents must enclose proof of their social security number.) Equifax charges $8 and Trans Union charges $15, except in states that have mandated lower limits: California ($8), Connecticut ($10), Louisiana ($8), and Maine ($2). New laws now allow Maryland and Vermont residents to get their reports for free. You can see your file for free if you've been denied credit in the past 60 days.

(When making a request by mail, be sure to include your full legal name, spouse's name, birth date, current address, social security number, any previous addresses over the past 5 years, daytime and evening phone numbers, and, for TRW, proof of ID such as a copy of a bill or driver's license. If you're asking for a free report because you've recently been denied credit, enclose a copy of the denial letter as well.)

One-Stop Shopping. Instead of sending away for three reports, you can get one merged file containing all information from the big three credit bureaus. Call Credco Inc. of Carlsbad, CA (800 637-2422), for an application. The cost is $24, or $1 more than most people would pay for their Equifax and Trans Union reports.

The Credco file is easy to read and identifies which bureau reported each item. Appropriately, it comes with a dispute form.

CREDIT-REPORT READING TIPS

The sample credit report on page 45 doesn't look exactly like what you'll receive from any of the big three credit bureaus, but it incorporates details from all of them. Here, proceeding from left to right, is what the entries mean:

The "Whose" column notes who is responsible for the account: "1" indicates the account is the sole responsibility of this individual; "2" indicates a spouse is an authorized user of the account; and "3" means it is a joint account with the spouse contractually liable.

The initial and numbers under the credit grantor's name represent the credit bureau's in-house identification or member number for the credit grantor. Occasionally, retail store accounts are listed under the name of the parent company (Tandy Corp.) rather than the store itself (Radio Shack).

"Date Reported" refers to the last time the credit grantor reported on the account's status.

"Method of Reporting" describes whether the data come from a computerized source ("Automtd."—abbreviated as "A" in most reports) or a non-computerized source ("Manual"—usually abbreviated as "M").

"Date Opened" tells a reader when the account was opened.

"Date of Last Payment" is self-explanatory.

"Highest Credit or Last Contract" refers to the credit limit on the account or the original amount of a particular installment loan.

"Balance Owing" is self-explanatory.

NAME AND ADDRESS OF CREDIT BUREAU MAKING REPORT

☐ SINGLE REFERENCE   ☒ IN FILE REPORT   ☐ TRADE REPORT

☐ FULL REPORT   ☐ EMPLOY & TRADE REPORT   ☐ PREVIOUS RESIDENCE REPORT

☐ OTHER_____

CREDIT BUREAU OF ANYTOWN
1131 MAIN ST.
ANYTOWN, ANYSTATE 12345

CONFIDENTIAL
crediscope® REPORT

Date Received: 4/11/86
Date Mailed: 4/11/86
In File Since: APRIL 1970
Inquired As: JOINT ACCOUNT

■ Member Associated Credit Bureaus, Inc.

FOR

FIRST NATIONAL BANK
ANYTOWN, ANYSTATE 12345

REPORT ON:	LAST NAME	FIRST NAME	INITIAL	SOCIAL SECURITY NUMBER	SPOUSE'S NAME
	CONSUMER	ROBERT	G.	123-45-6789	BETTY R.

ADDRESS: CITY	STATE:	ZIP CODE	SINCE:	SPOUSE'S SOCIAL SECURITY NO.
1234 ANY ST. ANYTOWN	ANYSTATE	12333	1973	987-65-4321

COMPLETE TO HERE FOR TRADE REPORT AND SKIP TO CREDIT HISTORY

PRESENT EMPLOYER:	POSITION HELD:	SINCE:	DATE EMPLOY VERIFIED	EST. MONTHLY INCOME
XYZ CORPORATION	ASST. DEPT. MGR.	10/81	12/81	$ 2500

COMPLETE TO HERE FOR EMPLOYMENT AND TRADE REPORT AND SKIP TO CREDIT HISTORY

DATE OF BIRTH	NUMBER OF DEPENDENTS INCLUDING SELF:			OTHER: (EXPLAIN)
5/25/50	4	☒ OWNS OR BUYING HOME	☐ RENTS HOME	

FORMER ADDRESS:	CITY:	STATE:	FROM:	TO:
4321 FIRST AVE.	ANYTOWN	ANYSTATE	1970	1973

FORMER EMPLOYER:	POSITION HELD:	FROM:	TO:	EST. MONTHLY INCOME
ABC & ASSOCIATES	SALES PERSON	2/80	9/81	$ 1285

SPOUSE'S EMPLOYER:	POSITION HELD:	SINCE:	DATE EMPLOY VERIFIED	EST. MONTHLY INCOME
BIG CITY DEPT. STORE	CASHIER	4/81	12/81	$ 1200

CREDIT HISTORY *(Complete this section for all reports)*

WHOSE	KIND OF BUSINESS AND ID CODE	DATE REPORTED AND METHOD OF REPORTING	DATE OPENED	DATE OF LAST PAYMENT	HIGHEST CREDIT OR LAST CONTRACT	BALANCE OWING	PAST DUE AMOUNT	NO. OF PAYMENTS	NO. MONTHS HISTORY REVIEWED	30-59 DAYS ONLY	60-89 DAYS ONLY	90 DAYS AND OVER	TYPE & TERMS (MANNER OF PAYMENT)	REMARKS
2	CONSUMER'S BANK B 12-345	2/6/86 AUTOMTD.	12/85	1/86	1200	1100	-0-	-0-	2	-0-	-0-	-0-	INSTALLMENT $100/MO.	
3	BIG CITY DEPT. STORE D 54-321	2/10/86 MANUAL	4/81	1/86	300	100	-0-	-0-	12	-0-	-0-	-0-	REVOLVING $ 25/MO.	
1	SUPER CREDIT CARD N 01-234	12/12/85 AUTOMTD.	7/82	11/85	200	100	100	1	12	1	-0-	-0-	OPEN 30-DAY	

PUBLIC RECORD: SMALL CLAIMS CT. CASE #SC1001 PLAINTIFF: ANYWHERE APPLIANCES
        AMOUNT $225 PAID 4/4/82
ADDITIONAL INFORMATION: REF. SMALL CLAIMS CT. CASE #SC1001--5/30/82 SUBJECT SAYS CLAIM PAID
        UNDER PROTEST. APPLIANCE DID NOT OPERATE PROPERLY.

The crucial "Past Due" section tells a creditor how you're currently handling your credit obligations.

The "Historical Status" portion of the report describes your repayment track record (the period under scrutiny is specified in the "No. Months History Reviewed" column).

"Type & Terms (Manner of Payment)" refers to the three types of payment options: "Installment" would apply to a credit obligation such as a car loan, which has fixed monthly payments. "Revolving" would describe a typical credit card, whose balance you may pay off in full or not, as you choose. "Open 30-day" would indicate an account like American Express, which requires the consumer to pay the balance in full each month. (Sometimes these account types will be abbreviated as "I," "R," and "O.")

All public record information and explanatory statements by consumers should appear at the bottom of each report.

Most creditors do not report consumers as delinquent until they are 60 days overdue, although the reporting of 30-day delinquencies is becoming more common. But beware: under our credit-reporting system, a payment that arrives one day late may be considered 30 days late for scoring purposes. (Just because you've been assessed a late fee does not mean that a credit bureau has been notified. Late fees per se are never reported.)

Pay close attention to the "Inquiries" section of the report, even though it does not appear on the sample included here. The category "Number of Inqs with this SS#" tells how often you've applied for credit in the past three or six months. If the number is three or higher, many creditors will think you're overly eager for additional credit. Be sure the listed inquiries relate to actual applications for credit; if they don't, ask that they be removed.

But what about all those prescreened credit offers that arrive in your mailbox every other day? They should be listed as "Promotional" or "Prm," and they're not supposed to count against you as inquiries—unless a mix-up occurs.

(Note: A second inquiry category on a TRW report, "Number of Inqs with this ADDR," refers to all credit applications emanating from your street address. It helps creditors screen for fraud. If you live in a high-rise, this Inqs number might be unnervingly high—mine once hit 34—but there's no need to worry.)

WHAT'S MY "CREDIT RATING"?

Not too long ago, this was a trick question. A credit rating was like a unicorn or a warm-hearted banker—a purely hypothetical creature. Credit bureaus didn't judge consumers; they accumulated information for credit grantors, who then analyzed it according to a highly individualistic blend of statistical analysis, gut feeling, and lender voodoo.

In the last few years, that's changed. The major credit bureaus now offer ratings to subscribers willing to pay extra for the service. In literature touting an oracular rating product called DELPHI, Trans Union claims that it is nothing less than the "answer to the crystal ball! DELPHI predicts your customer's financial future. This statistically tested system scores the potential risk of bankruptcy and delinquency."

TRW has less poetic products; one of them is simply known as the national risk score, which uses a scale of 0 to 1,000. Neither TRW nor Trans Union will tell consumers what their ratings are. You have to use your own crystal ball, apparently.

At the moment, though, the computerized scoring systems of creditors are more important than credit-bureau ratings. While lenders pride themselves on their individual systems, the scoring mechanisms are really very similar. The systems smile upon people who own their homes, rarely move, and have checking and savings accounts. They dislike those who rent, move frequently, and have high monthly loan or credit-card payments.

In assessing similar scores, two lending institutions may impose entirely different credit criteria. Some, like Arkansas Federal Savings, which in recent years has offered one of the lowest credit-card rates in the country, will reject any applicant with a single late payment. Other creditors may tolerate a bankruptcy or a string of bad debts.

Like horse players, financial handicappers are far more interested in the recent past than in ancient history, which, at least theoretically, is good news for you. If unemployment, illness, divorce, or bad judgment caused you to miss some payments several years ago, many creditors will be forgiving. Some focus almost exclusively on your payment history for the last 24 months.

So don't lose any sleep if you were late with one payment three years ago—especially if you were late paying Sears. (Sears is known for being trigger-happy when it comes to reporting late payments. "If a report says someone was 30 days late with a Sears payment, we ignore it," says Sidney Lenz, at Countrywide Funding.)

Several years ago, Sears took this curious habit to its logical extreme, according to Ken Yarbrough, former head of security for TRW. The store wished its customers a happy holiday season, and with a what-the-hell-it's-Christmas kind of a gesture it invited them to skip the January payment due on their Sears cards. Naturally, millions did so. On February 1, Sears's computer decided to play Scrooge, telling the nation's credit bureaus that some who accepted the offer were 30 days delinquent.

EXERCISING YOUR RIGHTS

Though an overhaul of the laws regulating credit bureaus is urgently needed, consumers already possess important weapons to help them combat credit-bureau errors and abuse. Under the Fair Credit Reporting Act, you have the right to obtain your credit report at any time and to find out exactly why you were denied credit (or employment or insurance, for that matter, if the denial was related to information in a credit file). You also have the right:

- to dispute any information in your credit file
- to ask that information be added to your report
- to have potential creditors or employers who've recently seen your file notified when errors have been corrected
- to include a 100-word statement explaining your side of a dispute
- to have negative information removed from your file after seven years (ten years in the case of bankruptcy)

DISPUTING INFORMATION

You have the right to ask a credit bureau to reinvestigate any item in your file. This must be done in writing. Either make the changes on the report itself or use one of the bureau's consumer-dispute forms, which you can request when asking for your report.

Challenge all mistakes, no matter how benign they may appear. When demanding changes, always request a complete *corrected* copy of your report; otherwise, you probably won't get one. (Also request that the bureau send corrected copies to the many smaller credit bureaus with whom they do business.)

Alas, there's a good chance that the "corrected" copy will still be wrong. For one thing, credit bureaus aren't very good at fixing mistakes. "The credit bureaus don't make money from clearing up mistakes," says Davitch, the mortgage banker. "They make money from selling credit reports."

Mistakes, though, often originate with the credit grantor. In such cases, the credit bureau's "reinvestigation" will probably be of no help whatsoever. It will simply "reverify" that Saks thinks you owe $2,900. Then the case is closed—unless you fight to keep it open. It's your job to convince Saks that it's wrong *and* to compel it to communicate that information to the credit bureau.

(Note: If you trace an error to a credit grantor, be sure to find out if it reports to any other credit bureaus. The same mistakes will likely reside there as well.)

ADDING POSTITIVE DATA

In his best-selling *Financial Self-Defense*, Charles Givens suggests that consumers have the right to have missing positive information added to a credit file. Perhaps you *should* have this right, and maybe eventually you will, but as of now you don't. All you can do is ask.

Trans Union and Equifax may accommodate you, for a small fee ($5 or $10 in most cases). TRW will not, no matter what you offer to pay. The company's position is, more or less: If it should have been reported, it would have been reported.

For closed accounts, such as paid-up car loans, TRW's stance makes absolutely no sense. But for current unreported accounts, its posture is perfectly logical. If the account is not routinely reported, then all you'd be able to add is a one-time listing. Eighteen months later, a potential creditor won't know if you're still current, so it won't be overly impressed. (If you're going to pay Trans Union or Equifax to add positive information, do so only for paid-off loans.)

NOTIFYING CREDITORS OR EMPLOYERS

If you've successfully fixed an error in your credit file, request in writing that the credit bureau communicate all changes to any potential creditor who has looked at your file in the last six months or any potential employer who has checked it in the previous two years.

EXPLAINING YOUR SIDE OF THE STORY

You have the right to demand that a credit bureau include a 100-word explanatory statement from you in your file. It's very important to take advantage of this opportunity when:

• a dispute is pending
• you've fought the good fight and lost (for instance, a merchant says it will charge you for an item that arrived broken and unusable)
• you want a future creditor or employer to understand exactly why your financial affairs were in disarray two years ago (credit bureaus don't have to include sob stories about unemployment and illness but often will)

If you ask, the credit bureau must help you write the statement. Just don't assume that the statement will always pack the punch you think it should. These days, when most credit reports are "read" by computers, the most moving prose in the world may not help your case. What you'll need is either a very unusual computer system or a human loan officer who can read.

REMOVING NEGATIVE INFORMATION

Be prepared to police this matter yourself. On the seventh anniversary of a bad debt or late payment, or on the tenth anniversary of a personal bankruptcy filing, send all three major credit bureaus a clear note explaining that the negative data should now be removed from your file.

Mark your calendar. The 7-year period starts from the date of the last regularly scheduled payment you made before the account became delinquent—unless the creditor eventually either charged off the account or obtained a judgment against you for the amount due. In those cases, the meter would start running on the date of either event.

Technically, the statutes of limitations have three exceptions:

1. if you borrow $50,000 or more for any reason
2. if you apply for a life insurance policy with a face amount of $50,000 or more

3. if you apply for a job with an annual salary of $20,000 or more (and you wonder why some people contend that the Fair Credit Reporting Act of 1970 has become outdated)

Credit bureaus say they don't disclose this information voluntarily after so much time has passed. But a potential creditor or employer with a less forgiving nature may request the data.

Occasionally, you can remove derogatory information more quickly. If you were late in paying a creditor but have since paid in full, you can ask to have that information stricken from your file. A favorable response is rare, but it's worth a shot.

GUERRILLA TACTICS

Credit bureaus are the leading subject of consumer complaints to the Federal Trade Commission. In 1990, more than 8,700 people brought grievances about credit bureaus to the attention of the FTC.

In 1991, a study of 155 of these cases by the U.S. PIRG (released under the objective title "Don't Call; Don't Write; We Don't Care") revealed some distressing statistics:

• Sixty-three percent of consumers had contacted the credit bureaus five times or more before turning to the FTC.

• The average duration of a complaint against a credit bureau prior to contact with the FTC was 22.5 weeks.

• Twelve percent of consumers who were denied credit alleged that the credit bureau either refused to reinvestigate their complaint or wouldn't allow them to include a dispute statement.

While no specific actions can guarantee that a credit bureau will treat you with decency and dispatch, techniques exist for easing the pain and speeding the process. Don't ever let yourself be bullied. Yes, credit bureaus are rigid. But they're not omnipotent.

First, keep dated copies of all correspondence with the credit bureau. Certified mail isn't essential but should be considered. In every letter or conversation, make it clear that you know your rights under the Fair Credit Reporting Act.

When speaking with credit bureau employees, get first and last names. Pin people down about when you can expect a response. (As part of their settlement of civil lawsuits, TRW and Equifax have agreed to respond within 30 days. Trans Union has made no similar agreement and, legally, has 60 days to respond. Ask for a faster answer anyway.)

If a mistake in your file led to a credit denial, it's probably wise to send copies of all letters to consumer-protection groups and government agencies, including the state attorney general's office of consumer protection, your state's Public Interest Research Group (PIRG), the U.S. PIRG, the Better Business Bureau, and the Federal Trade Commission. For $18 a year, Bankcard Holders of America routinely helps its members resolve such disputes. (See Appendix A, "Resources," for addresses and phone numbers.) Remember, three of the most powerful keystrokes you can make are *cc*: Let credit bureau personnel know that their conduct is being monitored.

At the first hint of being stonewalled, demand to speak to someone in authority. Find out what he or she thinks you need to do to fix the problem. Give the person a chance to help you.

If all this is getting you nowhere, write to your congressman. Go to the press. Threaten the credit bureau with a lawsuit. Although this isn't exactly a bluff, it's not the course many sane people would want to pursue. You may win, but you won't win much. One California developer who lost hundreds of thousands of dollars because a credit bureau refused to remove an inaccurate foreclosure item from his file eventually settled for $50,000.

In your case, though, the bureau may not settle. If you go to small claims court, you may triumph (don't forget to sue for lost time as well as any other financial losses), but be careful. Credit bureaus sometimes have such cases remanded to a higher court (which means higher fees for you).

CREDITORS

Creditors are easier to handle than credit bureaus—if you know what you're doing. Traditionally, they've been much better at recognizing the stake they have in customer service.

If, following its reinvestigation, a credit bureau refers you to a credit grantor, ask for the name of a contact person. Lacking one, try the credit marketing department before you go to customer service.

Don't be complacent if you prevail. Demand that the creditor contact *all* credit bureaus with the corrected information. Ask for a copy of the creditor's letter to the bureaus.

If the creditor won't budge, threaten to go public with the dispute. Use your economic leverage. Say you'll tell all your friends to take their business elsewhere. In the case of a department store, casually mention that you were thinking of registering there for your wedding, but. . . . Again, think of contacting the press.

Make a scene. Slice up your credit card. If you're right, you will win eventually.

IT AIN'T OVER TILL IT'S OVER— AND SOMETIMES IT STILL AIN'T OVER

When you think about a recently resolved credit dispute, let your mind briefly consider one of the terrifying conventions of horror or suspense films: the false ending. Remember the stories of Steven White and Mary Davis?

• If someone else's information has entered your credit file once, it may make a return visit. So be vigilant about checking your credit report.

• A double listing in your file—for example, the same $7,000 Chemical Bank gold Visa card listed twice—looks like a very simple problem but could be particularly hard to cure. Letters, phone calls, and legal threats may prove insufficient. A trip to the local office of the credit bureau might be required to clear things up.

CREDIT-REPAIR CLINICS

Your guerrilla tactics should probably never include a visit to a credit-repair clinic or credit "doctor." Most of them are either crooks or charlatans whose stock appeals in the classified sections of the tabloids and on late-night TV ("Credit problems? No problem!"; "Erase bad credit! 100% guaranteed"; "Remove bankruptcies from your credit file NOW!!!!") have cost unwitting consumers tens of millions of dollars in the last few years alone.

Legally, credit-repair clinics cannot do a single thing that you can't do yourself for far less money. That's the law. The issue is really very simple. You can't remove legitimate derogatory information from your file until 7 or 10 years have elapsed. You can, on the other hand, erase genuine mistakes without such high-priced, and generally ineffective, intervention.

Many credit-repair clinics try to back up their outrageous marketing claims by challenging every negative item in a credit file without regard to its validity. Sometimes, this may actually be effective—in the short run. The besieged credit bureau, and the creditors it contacts, may not be able to handle all the paperwork within the legally allotted period of time. As a result, some negative items may temporarily disappear from the file. But when the creditor does finally respond to the verification request and reconfirms the negative information, the black mark is reinstated.

Perversely, this kind of activity ends up hurting consumers who have legitimate grievances. Credit bureau officials assume that credit "doctors" are almost always in the wrong. In fact, from 1985 to 1989, according to a TRW executive, TRW used to ignore almost all credit-repair clinic requests, dismissing them as "frivolous or irrelevant." (In doing so, it was taking a rather aggressive anticonsumer view of the FTC's interpretation of part of the Fair Credit Reporting Act.)

The result? Once you went to a credit "doctor," the facts no longer mattered. You had, in effect, pleaded guilty.

Although some legitimate credit-repair clinics exist, none can perform miracles. There's nearly always a better alternative. It will be much cheaper to contact any of the resources listed in Appendix A.

I do disagree, however, with those who say credit "doctors" serve absolutely no purpose. They do. They make everyone else involved in the credit industry look noble by comparison.

CREATING YOUR OWN CREDIT REPORT

Let's say you've spent months trying to get inaccurate information removed from your credit file. The credit grantor is backing you up, but the credit bureau remains adamant. As for you, you're starting to panic because you want to apply for a large loan soon.

Solution: Get the credit grantor to write an explanatory letter that you can take to lenders. By now, most lenders have seen so many credit-report errors that they're often willing to override the credit bureau's "opinion" when they see exculpatory evidence. (Note: This approach is smart whether or not the credit bureau is making a good-faith effort to clear up your file. If you're in a hurry, the creditor may be able to give you the fast response you need.)

Occasionally, of course, a lender will simply accept your side of the story without documentation. Don't blame the lender, though, when this option isn't available. Most mortgage lenders *can't* simply trust you—not if they want to sell your mortgage in the secondary market. The major purchasers of mortgages—the Federal National Mortgage Association (Fannie Mae) and the Federal Home Loan Mortgage Association (Freddie Mac)—don't require flawless credit reports, but they do demand letters from creditors explaining away any "significant" problems in the files.

Similarly, when a credit bureau exercises its right not to allow you to add positive information to a report, you can take a do-it-yourself approach. Assuming you've been an impeccable customer, go to some of the lenders *not* mentioned in your report and request enthusiastic reference letters. Some will help. Don't be bashful about showing the reference letters around.

This strategy can work for three good reasons:

1. You'll be giving a potential lender powerful new information about your value as a customer.
2. The lender will do its own due diligence on some of these accounts—obviously, it won't just accept a letter saying that you've always made the payments on your $500,000 mortgage early—but the personal touch can be helpful nonetheless. A flattering letter written by a human being who seems to know you can be a real asset. ("My wife has a glowing reference letter from Bank of America, which holds her mortgage," says Ken Yarbrough. "She and I send that to any future creditor.")
3. Just making the effort will impress some lenders. Deadbeats don't do these things.

IF YOU'VE BEEN DIVORCED

People who have been divorced sometimes emerge with joint custody of their debts, which can be both awkward and risky.

A judge may divide the obligations down the middle, but a late payment or default by either party will damage the credit status of the ex-spouse. So you have to monitor your ex's payments. (Whenever possible, you should pay off and cancel all joint accounts immediately after the divorce.)

A good credit history can be shared as well. Let's say that Mr. and Mrs. Bliss had several joint accounts before they divorced. Following the divorce, the woman has the legal right to request that creditors report all joint accounts in her name as well, whether her post-divorce name is Bliss, Jones, or whatever. But beware: this rule applies only when both parties were jointly liable for the account. Additional credit cards don't count. For example, if Mr. Bliss got a Discover card for himself and later had a second card issued to his wife, only Mr. Bliss is liable for the payments, and only he can legitimately list the account on a future credit application.

DO YOU NEED A
CREDIT-REPORT MONITORING SERVICE?

In the last four years, the major credit bureaus introduced services that allowed consumers to keep tabs on their credit files for $20 to $44 per year. The credit bureaus then used the defects of their systems to sell the services. A TRW brochure advocated signing up for its Monitor service "so you can check any errors easily and quickly . . . before any damage is done."

A marketing piece for Trans Union's CreditWatch service boldly stated: "You should know if unauthorized people have inquired about your file." Clearly, under the law, Trans Union wasn't supposed to permit such "unauthorized" access, but since it did, it would admit its mistakes—and sell you information about its slip-ups.

In early TV ads for TRW Credentials, the actor Peter Graves gave viewers the fly-on-the-wall hard sell, saying that subscribers could now find out what others were saying about them. Congressman Charles Schumer of New York says one of the common consumer misconceptions about Credentials, which now has almost 1 million subscribers at $44 per year, is that it represents the *only* way to get access to a credit file.

At the very least, it's fair to say that the bureaus had found a way to profit from public fear and confusion about credit reports. Now that the three major bureaus have vowed to make substantial improvements, however, and TRW has offered its reports for free, the monitoring service concept has lost a lot of its value. That's why only one service—TRW Credentials—remains. Still, subscribing isn't necessarily a terrible idea.

For $44 Credentials offers unlimited access to credit reports. That's nice, but by itself it's not enough to justify the cost. TRW reports that the average Credentials subscriber asks to see his or her report twice a year.

But the extra payments do get you something. Only subscribers can order reports by phone, which is a definite convenience. Subscribers also seem to get reports faster than other people. (For an extra $5, TRW will send the file via overnight mail.) The bureaus' reputation for slow service (Consumers Union found that 6 percent of consumers waited much longer than 30 days for reports) also constitutes an argument in favor of membership.

Credentials notifies you whenever anyone, authorized or not, checks your file. This is particularly helpful for people who are worried about, say, a scheming business partner or spouse; otherwise, it may not be very beneficial.

It's more important to be notified whenever new negative information burrows its way into your file. Credentials updates you every quarter—which may not be fast enough. (A labor-intensive alternative to get more timely information: Order your credit report every month or two, and look for new entries.)

TRW Credentials also offers a personal "Financial Profile." Essentially, this is a detailed financial-disclosure form, similar to what you'd fill out if you were applying for a large loan. TRW doesn't fill it out; you do.

In its early marketing efforts, TRW said the profile would make it easier for subscribers to apply for loans. It has since backed away from that claim—wisely, too, since almost every lender in the country will demand that you fill out *its* application, whether or not you've already performed the same chore for TRW.

So what *is* the benefit? "It's a way for you to put all your financial information in one place," says a TRW marketing executive. "I know when I try to get all my financial stuff together I go nuts."

Needless to say, you could put all your informational eggs in one basket *without* paying TRW. Then TRW wouldn't be able to take all that valuable information and sell it to direct marketers. (Welcome to the information society!)

Even if you do subscribe to Credentials, you should examine your files at Equifax and Trans Union before applying for a major loan or a new job. You want to see what, if anything, the gremlins have been up to.

Major credit grantors such as Citibank pay $1.50 to $2.00 per credit report.

6

THROUGH THE
LENDER'S EYES

$The "people" part of the lending business isn't quite what it used to be. As in many other enterprises, computerized systems have largely supplanted the human factor. Your "lender" may really be an IBM mainframe stocked with customized software.

Usually, though, your credit report and your immediate financial needs will be evaluated by some form of human being/machine nexus—complex credit-scoring systems and flesh-and-blood lending officers who have the ability to overrule the machines, if they care enough about you or feel that the electronic beasts have not grasped the subtlety of your particular case.

THE MACHINES ARE WATCHING

When you apply for a credit card or a loan, your application is almost invariably assessed by an automated credit-scoring system. Most credit grantors will judge you based on 10 to 30 different criteria. Some create their own systems, while many lenders rely on third-party financial analysts and software developers such as Fair, Isaac Companies of San Rafael, California, and the MDS Group of Atlanta.

Below is a relatively basic credit-scoring profile that a bank is using to rate Alice, a 36-year-old teacher who is applying for a $12,000 new-car loan. Alice needs a score of 75 to qualify. (An asterisk marks her score in each category.)

CREDIT FACTORS	POINTS AWARDED
Age	
18–27	10
28–34	7
35–48	2*
49–60	11
61–64	12
65 and over	15
Monthly Income	
Less than $1,000	0
$1,001–$1,800	2
$1,801–$2,500	7*
$2,501–$2,999	10
Over $3,000	13
Time at Job	
0–1 year	5
1–4 years 6 months	10*
4 years 7 months–10 years	15
Over 10 years	18
Occupation	
Professional	12*
Clerical	11
Sales	10
Military	12
All other	10
Home Ownership	
Own/Buying	12
Rent	6*
All other	6
Time at Current Address	
0–1 year	3
1–3 years	5*
Over 3 years	12
Listed Telephone in Borrower's Name	
Yes	7*
No	0
Number of Major Credit Cards	
0	0
1–3	8
4–7	6*
More than 7	2

CREDIT FACTORS	POINTS AWARDED
Monthly Nonmortgage Debt Payment	
$0–$500	10
$501–$750	9*
$751–$1,300	6
More than $1,300	4
Bank Accounts	
Checking	10
Savings	12
Checking and savings	13*
Payment History	
Never more than one time 30 days late	10*
Never more than one time 60 days late	7
Never more than one time 90 days late	2
Collection or bankruptcy	−15

Alice scored an 87 and got the loan.

Comments:

• Not all systems are so forgiving about 60-day late payments.

• Some systems may grant many more points for a perfect payment history—perhaps as many as 25 percent of the total needed to qualify.

• The system doesn't usually distinguish between a person who makes $3,001 a month and one who earns $6,002 or $9,003. Most computers consider you rich if you earn $35,000 or $40,000 (which shows you how much computers know).

• Note the prejudice against a person who has "too many" bank cards. This is a growing trend in scoring systems. Many borrowers, unfortunately, are still living in the past, assuming that lenders are very impressed with people who have already shown that they're extremely good at borrowing. ("Lenders are far more impressed with people who've shown they're good at *saving*," says S. A. Ibrahim, senior vice-president and chief of staff for financial and technology services at Chemical Bank.)

• Note, too, the perfectly legal bias against someone between the ages of 28 and 48. Why? Because that's when people typically have the most financial obligations. And baby boomers, in particular, have shown a penchant for taking on more debt than they can repay. (This scoring system doesn't ask whether the applicant has children, but it clearly doesn't like a person who is of an age when he or she is most likely to have a child.)

• More sophisticated systems may penalize you less for moving recently if you live in a highly mobile area such as Washington, D.C.

• If you just relocated to take a great new job, a system like this is going to count your smart career move as a sign not of upward mobility but of instability. That's why it is vital for you to address this point on your application or in conversation with the lender. The human factor becomes important here.

• If the scoring system rejects you, and you really think it has overemphasized your defects and neglected your virtues, politely raise hell with the lender. Over the years, many lenders have learned that the rejected borrowers who gripe the most are usually pretty good credit risks. An intelligent, rational appeal may score you a lot of points—maybe just enough to overrule the software that's been so blind to your merits.

• Warning: The computer that was kind enough to allow you to borrow may someday revoke or limit your privileges.

This but-what-have-you-done-with-your-debts-lately analysis is an emerging trend in the credit industry.

"Lenders are looking for more dynamic risk-assessment information," says one credit analyst. "An applicant's data may have looked great when he received credit five years ago—but now lenders want to know, 'What kind of shape is he in today?' "

First Chicago used such a model in 1991 to yank thousands of credit cards from customers in the Northeast and sharply reduce the credit limits of thousands of others.

RATIOS

To many lenders, you're also a ratio—at least when you apply for large loans, such as a mortgage or a home-equity loan or line. Throughout the eighties, lenders showed a growing willingness to stretch the debt-to-income ratios they would tolerate—which might help explain why the annual number of personal bankruptcies almost quadrupled from 1980 to 1991. Today, a typical acceptable debt-to-income ration for a home-equity line might be as high as 43 percent or 44 percent. (The ratio will be higher in California, where homes are so much more expensive. It can also go higher for people who have a lot of equity in their home.)

Loan officers and branch managers can expand the ratios for personal loans, home-equity loans and lines, and some mortgages, if they like you or have reason to believe you're a better risk than the raw numbers indicate (they won't *know* that, though, unless you tell them).

Sometimes the ratios are immutable. For conventional mortgages, almost every lender in the country tries to conform to the standards established by Fannie Mae and Freddie Mac, so it can sell the mortgage in the secondary market. If the lender gives you a mortgage that puts your front ratio above 28 percent or your back ratio above 36 percent, it may be stuck with the mortgage forever—and that's not the way institutions like to do business these days, no matter how much they love you. (The front ratio refers to the percentage of your gross income that can be devoted to mortgage principal, mortgage interest, property taxes, and property insurance, collectively known as PITI in the lending industry. The back ratio is the percentage of income devoted to PITI plus all other monthly debt payments.)

HUMANS

Just because the computer rejects you doesn't mean a human lending or credit officer will—if, that is, a human being ever sees your credit report at all.

That's another reason it's so important to know what it contains. That way you can alert the lender to anything that might initially be *perceived* as a problem.

Although you should do this as a precaution, it's not always necessary. Lenders have become so accustomed to seeing errors on credit reports that occasionally they'll simply assume that a seemingly anomalous item—a $200 bad debt or a 90-day delinquency in an otherwise pristine file—is a mistake. They may not even bother to ask you about it.

Do lenders care about those 100-word explanatory statements in your credit file? If they ever get to read them, they often do care. When he was a loan officer, Ross Richardson, now a financial planner in Houston, paid close attention to the statements.

"The very fact that they were there was positive," he says. "An applicant concerned enough to put one in was probably going to be concerned about paying on time. Of course, as always, you'd see some people who had learned to play the game. They'd use any excuse to 'explain' why they couldn't make certain payments. Their grandmother had cancer, the sun was in their eyes—whatever."

You can also do your explaining on the phone, in person, or on a piece of paper attached to the application. If you couldn't pay some bills 18 months ago because of a medical emergency, a layoff, or some kind of personal crisis, *let the lender know*. If you allow your credit report to do all the talking on your behalf, it may say some very unflattering things. (Almost all lenders will check out your story, so besides being unethical and illegal, lying will probably be a waste of time.)

It's easiest, and potentially most beneficial, to establish a relationship with a lending officer or branch manager at a small bank, or at a fairly small branch of a larger institution. That doesn't mean it's impossible at a midtown branch of Citibank, Chemical Bank, First Chicago, Bank of America, or Wells Fargo; it just takes more luck, and often more perseverance.

It also helps, in such cases, if you're a bigger-than-average fish. An accountant friend of mine who invests in a lot of real estate spends a half hour every month chatting in person with his lending officer at Citibank, regardless of whether he'll soon be asking the bank for some of its money. "When I do bring up specific potential deals," he says, "I get a sense of what the bank will and won't go for. That helps me plan my strategy."

Rapport helps, but it's not magic. The lending officer still has to have reason to expect you'll return his institution's money, with interest, when you say you will.

For instance, a loan officer can't exceed his lending, or floor, limit no matter what kind of relationship he or she has with you. At some point, ask what that limit is, so you don't spend time talking to your friend about a deal he can't possibly approve.

TIPS

• Always come prepared with the appropriate documents, and then some. Ask the bank what you should bring. Generally, this will include several recent pay stubs (or two years of tax returns, if you're self-employed), two or three proofs of identification, and information about your outstanding balances with various creditors. Doing this saves time and impresses the lender. If you're applying for a personal loan, consider bringing an updated net-worth statement (which you'll prepare yourself).

• When applying by mail, send in copies of your proof of income (recent pay stubs or past tax returns) with the application. Lenders are always going to ask for proof; there's no need to wait for them to do so officially. This will only delay the loan process by a week or two. (*Never* send originals.)

• If you're ever turned down for a loan, ask the lender exactly what it would take for you to qualify.

• If there's a serious problem with your credit, don't let yourself get stuck with a young loan officer. Often, they can't lend to people with bad credit. Find a senior officer instead.

• Don't worry too much about being nervous. Nervous is okay. You're supposed to be somewhat intimidated. Nervous is better than slick.

• When applying for a loan, don't ever bring your children. "We hate that," says one lender. "I know applicants who have been turned down because their kids were bothering everybody. The lending officer just wanted to get rid of them."

But even this response has a bright side. It's *human*. It's understandable. While it may not represent the personal touch you long for, it is a sign that the machines are not yet in complete control.

7

HOW TO ESTABLISH CREDIT

$A few years ago, Eran Rosenthal was working 30 hours a week at two jobs while he was a part-time student at the University of North Carolina. Like any red-blooded young American, he applied for a credit card—five of them, in fact—but he was turned down each time.

Then Eran decided to reduce his income. He became a full-time student. As he struggled to meet his monthly expenses, Eran applied for yet another credit card. Now he really needed it. And a curious thing happened. He got it.

Although halving your income is rarely a smart credit-seeking maneuver, it works beautifully when you combine it with a second step: becoming a full-time college student. While you may be skeptical about the value of a college education, credit-card issuers most emphatically are not. They love college students. They definitely prefer them to 20-year-olds who already have stable jobs.

Let's face it: the rules lenders use when considering whether to extend credit to a virgin borrower or deciding how to rate the payment habits of a fledgling consumer don't always seem logical. Still, if you're a young credit-seeker, or if you have children who might someday grow up to become borrowers (and you don't want them turning to you), it helps to know the ropes.

Actually, the bias in favor of college students over the gainfully employed has some economic validity. As credit risks, college kids are just like employed adults: 4 to 5 percent default on credit-card debts. Of course, the rate would be far higher if the parents of the students didn't act as de facto co-signers—or real co-signers—for the cards.

Card issuers also like college students because they're young and impressionable. Marketers always love a chance to establish early brand loyalty. Issuers also know that college graduates will *eventually* earn more, charge more, and default less often than those who never go to college.

Luckily, there are ways to beat the system that do not entail tuition payments.

WHAT WORKS

Little things count. The best way to begin your quest for recognition as a creditworthy adult is to get a phone in your own name, pay for your utilities, and, most important, open a savings and a checking account.

THE BANKING RELATIONSHIP First, shop around to find a conveniently located institution that will serve your needs well. Ask several banks, S&Ls, or credit unions about their monthly fees and minimum-balance requirements before making your selection. Eliminate any institution that doesn't issue its own credit card. Then ask all the finalists what chance you would have of getting such a card now or in the near future.

You may not be able to obtain a card until you've been a customer for a while. If so, wait three or four months, then make an appointment to see the bank's credit manager and request a credit card. If you're told that you still don't meet the institution's credit-card standards, find out exactly what you have to do to qualify. If the terms seem reasonable (compared with the alternatives discussed below), smile and agree to comply.

THE TRADING-UP METHOD Open a checking account with overdraft privileges and use them. Gently. Then get a credit card from an oil company that reports positive credit information to credit bureaus. Unocal will report if you give the company written permission (and Mobil may soon do so), but most oil companies—including Exxon, Chevron, and Amoco—do not report. That makes their cards fairly useless for establishing credit, unless you expect to charge nothing but gas, tires, and lube jobs for the rest of your life. (Call the oil company to find out if it reports to credit bureaus.) Oil-company cards tend to charge high interest rates but no annual fees. If you get one, use it and pay off the bills in full each month.

The oil-company plastic will help when you apply for a card with a large local retailer—or JC Penney or Sears—which is what you should do next. Starting local is the most certain solution, although it is labor-intensive. But you can go directly to the big national chains if you like. If they reject you, you can always go local.

Again, make sure the retailer reports to credit bureaus. Retail cards, which often have higher interest rates than bank cards, seldom have annual fees. Use the card judiciously, and pay the bills in full each month.

Now, at last, you're ready to apply for a Visa card or MasterCard. With a spotless, albeit meager, credit record and an income of at least $15,000 a year, you should be able to get a card from a giant issuer such as Citibank, Chase Manhattan, First Chicago, or Bank of America. As cards go, they're all fairly expensive. Should that worry you? No, because with a clean payment record, you'll be able to trade up to a less expensive card in six months or a year.

THE CO-SIGNER ANGLE A parent or a very good friend can co-sign a loan or a credit-card agreement for you. Since you're partly liable for the debt or the card (remember this), you get points for handling either one like a good citizen.

If you make every payment on time, a co-signer arrangement can be a valuable stepping stone. The next time around, a lender probably won't demand that you have someone with deep pockets in your corner. After using a co-signed card for a year, or after you graduate from college, request that the co-signed card be transformed into one for which you have sole responsibility.

Warning: If you can't make the payments, your co-signer will be forced to come up with the money. (In the business world, co-signing is sometimes called "suicide by fountain pen.")

THE SECURED-CARD MANEUVER If the first two approaches don't work and you can't find, or choose not to use, a co-signer, consider a secured credit card. (Chapter 26 has details and a list of good cards.)

Secured cards are credit cards backed by collateral (almost invariably a savings account or CD). Because you can't borrow more than you have on deposit, the lender can't lose.

Secured cards were once a tool solely for people with very bad credit, and these cards are still trying to shed their déclassé image. But secured cards can be great for people with no credit. Although they typically have high set-up and annual fees, they're worth the money if you can't find a better deal elsewhere. After a year or so of responsible use, you may be able to graduate to an unsecured card.

(Note: You usually have to be employed to qualify for a secured card.)

THE BORROW-AND-BORROW-SO-YOU-CAN-BORROW-PLOY This is one of the oldest tricks in the book. You deposit money in a bank, S&L, or credit union and borrow against your savings. Then you pay off the loan on time—or, better yet, repay it early to save on the interest charges—and you've enhanced your credit standing.

Although this strategy can be effective, it is also expensive and time-consuming. You lose money on the spread between the savings rate and the loan rate (usually the differential will be two to six percentage points), and you'll probably have to get the loan in person. In addition, most institutions won't do the deal unless you borrow at least $500. (Some credit unions will let you borrow as little as $50, however.)

But the approach does demonstrate a degree of discipline and a willingness to go through contortions to get credit—two things credit grantors love. It will get you points on many credit-scoring systems.

In fact, even after you have all the credit cards you need, taking out an unnecessary bank loan and repaying it promptly may help you when you apply for a *real* loan sometime in the future.

As always, find a lender who will report your loan to credit bureaus; approximately two-thirds of them do.

WHAT DOESN'T WORK

• Dealing with credit grantors who don't report to credit bureaus is almost a complete waste of time. Always ask the credit grantor if it will report your transaction. If not, go elsewhere.

• Similarly, be aware that some perfectly nice parental gestures won't do you any good. If your parents give you an additional credit card linked to an account in their names, this does nothing for your credit status.

• Don't apply for too much credit at once. Too many requests can spook lenders and trigger alarms in credit-scoring systems.

• Whenever possible, resist applying for a credit card or loan if your chances of being approved are minimal: a rejection looks bad on your credit report. How can you determine the odds in advance? Make it a habit to call the credit manager before you fill out the application. Present your financial credentials honestly and ask what chance you have of being approved.

TIPS FOR THE CREDIT NOVICE

• Don't get too much credit. With credit, less is usually more, especially when you're starting out.

• Don't make the classic new-cardholder mistake of forgetting that plastic is just like cash, only more expensive. The card issuer *will* send you a bill—they never forget—and you will have to pay it.

• Realize that your first credit-card bills will probably be larger than you anticipated.

• Don't make the second classic new-cardholder mistake: quickly reaching your credit limit on your first card and then scurrying to find another.

• Remember that there is an enormous difference between being able to charge something and being able to afford it.

• Don't *ever* pay late. If you do, you may wind up with a credit report filled with "derogs." Having a bad credit record can hurt you when you try to rent an apartment or buy a car.

GET OFF TO A GOOD START

While it's important to know how to get credit when you don't have any but want some, it is also crucial to be aware that you'll be offered some pretty awful credit deals. "Money often costs too much," said Ralph Waldo Emerson, and this is especially true if you're young or new to the game.

So don't be too eager. And don't be too grateful when some seemingly kindhearted institution welcomes you to the world of credit. Consider the motivation underlying the offer to rent money to you. If a card issuer thought you'd just carry your card around in your wallet in case of emergencies but never actually use it—sort of the way some young men handled condoms in the fifties—then it wouldn't give you a card in the first place.

If someone gives you access to credit, you'll probably use it. You may even wind up paying interest, perhaps for many years. Given this possibility, it makes sense to take a little extra time at the start of your credit career to search for a favorable deal. You'll be rewarded for not leaping at the first offer you get.

8

PLASTIC EXPLOSIVES: HOW TO PROTECT YOURSELF FROM YOUR CREDIT CARDS

$Credit cards can be wonderfully powerful tools for the modern consumer. Used wisely, they can save time and money. Used very wisely, as we'll see, they can even allow you to earn hundreds of dollars a year, every year.

Yet consumers probably make more mistakes with credit cards than with any other financial instrument. Sometimes the mistakes do enormous harm. It is not for nothing that one of the rituals in any credit-counseling office is the systematic destruction of a client's credit cards.

Most card issuers assume that the majority of consumers will not use plastic in a manner that is most advantageous to them. The card issuers' conviction that human nature will triumph over both common sense *and* self-interest has led to enormous profits. Based on many financial yardsticks, issuing credit cards is one of the best businesses in America. (The FDIC reports that between 1985 and 1990 the average return on assets for all bank loans was .5 percent. For credit cards, net margins are 3.4 percent, almost 7 times greater.)

PLASTIC NATION

The credit card, like the computer, is one of those symbolic products that helps define an age. For most of us, credit cards are more important

TOTAL ANNUAL CHARGES ON VISA, MASTERCARD, AMERICAN EXPRESS, AND DISCOVER (IN BILLIONS)

1980—$67.4	1986—$188.1
1981—$79.3	1987—$222.0
1982—$90.1	1988—$258.7
1983—$109.1	1989—$303.5
1984—$139.7	1990—$348.5
1985—$167.7	1991—$370.4

(Source: *Credit Card News*)

than we think. If you don't believe this, try leaving home without plastic for a few days. The experience will probably make you feel disoriented, alien, and befuddled—as if you had traveled back in time. It might also make you feel poor.

In America, where people have an affinity for plastic that is unmatched anywhere in the world, credit cards outnumber people by almost five to one. (In Australia, the human population is dwarfed by sheep; here it's by plastic.) The average American household has more than 10 credit cards. The average "creditworthy" household has twelve. In 1990, Americans used their more than 1 billion credit and charge cards to make purchases of about $500 billion, according to *Credit Card News*.

Throughout the 1980s—the Debt Decade—the volume charged on the "big four" cards (Visa, MasterCard, American Express, and Discover) exploded, growing by at least 12 percent every year. In 1984 it rose by an extraordinary 28 percent. (See chart above.)

Only a fairly small portion of this amazing rise can be explained by inflation. So what caused the rest?

For one thing, the cards become much easier to use, sometimes in fairly subtle ways. Credit-card validation at retail outlets can now take as little as two seconds—literally—so paying with plastic may be faster than paying with cash.

Furthermore, the opportunity—or temptation—to pay with plastic has grown dramatically. Today, credit cards are widely accepted by supermarkets. Their acceptance is growing in fast-food outlets, movie theaters, hospitals, taxicabs, and parking lots, and with doctors as well. In Alabama, Arkansas, California, Indiana, Maryland, Minnesota,

Missouri, Montana, Oklahoma, Texas, Vermont, and Wisconsin you can, in some cases, pay state taxes, property taxes, or state fees with credit cards. If the IRS gets its wish, Congress will soon allow it to accept credit cards as well. Given the trend, lemonade stands may someday be the sole holdouts against plastic.

Today, 71 percent of the Americans who wield credit cards use them to borrow money (that is, they carry balances). Since 1980, the amount Americans owe on credit cards has risen over 300 percent, to more than $230 billion, or about $2,500 per household.

When the eighties began, credit cards accounted for 18 percent of total consumer nonmortgage debt. By the end of the decade, the figure had swelled to 29 percent. Collecting exorbitant interest on that debt is how the industry earns the bulk of its money, but it is by no means the only source of profits.

INSIDE THE CREDIT-CARD INDUSTRY

Merchants are more aware than consumers that plastic is not the same as real money. If you buy $100 worth of shirts at Lou's Clothes and pay by credit card, Lou may surrender as much as $5.50 of the sale to the card issuer. On every credit-card purchase, the merchant must pay a fee, called the discount fee.

For Visa and MasterCard, the fee ranges from 1 percent to 4.5 percent of the purchase amount, depending on the establishment's annual volume and type of business. The average is 2.15 percent. For American Express, the fee is significantly higher, ranging from 2.5 percent to 5.5 percent and averaging about 3.375 percent.

The discount fee is split between the merchant's bank, which transforms Lou's Clothes credit-card slips into cash, and the bank that issued the credit card. The card-issuing bank or card-issuing company gets almost 70 percent of the haul. This is called the interchange fee. Tiny though these percentages are, they do manage to add up. In 1990, discount fees generated more than $5.5 billion for credit-card issuers.

That year, the issuers also collected more than $35 billion in interest charges (those small monthly payments add up, too). This is the kind of financial tribute that issuers have come to see as their due. In fact, industry officials regard cardholders who don't ever pay interest with scorn, calling them "30-day wonders" or "deadbeats."

To discourage such behavior, most issuers invite customers to skip a payment once or twice a year. Needless to say, they don't always prominently explain that interest continues to accumulate at its normal relentless pace. Accepting this kind offer of a month's forgiveness simply increases the cost of borrowing. It's the opposite of prepayment; you're agreeing to pay back the principal more slowly, which will cost you more in finance charges.

In 1990, credit-card issuers took in another $2.25 billion in annual fees, plus hundreds of millions of dollars in assorted late fees, over-the-limit fees, and bounced-check charges.

All told, the industry raked in approximately $45 billion in that year. Not all of this was profit, of course. In 1990, issuers wrote off about $7 billion in bad debt; they lost another $500 million to credit-card fraud. And there are the salaries, the overhead, and the staggering direct-mail costs. Still, when you're lending more than $230 billion at an average rate of 12 points over prime, it's hard not to have something left over. In 1991, the profits of Citibank's credit-card division were more than $600 million.

THE RISE OF THE CREDIT CARD

The first credit card appeared in 1914. That year, several department stores, as well as Western Union, began to issue cards to their wealthier customers so they could run up a tab in an organized fashion. (Technically, these were all "charge" cards; no interest was levied, and the balance had to be paid off each month.) Though the cards were only made of paper, they had considerable prestige value. If you weren't either rich or a very good customer, you couldn't get one.

In the early 1920s, oil companies introduced "courtesy" cards, allowing an increasingly mobile population to use credit far from home. Some hotel chains followed suit. By the end of the decade, the formerly flimsy credit card was being made from more durable stuff, as retailers pioneered embossed metal "charga-plates," similar to military dog tags.

In the 1930s, retailers in selected cities began to accept cards issued by their neighboring competitors. By 1936, the Retail Service Bureau of Seattle had 1,000 member retailers who accepted charges made by joint customers (according to Lewis Mandell's *The Credit Card Industry: A History*). Several years later, retailers introduced the revolving credit system, with its familiar feature of monthly finance charges. The trail-blazer in this effort to get consumers to buy more with less was probably L. Bamberger & Company of Newark, New Jersey (now owned by Macy's).

The first "universal" bank card was issued in 1947 by the Flatbush National Bank of Brooklyn. It was accepted by a variety of different merchants, but it had an obvious flaw: every merchant was located in a two-square-block area of Brooklyn. You had to possess a marvelously parochial world view, even by Brooklyn standards, to consider the card truly "universal."

In 1950, the Diners Club card finally changed all that, altering the history of twentieth-century finance. Created by Frank McNamara, Ralph Snyder, and Alfred Bloomingdale (heir to the Bloomingdale department store fortune), Diners Club was the first card that could really travel. It was the first credit instrument that could be used as a cash equivalent with many different providers of goods and services all over the country, and eventually throughout much of the world.

The card's developers also deserve credit for finally figuring out how to make the industry profitable. It was they who invented the discount fee, which was originally 7 percent.

In the fifties, banks began rolling out similar charge cards. By the end of the decade, many had discovered that the inauguration of a revolving-credit feature increased both consumer acceptance and profitability—clearly a fortunate combination.

In 1958, the American Express card (which was originally purple and made out of cardboard) and Carte Blanche (a souped-up version of the private card issued by Hilton Hotels) made their initial appear-ance. Life was certainly different then. Like the first charge cards offered in 1914, the American Express card was actually a genuine status symbol. Only 232,000 cards were issued that first year. Then, most of the people who had the card really needed it.

In 1966, Bank of America, the nation's leading bank-card issuer, began licensing its BankAmericard to issuers around the country. Alarmed, a group of rival banks quickly formed the Interbank Card Association and began pushing its new card to all banks that would have it. Today, BankAmericard is known as Visa, and Interbank as MasterCard; their battle is still being waged nightly in TV commercials.

In the late sixties, both companies came up with an exciting and dangerous new marketing idea. They sent out tens of millions of free, unsolicited credit cards to normal folk all over America. You didn't have to be a Rockefeller to qualify; if you could sign your name and identify where you lived, you were golden. Any college student taking at least three courses was entitled to a free credit card.

This indiscriminate dumping of millions of credit cards led to some abuse. People who might not normally qualify for credit suddenly had it. Some less noble citizens stole the cards from the postal system and ran up monumental charges. The next month, innocent consumers who had never received their cards got appalling bills. In 1970, Congress determined that the marketing gimmick was driving a lot of people crazy; it banned the practice of sending out unsolicited credit cards. (Yes, you still get unsolicited plastic in the mail, but mailings no longer contain "live" ammunition. Without returning a signed and completed application, there can be no detonation.)

THE ART OF MANAGING YOUR CREDIT CARDS

By my calculations, the average American family wastes well over $200 on credit-card interest and annual fees every year, or more than $4,000 over 20 years.

Why? Because few important personal possessions are acquired as haphazardly as credit cards. Most of us do not assemble our motley credit-card portfolios by thinking ahead or making carefully considered choices.

Instead, we react to offers from creditors, most of which arrive through the mail. The pitch letters probably constitute the most fawning correspondence any of us will ever receive.

The letters are marvelous reminders that the world is full of possibilities. And the letter writers don't seem to be selling debt at all. Instead, they sell *life*. Abundance. Happiness. Fulfillment. Status.

When your dreams—or your existing debts—are running particularly wild, you may succumb to an offer. It's so easy. Millions of normally smart consumers do this sort of thing all the time.

But there's a reason people refer to such solicitations as "junk mail." Virtually any credit card offered by mail is a bad deal. The largest and sleaziest credit-card issuers dominate the direct-mail field. Almost all charge interest rates and annual fees well above the national average. While the average interest rate for credit cards is now 18 percent, most of the ten top credit-card issuers, who control well over 40 percent of the market, charge 18.9 percent or more to at least some of their customers. These higher rates help subsidize more direct-mail bombardments, thus creating the perfect vicious circle for consumers.

In 1992, however, big card issuers finally began to perceive some growing consumer antipathy toward high credit-card rates. Both Citibank and Optima introduced three-tiered programs that offer low rates (13.4 percent and 12 percent, respectively) to their most dependable and most active customers. Discover initiated a similar program in 1992, and many other large issuers have begun offering lower rates on a formal or informal basis.

These lower rates are clearly an improvement. Nonetheless, it remains true that the institutions offering the best credit-card deals in America hardly do any marketing at all. Generally small and obscure, they're so intent on keeping overhead low that they can't afford to advertise. It generally pays *not* to trust the names you know. In such cases, familiarity should breed suspicion, if not contempt. (See the lists on pages 87 and 91 for the best credit-card deals in America.)

TELL THE TRUTH, NOW

Before you can choose the ideal credit cards, you have to be honest with yourself about how you use them. Unfortunately, most consumers aren't. They spend a lot of time—and money—kidding themselves.

First, they fool themselves about the very nature of the cards. In research studies, most consumers insist that they won't use a new credit card to borrow money. They say they're getting the card for convenience or for emergencies. *Then they use it to borrow money.* The most insidious thing about credit cards—and one reason most Americans are on a credit-card debt treadmill—is that the penalties for carrying a balance can seem negligible.

Because the minimum monthly payments are so low—usually 2 percent to 3 percent of the outstanding balance—you have to engage in some heavy-duty consumption before you begin to feel any pain on a cash-flow basis. You can carry a debt of $1,000 with a monthly payment of less than $30; a $2,000 load for under $60; and a $5,000 burden for less than $150. It's still probably a much smaller nut than your car payment.

But with a car loan, you know exactly when your payments will end. With some credit cards, you may not live long enough to see that day. The worst deals have minimum payments as low as 2 percent of the outstanding balance, including the finance charge. At this rate it would take you 25 years and 5 months of minimum payments to rid yourself of a $2,000 debt at 19.8 percent. During this time you'd also rid yourself of $5,844.03 in interest, on top of the $2,000 in principal.

Nor is this the worst-case scenario. With those credit cards having interest rates of 24 percent or more, making only the minimum payment could mean you will never discharge the debt. On the contrary; the amount outstanding will grow each month.

Adhering to a minimum-payment plan is one of the most devastating financial strategies you can employ. Even if you do it with an average credit card (18-percent interest rate, 2.5-percent minimum payment), it will take you 12 years and 9 months to retire a $2,000 debt. Your finance charges will total $2,230.83.

THE RATE I'M PAYING IS . . .

People also kid themselves about credit-card interest rates, which can range at least as high as 29 percent. Surveys reveal that most people can't tell you the rate they're paying. But ask them about their CD rates and they'll be right on the money. What's going on here?

Two of the culprits are fatalism and complacency. Many consumers figure that they can't get a good credit-card deal, while others assume that if they're making the minimum monthly payments things are more or less under control.

Any borrower who expects to be fleeced will have no trouble finding a lender willing to do the shearing. Nowhere is this more true than in the world of credit cards.

The conviction that all credit cards charge obscenely high rates is logical, though, especially for people who read their mail. It even reveals an intelligent prejudice against credit-card debt. Nevertheless, it's an unfortunate half-truth, and it costs consumers billions of dollars every year.

THE SIMPLEST IDEA IN THIS BOOK

If you are now carrying, or often carry, a lot of high-interest credit-card debt, you should switch to a cheaper credit card. Or you should call the issuers of your cards and ask them to reduce their rates. Some will.

If you already know about cheap credit cards but just haven't taken advantage of them, you're not alone. Inertia is a very powerful enemy for cardholders. (That's one reason it's so important for people just starting out to pick the right card.)

What else, besides a lack of knowledge, stops people from making the switch?

• The fear—often unfounded—of being turned down for new credit cards.
• The hope that the problem will magically disappear if it is ignored long enough. (It won't.)
• A reluctance to admit having made a financial error. This isn't just an ego problem. It's common to have a mental block that prevents the acknowledgment of a major money-management mistake. Why? Because it hurts to confront the fact that in the past you squandered a lot of your hard-earned money. (Don't let regrets about the past undermine your borrowing future.)
• The belief that switching cards is too much of a hassle—that it just isn't worth it. (On an hourly basis, making the switch is probably one of then most lucrative things you can ever do.)

$5,210 AN HOUR

Skeptical about that last point? Let's imagine that you're the average American family. You owe $2,500 on your credit cards and are paying 18-percent interest. If you lowered the interest rate to 13 percent (by no means the best in the country), you would save $125 a year. Once you have a toll-free number in front of you, it takes about twenty minutes to request, complete, and mail a credit-card application. So by switching, you could save the after-tax equivalent of $375 an hour (if you're in the 28-percent tax bracket, that's $521 an hour before taxes) for doing this twenty-minute chore.

If you maintain the same level of debt for 5 years, you'd actually have made $2,605 an hour. Keep it for 10 years and you've made $5,210 an hour. Nice work if you can get it.

Switch cards and you'll feel as if you've taken an enormous step in the right direction. Because you have.

Before you apply for a new card, however, carefully consider the criteria each issuer uses, as well as the credit limits it is likely to impose. Consider the approval rates of each issuer. Apply for one card at a time. (It sometimes pays to call the issuer to assess your chances of being accepted. Some might have scoring systems that make it especially difficult for self-employed people, for instance, to get credit.)

If you're rejected, don't be discouraged. Find out why (as explained in chapter 5 on credit reports) and apply somewhere else. Just realize that you don't have an unlimited number of chances. This isn't the lottery. If you apply for three credit cards within six months, many lenders will hold that against you. If you try to get six different credit cards in one year, almost every lender will become suspicious.

WHAT'S WRONG WITH ARKANSAS FEDERAL?

But please don't despair just because you've already applied to Arkansas Federal of Little Rock for a cheap card and been turned down. Notwithstanding its impressively low rates—8 percent as we went to press—Arkansas Federal may have frustrated as many consumers as it has helped. Because it is featured in almost every article on cheap cards, many people apply to Arkansas Federal for credit. But the issuer rejects most people who apply (between 70 percent and 90 percent of applicants, according to industry sources).

To be accepted, out-of-state applicants must have no late payments on their credit report. Actually, being accepted may not be so great, either, considering that for new customers Arkansas Federal often sets $800 or $1,000 credit limits (the borrowing equivalent of training wheels). That may not be exactly what you're looking for.

CREDIT-UNION CARDS

Before applying for any card on my list, check the offerings of your credit union (see chapter 13 for tips on which credit unions you can join). Credit unions are terrific financial resources, with some knockout credit-card deals. The Pentagon Federal Credit Union, for example, offers a no-fee Visa or MasterCard with a 12.9-percent rate. Its gold cards have the same rate and an annual fee of only $15. Both cards have standard 25-day grace periods. (See chapter 13 for membership information.)

Other appealing card offers from credit unions include:

• Boeing Employees Credit Union (Seattle; 206 439-5700)—12.4-percent standard card, $12 fee (first year is free)
• Iowa State University Credit Union (Ames; 515 232-6310)—13-percent standard card, $10 fee (first year is free)
• Mission Federal Credit Union (San Diego; 619 697-5977)—12.59-percent standard card, no fee (applicants must be teachers, parents of students, or students)

Although most small credit unions do not offer cards, 75 percent of credit-union members belong to one that does. Credit unions charge 4 points less in interest than the national bank-card average; their annual fees are about 50 percent lower as well.

How can they do this? Being nonprofit and tax-exempt helps. Equally important, says Bill Hampel, chief economist of the Credit Union National Association, is the fact that "credit unions don't send preapproved credit-card applications to anyone who passes a warm-breath test." As a result, their credit-card chargeoffs are 1 percent, compared with 4 percent to 5 percent for bank cards.

It's a shame that more people don't take advantage of the credit-union deals. Of the 6 million folks eligible for those Pentagon credit cards, only 100,000 have them. It's hard to believe the rest are all getting a better deal elsewhere.

MAKING THE SWITCH

When you get your new card, use it immediately to pay off your existing balances. Either get a cash advance from your bank, or use one of the checks that are often provided by the new-card issuer. Technically, the check is also considered a cash advance, and you'll have to pay the appropriate fee. (To encourage switching, some issuers have made the process even easier. You can shift debt to your new Wells Fargo credit card simply by slicing up your old higher-rate credit card and mailing it to Wells Fargo, which will then take care of all the paperwork.)

But what if the timing is off—if the new card arrives just after you've sent in the minimum payments on your other cards? You don't have to wait until next month's statements arrive to make a payment and stop that high-interest-rate meter from running. Send a check with your account number and a brief note explaining that you want this payment credited to your account. You are, in effect, prepaying your credit-card debt, just as you would prepay a mortgage.

Most people don't know this, but you can prepay credit-card debts anytime. A word of caution: When you prepay, be sure to send the check to the same address you've been using each month. Send it to headquarters by mistake, and your money will spend days wandering around the United States before it finds the right department in South Dakota or Delaware.

When you've paid off the old card, cut it in half; then mail it back to the issuer with a note requesting that the card be canceled.

THE ANNUAL-FEE TRAP

Credit-card researchers know that consumers are sometimes so passionate about annual fees that they will switch cards to save $10 or $20 a year on the fee, but not to save $100 or $200 a year in interest charges. The intelligent money manager should recognize when such emotional behavior is financially self-defeating.

Why such loathing for annual fees? One reason is that people become accustomed to using cards without fees. Before 1980, only travel-and-entertainment cards imposed any annual tariff. On a more visceral level, people resent paying for the privilege of being charged high interest rates.

But your ideal card might have a fairly high annual fee (First Wachovia's 8.9-percent gold card has a hefty $49 annual fee, yet for some people it's still a wonderful deal), or a no-fee card could turn into a financial disaster (the "free" variable-rate AT&T Universal card could charge 21.9 percent if the prime rate rises).

Luckily, you now have more leverage on this issue than at any time since fees were introduced. Today, each kind of credit-card user, both the borrower and the "transactor" (a person who never uses the revolving-credit feature), can save on annual fees. No-fee issuers such as Discover, AT&T, Ford, GM, and GTE have forced many competitors to adjust their fees or to make them more flexible.

There are now many different ways to get a no-fee card, among them:

• Select an issuer that never charges a fee.
• See if your bank offers no-fee cards to customers with checking and savings accounts (more and more are doing so), or switch to a bank that does.
• Find an issuer that waives the fee if you charge a certain amount per year (the most common magic number is $2,300). More than three hundred card issuers offer this feature.
• Negotiate. One of the best ways to save money on your credit cards is to haggle. These days, issuers are increasingly likely to cave in. A good approach is to tell the issuer that you recently received an offer in the mail for a no-fee card and you're thinking of switching, although you'd really rather not. Is there anything they can do to help?

I've successfully used the last approach. Each year, Chemical waives the $45 fee on my gold card. American Express slashed my $55 fee to $30 when I complained. (As we went to press, Amex had ceased making such accommodations. But it will sometimes charge senior citizens only $35.) Squawk loudly enough and Discover will waive the $40 fee on its Private Issue premium card, and the $15 fee on its regular card in those states (North Carolina and Wisconsin) where annual fees apply. Many of the big banks may also relent. Often, they'll begin by lifting the fee for only one year—or so they say. In such cases, make a note on your calendar; you'll have to spend another two minutes next year to save the $45. Seems worth it to me.

In a recent survey, 65 percent of top credit-card issuers said they would waive annual fees under certain conditions. (Citibank, though, is not one of them. It won't budge no matter what you do.)

If you're a consumer who doesn't care much about annual fees, perhaps you should. On an annual per-card basis, the potential savings may not seem so impressive. According to RAM Research, the average fee for regular bank cards is $17.13; for gold cards, it's $34.68. But if you have one regular card and two gold cards, that's $86.49 a year, every year, or $864.90 every 10 years.

OTHER FEES AND HIDDEN CHARGES

Card issuers extract money in several other ways. All penalize a card-holder who is careless, overextended, or simply inattentive, so beware.

NO GRACE PERIOD

Most credit cards have a "grace period"—a window during which no finance charges can accrue. The most common grace period was once 30 days, but, following the inexorable modern trend in which more inevitably seems to become less, it has since shriveled to 25 days. (All information on grace periods, interest rates, and annual fees must be listed on any credit-card application.)

About 20 percent of all credit cards have no grace period, and for consumers this can be an expensive omission. If you charge $3,000 a year, this could cost you an extra $37.50 to $75.00 a year on an 18-percent card, depending on when you make your payments and purchases. (Note: I'm assuming all payments are timely.)

With so many cards to choose from, it almost never makes sense to subject yourself to such excessive charges. The only exception is a low-rate card, such as Arkansas Federal's, which remains a good deal even after factoring in the lack of a grace period. (Because they have no grace periods and charge high annual fees, Arkansas Federal's cards are terrible choices if you don't carry a high balance from month to month.)

CREDIT LIFE, DISABILITY, OR UNEMPLOYMENT INSURANCE

Never under any circumstances accept an insurance product offered by a credit-card issuer. The insurance terms are generally among the worst available anywhere. Furthermore, some of the insurance is un-necessary, or even worthless. (See chapter 21 for more information.)

CREDIT-CARD REGISTRATION SERVICES

You're probably familiar with the offer: if your credit cards are lost or stolen, make just one call and every card you've registered will be canceled, thus avoiding any hassles or additional stress. The cost for the service seems small—usually $12 a year—but it's really not, unless you lose your cards a few times a year, every year. Then it's a steal.

Only the most absentminded or criminally alluring people will lose their wallets or purses on more than a handful of occasions over a lifetime. If you figure that an average human spends 55 years as a consuming adult, then a lifetime of cheap registration comes to $660 —an exorbitant sum for a few dozen toll-free phone calls.

In addition, the services are not necessarily the great time-savers they're made out to be. Whenever you add a card to your portfolio, you have to contact the registration service by mail. For most people it's easier, smarter, and cheaper to keep a file filled with the vital information. (When traveling, be sure to take along a record of the relevant account numbers and toll-free telephone numbers. Carry this apart from your credit cards.)

Credit-card registration is perfectly fine when it's free, though. Some gold-card issuers offer it as part of their package (see chapter 10), as do some credit unions and affinity-card programs (the American Automobile Association, for one). If you're diligent about registering all your cards, this can be a nice benefit. If you're not, you may *think* you've canceled all your cards when, in fact, you haven't.

LATE CHARGES, OVER-THE-LIMIT FEES,
AND RETURNED-CHECK CHARGES

Most credit cards levy charges for late payments and bounced checks, and most also hit you with fees for exceeding your credit limit. If you're sloppy about keeping on top of your bills, monitoring your total indebtedness, or balancing your checkbook, credit-card issuers will profit at your expense.

In recent years, these fees have risen sharply. Banks everywhere have discovered that penalties and assorted transaction charges—on everything from credit cards to checking accounts—offer exciting new profit opportunities in an era when traditional sources of revenue have become less dependable.

Issuers typically charge $10 or $15 for a late payment, $15 for exceeding a credit limit and $15 for a check that doesn't clear. If you go over the limit and then pay late with a rubber check, that alone could cost you $45 or more, without factoring in the finance charge. Actually, it will cost more, because your *bank* will also impose a charge (usually $10 to $20) for the bounced check.

THE RIGHT CARD FOR YOU

Picking the perfect mutual fund may be impossible, but selecting the perfect credit card is not—if you can anticipate how you'll use the card in the future. (Even though foresight is limited, it's easy to make adjustments if habits change.)

If you never carry a balance, obviously you should stick to cards with no annual fee and a standard 25-day grace period.

According to RAM Research's CardTrak, some of the best *no-fee* standard cards are offered by the following institutions:

- *Oak Brook Bank* (Oak Brook, Illinois)—11.9-percent variable rate, 25-day grace period; 800 666-1011
- *Armed Forces Benefit Association Industrial Bank* (not at all restrictive, despite what its name suggests; Alexandria, Virginia)—12.5-percent variable rate, 25-day grace period; 800 776-2322
- *USAA Federal Savings* (Tulsa, Oklahoma)—12.5-percent variable rate, 25-day grace period; 800 922-9092
- *Amalgamated Bank of Chicago* (Chicago)—12.5-percent variable rate, 25-day grace period; 800 365-6464, 312 822-3130 in Illinois
- *Wachovia Bank* (Wilmington, Delaware)—15.9-percent variable rate, 25-day grace period; 800 842 3262
- *Abbott Bank* (Alliance, Nebraska)—16.3-percent variable rate, 25-day grace period, loaded with enhancements; 800 999-6977

And for consumers with excellent credit records and annual incomes of at least $25,000, some of the best *no-fee* gold cards are offered by the following:

- *Amalgamated Bank of Chicago* (Chicago)—11-percent variable rate, 25-day grace period; 800 365-6464
- *Armed Forces Benefit Association Industrial Bank* (Alexandria, Virginia)—12.5-percent variable rate, 25-day grace period; 800 776-2322
- *Oak Brook Bank* (Oak Brook, Illinois)—12.9-percent variable rate, 25-day grace period; 800 666-1011
- *Security Bank* (Southgate, Michigan)—13-percent variable rate, 25-day grace period; 800 444-8060

- *Union Planters Bank* (Memphis)—13-percent variable rate, 25-day grace period; 800 628-8946

(Note: Issuers on both lists accept approximately 30 percent of all applicants.)

Since finance charges don't concern you (after all, you pay off your balances each month), you're in the enviable position of being able to profit from being a credit-card user. Both the Ford and Discover cards will pay *you* every time you use their cards. Both have high interest rates, but you don't care. You should care more about what you get back at the end of the year.

For most people, Ford's Visa or MasterCard is a much better deal than Discover. Not only does the card offer a higher maximum rebate rate (see table below) but it is much more widely accepted.

REBATE PERCENTAGES ON FORD AND DISCOVER CARDS, BASED ON ANNUAL CHARGE VOLUME

Ford	Discover
Less than $1,000—.5 percent	Less than $1,000—.25 percent
$1,000–$2,000—.75 percent	$1,000–$2,000—.50 percent
$2,000–$3,000—1 percent	$2,000–$3,000—.75 percent
$3,000 or more—1.5 percent	$3,000 or more—1 percent

Almost no one needs both cards. Clearly, charging $1,500 a year on each card is a mistake. If you spent $3,000 on one of the cards, you'd be in the top rebate category. Split the charges between the two cards, and you won't get the maximum rebate, so you're cheating yourself. You're also wasting time and money (on postage) by paying two bills a month instead of one.

DO YOU REALLY GET CASH BACK?

The cash-back programs are legit; it's easy to collect. Spend $10,000 a year with a Ford card and you'll receive a check for $150 every year. Granted, that amount won't change your life, but it could buy an extraordinarily nice dinner or several very cheap suits. Best of all, when the rebate check arrives, it feels like found money—the best kind.

For less extravagant spenders, such as myself, the year-end bonus may be a bit skimpier—more in the neighborhood of $7.07, the sum I received after charging $1,915.88 on my Discover card during my first year as a cardholder.

But oh, the fanfare that accompanied that paltry check! It came in a large folder titled "Your Annual Cashback Bonus Report." The cover informed me that I had made my $7.07 the old-fashioned way— "You've earned it!"

Inside, in addition to a check made out to me in the mid-to-high single figures, there were convenience checks to encourage additional spending and an order form for more convenience checks to stimulate still more spending. Then, to my surprise, there was a detailed description of what I could do with my newly accumulated riches.

The choices? I could cash the check, donate it to the Make-a-Wish Foundation (which grants wishes to children suffering from life-threatening diseases), or use it to open a Discover Savers' Account. Only the savings account would produce additional revenue for Discover, but there was a problem: you needed a minimum deposit of $1,000 to open the account. I was $992.93 short. (Actually, the savings rate wasn't bad, but you can do better. The 30-day teaser rate was terrific; the regular rate fell between the average savings account and money-market fund).

Discover can be a very good card if you avoid being mauled by its 19.8-percent interest rate, the top bracket in its three-tiered system. One month's interest on $428.48 would have wiped out my $7.07 Cashback Bonus. Discover also has a nice automatic-payment feature (discussed in the section on float at the end of this chapter). But the card has a major drawback. Approximately 2.8 million establishments in the United States accept Visa and MasterCard; only 1.46 million honor Discover. This mars the beauty of the cash-back provision, forcing you to exert some extra energy to get something for nothing.

OTHER WAYS TO PLAY THE REBATE GAME

You can also profit from the GM, GE, and GTE cards, but it takes some work. Beware: The cards aren't cheap if you carry a balance. GE

Rewards has a rate of 18.4 percent and an annual fee of $25. GM and GTE have no annual fees and a rate of 16.4 percent.

Nonetheless, if you yearn for a GM car or truck and can avoid monthly finance charges, the GM card could provide you with a legitimate rebate of $3,500 after 7 years (the rebate equals 5 percent of your charges, with a $500 annual cap).

The GE card could let you "save" $800 a year if you buy GE appliances and patronize two dozen companies (including Kmart and Macy's) virtually nonstop, but you have to spend a lot—and within a very narrow time frame—to score big.

If GTE provides your local phone service, its card gives you a 10-percent annual discount on calling-card calls—up to $50 a year—plus 10 percent off GTE phone-store products.

Clearly, a new trend has emerged. Consumers who are smart about credit cards will have more and more chances to profit from plastic.

IF YOU CARRY A BALANCE

People who carry balances occasionally or chronically have to do a little math to make the optimal credit-card choice. But the calculations are fairly painless, and you may only have to do them once. Don't be intimidated by the numbers.

Be aware that you'll probably have to compromise. If you want the lowest rate, you'll typically have to pay an annual fee. If you want to avoid an annual fee, you'll generally have to accept a higher rate. You can determine with mathematical certainty which alternative is the better deal. (Unfortunately, most Americans have opted for the worst of both worlds: the most popular cards in the country have high rates *and* high fees, which is ridiculous.)

All you need to know to begin the calculation is the average monthly balance on your cards. To determine this, find your statements for the last twelve months, add up the monthly-balance figures, then divide by twelve. (If you can't find all the statements, just make a good-faith estimate.)

Let's say the figure is $2,500. One quick way to compare two credit cards is to convert the annual fee into its interest-rate equivalent. Divide the annual fee (say, $35) by the average monthly balance ($2,500). The result is .014. So that annual fee is costing you 1.4 percent a year. Add that 1.4 percent to the card's stated APR (for example, 12 percent) for a *total card cost* of 13.4 percent. A no-fee card would have to have an interest rate below 13.4 percent to be a better deal for you.

But what if your average monthly balance is only $400? Dividing $35 by $400 reveals that you're paying the equivalent of 8.75 percent a year in interest for the fee alone. This means your 12-percent card is really costing you 20.75 percent a year—a terrible deal. A $20 fee (5 percent a year) is probably far too high for such a small balance.

Even if you acquire the perfect credit card, don't be complacent. It may undergo a horrifying transformation if the issuer is swallowed up by one of the industry giants. When this happens, both rates and fees inevitably soar. When Citibank acquired Connecticut Bank and Trust's credit-card portfolio, for example, rates rose from 15 percent to 19.8 percent. The acquirer has to notify you in advance of any changes, so be alert—and prepared to switch.

RAM Research's CardTrak says that some of the best *low-rate* standard cards are offered by the following institutions:

Oak Brook Bank (Oak Brook, Illinois)—10.4-percent variable rate, $20 annual fee, 25-day grace period; 800 666-1011

People's Bank (Bridgeport, Connecticut)—11.5-percent fixed rate, $25 annual fee, 25-day grace period; 800 423-3273

Bank of Montana (Great Falls, Montana)—11.75-percent variable rate, $19 annual fee, 25-day grace period; 800 735-5536

Armed Forces Benefit Association Industrial Bank (Alexandria, Virginia)—12.5-percent variable rate, no annual fee, 25-day grace period; 800 776-2322

USAA Federal Savings (Tulsa, Oklahoma)—12.5-percent variable rate, no annual fee, 25-day grace period; 800 922-9092

Among the outstanding *low-rate* gold cards for people with excellent credit histories and incomes of at least $25,000 are the following:

Wachovia Bank (Wilmington, Delaware)—8.9-percent variable rate, $49 annual fee, 25-day grace period; 800 842-3262

Central Carolina (Durham, North Carolina)—9-percent variable rate, $20 annual fee, 25-day grace period; 800 672-2539

Amalgamated Bank of Chicago (Chicago)—11-percent variable rate, no annual fee, 25-day grace period; 800 365-6464

People's Bank (Bridgeport, Connecticut)—11.5-percent fixed rate, $40 annual fee, 25-day grace period; 800 423-3273

Armed Forces Benefit Association Industrial Bank (Alexandria, Virginia)—12.5-percent variable rate, no annual fee, 25-day grace period; 800 776-2322

(Note: Most issuers on both lists accept approximately 30 percent of all applicants, although the Bank of Montana is somewhat more finicky.)

HOW TO CARRY A BALANCE

If you carry a balance on a credit card, you can usually save money by making your payment as soon as you get the bill. When the card issuer receives your check, it immediately credits the account, thus reducing your average daily balance, the amount upon which next month's finance charges will most commonly be based. Wait until just before the due date, however, and your average balance will be higher—and you'll probably pay more interest.

If you pay in full, wait until just before the due date.

WHAT YOU SHOULD AND SHOULDN'T CARRY

Most people carry too many cards. As a result, they're either paying too much in annual fees or carrying too much impulse-buying firepower—or both.

If you're a typical consumer, two or three credit cards should be more than enough. Which two or three? For most people, a no-fee card with a grace period and a high credit limit for convenience purchases, perhaps a low-interest-rate card for borrowing and emergencies, and a gold card or travel-and-entertainment card for business purposes or for traveling (if you use the card for business, the annual fee is tax-deductible).

So what should you dump? Almost any card issued by a retailer is a good candidate for the trash. Although the cards don't charge annual fees, their interest rates are usually extremely high, even by credit-card standards. The nation's most popular single piece of plastic, the Sears credit card, charges an appalling 21-percent interest rate in some states—3 percentage points above the national average, and 15 points over prime as we went to press!

Five or ten years ago, some major department stores refused to accept Visa or MasterCard, so having a store card seemed logical. But the stores capitulated; they now accept bank cards. (Because of the discount fee, they'll never *welcome* them.)

If you use store cards to finance purchases, stop right now. Get another cheap bank card instead. The only good reasons to have a card are to stay on the store's mailing list (a quick phone call could accomplish this) and to take advantage of the occasional discounts and special promotions available only to cardholders.

Other smart discards might include affinity cards connected to charities, organizations, or sports teams (many make emotional but not financial sense), and T&E cards that merely duplicate one another (do you really need American Express, Diners Club, *and* Carte Blanche?). Also get rid of any cards whose presence and purpose seem mysterious. The "Today" show co-host Katie Couric once mentioned on-air that she had three American Express cards, although she had no idea *why*. Three of a kind often works well in poker, but it's rarely a winner for your wallet.

JUST LIKE MONEY—ONLY BETTER?

One good reason to weed your credit-card portfolio is that plastic can be hazardous to your financial health even if you never pay finance charges or annual fees. People who shop with credit cards spend more than those who pay by cash or check, no matter what the purchase price. A 1990 test conducted by Discover at Arby's—of all places—found that credit-card customers spent 40 percent more per meal than cash customers ($7 versus $5). (For years, American Express has defended its higher discount fees by flaunting research showing that Amex customers spend more than those paying with Visa or MasterCard.)

THE CASH-ADVANCE TRAP

Sometimes the combined finance charge and transaction cost of a cash advance can make you nostalgic for loan sharks. Yet some people use cash advances the way others use ATM cards—as the standard method of rapid cash acquisition. This is a big mistake.

If you're going to get a cash advance, be sure you know the rate you'll pay. It's often several percentage points higher than the normal credit-card rate. Optima, for example, charges some customers 12 percent for credit-card purchases but 16.9 percent for cash advances.

Recognize, too, that the "small" transaction costs can really mount up if you go to the well too often. Some cards assess a flat fee for all cash advances (usually $1 to $10), while others charge a percentage of the amount withdrawn (1 percent to 5 percent, with a cap usually, but not always, at $10). Realize as well that for more than 99 percent of the credit cards in America, there is no grace period for cash advances. You draw your advance one minute, then begin paying interest the next—no matter when you pay the money back.

Worse than that, though, is the fact that with many cards, taking a cash advance triggers finance charges on your *existing* balance as well. Consider this extreme—and extremely unpleasant—example. On Monday your balance was zero. On Tuesday you charged $1,000 worth of goods. On Friday you took out a cash advance for $50. If you did this with a 19.8 percent card, you could pay 19.8 percent interest on $1,050, not $50, as soon as you pocket the fifty bucks. That's $17.33 in interest for one month. Add in the transaction fee of $1 and your total interest cost for borrowing the $50 could be as much as 36.7 percent for the first month, or 440 percent on an annualized basis.

Let's tone down the example. Again, assume an interest rate of 19.8 percent. If your existing balance is $1,000 and you take an advance of $500, you'll probably pay a $10 fee (the standard fee is 2 percent) plus $24.75 in interest for the first month. That's a cost of $34.75 to borrow $500 for one month, or 83.4 percent on an annualized basis.

It's not hard to avoid those extra charges on pre-existing balances. Either call the credit-card issuer's toll-free number and ask about its policy, or, if you're feeling masochistic, read the fine print in your credit agreement.

(Note: Cash advances don't help you earn rebates.)

CREDIT LIMITS

Although the practice of sending unsolicited credit cards through the mail has been outlawed, it is still legal for card issuers to raise your limit unilaterally, without consulting you. This may be just what you need, or it could represent the kind of temptation you know isn't good for you. If you see the credit-limit increase as a potential liability, refuse it. Call the issuer and say, "Thanks, but no thanks."

If you do want more credit rather than less, however, be aware of one of the major misconceptions about credit cards—that only gold cards offer high lines of credit. True, standard cards usually start off with lower limits than their gilded cousins, but you can request that your limit be raised several times a year. In many instances, it can be raised to $5,000 or $7,000 fairly quickly. So if a high credit limit is the reason you've gone for the gold and are paying a significantly higher annual fee, think again. (Generally, when you ask to have your limit raised, the lender's follow-up procedure will register as an "inquiry" on your credit report, as discussed in chapter 5.)

Sometimes it may pay to maintain a higher credit limit than you think you need. It can be an important cushion, for instance, when you're traveling and using your card to reserve hotel rooms and rental cars. When they take your card number, hotels and rental-car companies place a hold on some of your spending power. To protect themselves, they tie up an amount greater than the charges you'll actually incur. But this doesn't protect *you*. If you're planning a long trip, these "holds" can gobble up all your available credit. The solution? A high credit limit or a second credit card.

THE RIGHT WAY
TO THINK ABOUT CREDIT CARDS

When interest rates shot up in the late seventies and early eighties, smart credit-card holders discovered a new way to mint money. Because many state usury laws then capped credit-card interest rates at 12 percent, people took out cash advances at 12 percent and immediately put the proceeds into money-market funds with yields above 12 percent—a classic no-risk arbitrage play.

Well, today every state except Arkansas has a usury ceiling of at least 18 percent. With money-market fund yields now far lower, the old cash-advance ploy won't cut it anymore. (Please don't try it.) But now there's a new wrinkle.

First publicized by Harvard Business School finance professor Michael E. Edleson in a *Money* magazine article, the technique works only with credit cards that have grace periods on cash advances and caps on cash-advance fees. The list of such cards is not long; in fact, it could hardly be shorter. It includes the AT&T Universal card (800 662-7759) and Visa and MasterCards issued by Fidelity National

Bank of Atlanta (800 753-2900). It included Discover, as well, until December 1991, when the issuer took the $10 cap off its cash-advance fee.

In 1991, Edleson, who had two Discover cards with $7,500 credit limits, earned about $800 in interest through creative cash advancement. A third of his Harvard finance students profited from the loophole as well.

Here's how it might work today. Fidelity National Bank of Atlanta charges no interest on cash advances repaid within its 25-day grace period. The only charge for the transaction is the 4-percent cash-advance fee, with a minimum charge of $5 and a maximum of $25. Such fees can make small advances ridiculously expensive (a $200 advance paid off in 25 days would have an $8 fee—and a 57-percent annual interest rate), but they are relatively insignificant on large amounts, especially if you maximize the time you get to use the money without paying a finance charge. (AT&T's fee is 2.5 percent, with a minimum of $2 and a maximum of $20.)

Let's say the closing date for your May statement is May 24 (the date appears on your monthly bill). On that day, you use one of the card's convenience checks to make a $10,000 payment to your money-market fund.

Six days later, on May 30, your monthly statement arrives. It will not mention the cash advance at all, but if there are any other charges outstanding, be sure to pay them off before the grace period ends on June 18.

A month later, on June 30, the June statement arrives, revealing that you owe $10,000, plus the $25 transaction fee. On July 10, write a money-market check for $10,025 to the credit-card issuer. It should clear about three days before the end of the grace period, thus averting all finance charges.

The annualized interest rate on this 50-day loan is a phenomenal 1.8 percent. So if you can find an investment yielding more than 1.8 percent, you can profit from the interest-rate spread, thus pocketing hundreds of dollars a year. (With AT&T, the rate would be 1.44 percent.)

Is the system foolproof? Yes, if you follow the timetable precisely and the post office does its part—and if your investment is a secure one. But beware: You have to pay off all purchases made the month before and the month after the cash advance or you'll get socked with a finance charge. If you can remember that detail, it's easy to put the Edleson plan into action six times a year on each card.

And a couple could do this with four cards, if each person had a regular card and a premium card. If all the cards had $11,000 limits, two people could earn over $1,400 a year in interest, after transaction fees, if they used the cards exclusively for cash advances and deposited the proceeds in a fund yielding 6 percent. (You watch: someday we'll see 6-percent money-market funds again.) At 4 percent, the couple could earn more than $700 a year; at 3 percent, over $400.

On an hourly basis, this money-making scheme offers fantastic returns, but that doesn't mean it's right for you. Adding more details to worry about to an already overcrowded life just may not be worth it. Furthermore, the returns won't be as impressive if you're at all careless.

Still, you can make money even if you take advantage of the loophole only once or twice. So keep it in mind if you ever need a short-term loan or have to cope with a temporary financial emergency.

Finally, if you sometimes pay checking-account fees because your monthly balance drops below the bank's limit of $1,500, $3,000, or $5,000, the cash-advance system could help you avoid those annoying charges while you earn additional interest.

CREDIT CARDS AND THE FLOAT

You can also profit from your cards without doing anything as complicated as the Edleson shuffle. If you pay off your credit-card balances each month, get in the habit of using plastic more often instead of writing a check or paying cash. By its very nature, plastic is a deferred-payment mechanism. It enables you to profit from the float without even trying. By adding just a little conscious effort, a consumer can save or make $50, $100, or more per year.

It helps to know the rules even if you don't intend to be fanatical about them. For example, to generate the greatest float time, you should make credit-card purchases at the very beginning of your billing cycle (as in the Edleson plan).

Some cards have staggered billing cycles (most notably American Express), so if you carry several it may make sense to use one card early in the month and another three weeks later. If you want to be truly methodical about this, you can write the billing-cycle dates on a piece of paper and tuck it in your wallet. (Don't try to play this game unless all your cards have grace periods of at least 25 days.)

Let's assume the time between the purchase date and the payment-due date ranges between 28 and 53 days and that you make your purchases randomly throughout the month. That means the average float time per purchase will be 40 days.

If your credit-card purchases total $1,500 a month and you invest that money in a money-market mutual fund (not an insured money-market account at a bank, which offers a poorer rate), you will earn interest of .25 percent a month if the fund yields 3 percent per year. But since you have the money for 40 days before paying off the bill, you're really earning .33 percent on the $1,500, or $59 in extra interest for an entire year. (At 4 percent, you'd earn an extra $79.)

You can increase your return by using a credit card (such as Discover) that will deduct payments from your checking account five days *after* your bill is due. Discover lets you set up an automatic payment program for either full payments or minimum payments (doing the latter locks you into a very nasty habit—and one which could have a 19.8-percent interest rate, to boot—so it's a bad idea).

Many people don't know how to float. Some, in fact, turn the tables on themselves with confused thinking. They shudder at using a credit card in a supermarket. "I don't want to pay 19-percent interest for my groceries," is how they reason. Well, no one should do that, but if you don't carry a balance, you're not paying 19 percent. Writing a check or paying cash means you're forgoing the opportunity to have your money earn interest. (Note: Floating with credit cards doesn't work if you carry balances from month to month. When you're paying finance charges, the grace period for new purchases is revoked.)

DEBIT CARDS

People who don't pay finance charges should shun debit cards. Debit cards are little plastic devices that look just like credit cards. They just steal your money in a different way. When you use a debit card, the purchase amount is instantly subtracted from your bank balance. You begin losing interest income faster than if you had paid by check. There's no waiting period for anything to clear.

On the other hand, debit cards may make sense for people who know they can't trust themselves with credit cards. The cards can be more convenient than checks and the money you'll lose on the float each year may not be worth worrying about.

Debit cards can save you a trip to the cash machine. They may be especially convenient for men, who are less likely than women to have their checkbooks with them when they're at a store.

But in the event of a dispute with a merchant, a consumer who used a credit card has more leverage than one who used a debit card.

NO SUCH THING AS A MINIMUM

Many merchants display signs announcing credit-card purchase "minimums" ($10, $15, $20, and $25 are the most common amounts). Did you know they can't do this? Requiring any minimum purchase is an explicit violation of the merchant's agreement with Visa and MasterCard. It is also clearly a violation of the spirit, if not absolutely the letter, of the pact with American Express.

The people who get hurt are those who live paycheck to paycheck and have exhausted their cash for the moment. They may be forced to buy some items they don't really need in order to cross the minimum-purchase threshold.

Clearly, Visa, MasterCard, and American Express have more pressing items on their agenda than policing the merchants whose sales keep them in business. Nonetheless, if you have some extra time, you might want to report the offending merchant to the bank that handles its credit-card receivables. If you have a credit-card receipt from the merchant, Visa, MasterCard, and American Express can tell you which bank to contact.

STATE REGULATIONS

Credit-card rates and fees vary from state to state. Consumers get a break in Maine, North Carolina, and Wisconsin, where credit-card interest rates cannot exceed 18 percent, and in Pennsylvania, where annual fees are capped at $15. Maine, Michigan, Minnesota, and North Carolina require that all cards issued to state residents have grace periods of at least 25 days.

Like many laws, however, these statutes can have a boomerang effect. Discover charges 18 percent (not 19.8 percent) on unpaid balances in North Carolina and Wisconsin but hits residents there with a $15 annual fee.

VARIABLE-RATE CARDS

In 1991 and 1992, many consumers with variable-rate credit cards benefited as the prime rate plummeted. The variable rate on AT&T's popular Universal card, which originally scared some consumer advocates because it could have jumped as high as 21.9 percent, instead headed south, hitting 14.9 percent. Does this mean that variables are a great deal?

If rates are still very low as you read this, be careful. Will the variable-rate card be a good deal if rates stabilize? What if they rise a bit? What if they soar? Is there a cap?

But don't spend too much time worrying, because card issuers can change the rules whenever they choose, as long as they give you 15 days' notice. For instance, as the prime rate dropped, some issuers of variable-rate cards raised their spread, or margin, over the prime rate. American Express's Optima card had an interest rate of 15.75 percent in December 1990. In December 1991, the prime was two and a half points lower, but Optima's rate had actually risen, to 16.25 percent.

How did this happen? In January 1991, Optima altered its rate formula from prime plus 5.75 points to prime plus 6.75 points. In October, it rose again, to prime plus 7.75 points. Since the rate adjusts only semiannually, customers have to wait a long time for rate reductions to be reflected in their finance charges.

9

THE GREEN MONSTER, OR WHY YOU SHOULD PROBABLY LEAVE HOME WITHOUT THE AMERICAN EXPRESS CARD

$One of the easiest and smartest ways to save money when you "borrow" is to get rid of your American Express card. You can save $55 a year on the annual fee, or $550 every 10 years. In truth, you can save much more if you count the interest earned on that money.

Granted, that won't make you rich, but the idea should prompt two important questions: Do I need the card? If I don't need it, then why do I have it?

Very few people really *need* the American Express card. Although Amex deserves a lot of credit for pioneering some fine customer services, that doesn't mean it deserves your business *today*.

Especially when almost all of those innovative membership privileges are available elsewhere for much less money—often for free. So why do I (a cardholder since 1983) and tens of millions of other consumers worldwide spend more than $1 billion a year in annual fees to carry Amex cards?

Habit and status seeking are probably the two leading reasons, but don't underestimate fear. Yes, fear. The marketing folks at Amex have done such a marvelous job—American Express ranks as the third-best-known brand name in the United States, behind only Coca-Cola and McDonald's—that many of us aren't sure what life would be like without the card. Carrying the card gives some of us that warm, fuzzy feeling marketers yearn to convey—when you like something without quite knowing why.

A brief confession. I was seeking status when I got my first American Express card. Back in 1983, when I was 28, I thought the green card was the proper piece of plastic to flash when entertaining clients or journalistic sources. I figured a bank card would make me appear cheap, second-class, and immature—a financial geek. I wanted to feel grown-up, to be a man of the world, a sophisticated consumer; and Amex's annual fee seemed a small enough price to pay.

It was largely a defensive social move. I didn't think an American Express card *proved* that I had made it. I worried, though, that displaying a bank card might convince people I hadn't.

Since then, the status gap between Amex and the bank cards has narrowed dramatically. Visa and MasterCard gold cards duplicate almost all Amex services. And sometimes they may actually be harder to acquire. (After all, you can get an American Express card without even having a job—just ask the hundreds of thousands of college students who receive card offers every year.)

Amex's most brilliant, and sometimes puzzling, achievement is that it has been so successful at mass-marketing status. There are *37 million* Amex cards out there—yet its cardholders' booklet states that "American Express Cardmembers enjoy a prestige that is associated with no other card. Cardmembers may feel this specialness as soon as they begin to use the card. When you use the card you may even notice that often you are served better and are accorded an added degree of respect."

In a delightful piece in *The New Republic* entitled "Leave Home Without It" (included in his book *The Money Culture*), *Liar's Poker* author Michael Lewis mocked Amex for its attempts to "manufacture" prestige at such high volume. To do so, he wrote, "requires 100 public relations specialists and (I am told) $350 million a year in ads and promotion. That's about ten dollars a year per card. Cardholders should know that nearly a fifth of their annual membership fee goes into ads to tell others: YOU CAN JOIN OUR EXCLUSIVE CLUB. Sort of defeats the purpose."

If overpaying for a label makes you feel better, and you can afford it, then be my guest. Just be aware, however, that in the 1990s, over-paying for anything has lost much of the cachet it had in the previous decade.

WHAT DO YOU GET BESIDES THE LABEL?

In the summer of 1991, Amex finally gave those who are seeking value a plausible reason for carrying the card. Not necessarily a good reason, mind you; just a plausible one. The Membership Miles program offers frequent-flier miles to cardholders, a perk matched by Diners Club and the airlines' own affinity cards.

Like the airline-card programs, Membership Miles gives you one mile for every dollar charged (charges of a spouse or other family member can be pooled with your own). Unlike the affinity cards, however, frequent-flier miles earned with Amex are good on five air-lines instead of just one. (Citicorp's Diners Club deal is even better—its miles can be used on any major airline.) The Amex-affiliated carriers, which control nearly half the U.S. traffic, are Delta, Northwest, Continental, Southwest, and MGM Grand Air. (Midway and Pan Am had been a part of the package, but they both went out of business.)

Miles accumulated under the Amex and Diners Club programs have a longer shelf life than those earned via the airline affinity offerings. Theoretically, they last forever. This makes the Amex and Diners Club programs preferable for people who don't spend enough—or travel enough—to earn free trips before their miles start expiring.

Membership in the Amex program, though, is not automatic. To be eligible, you have to charge $5,000 in 12 months. The annual cost is $25 a year after the first year. You must allow two or three weeks to transfer your Amex miles to an airline's frequent-flier program. All flights using frequent-flier miles must be booked through American Express Travel. (Call 800 297-1095 for further information.)

Many of the other supposed Amex benefits are really fairly hollow, although the company is known for providing extraordinarily good service to its "members" (at every step, Amex wants you to think you're part of a club).

• Many Amex cardholders can get a line of credit and pay an interest rate of prime plus 9 percent, but most people who do any credit shopping can find a better rate.

• The card allows you to get cash at more than 40,000 ATMs around the world (the per-transaction charge is $2 to $6), but if, like most people, you carry a bank ATM card and a Visa or MasterCard, you probably already have access to more than enough cash machines.

• By using Amex's Sign and Travel Account, you can pay off travel charges over a 36-month period, at an interest rate of prime plus 9. (This is a perk?)

• For $15 more per year, you can get the Optima card, which offers revolving credit at rates ranging from 12 percent to 18.25 percent. You could do worse; you could do better.

• Amex offers members a savings program as well. Select an amount between $50 and $5,000, and Amex will bill you each month for that sum, which it will then deposit in a savings account. The yield: one-half of one percentage point better than the average bank money-market account. A quick look at the leading yields in *Money* magazine will tell you that you can do far better on your own.

• Some establishments accept no other credit cards. This is true at very few places—and only because Amex has been so good at giving them financial and marketing incentives to shun all other plastic (selectively lowering its merchant discount rate and offering compliant merchants free advertising). Neiman Marcus and Bergdorf Goodman won't take Visa or MasterCard, but they'll quickly give out their own store cards if you ask.

Some top restaurants take only Amex, so if you entertain clients often you may really need the card. In pushing this "benefit," of course, Amex is not exactly leading from strength: it is accepted by 3.5 million establishments worldwide; Visa and MasterCard, by 9.2 million. If you carry nothing but Amex, make sure you've always got a barrowful of cash as well.

• With Amex, there's no preset spending limit. But try to charge a Mercedes and see what happens. Every card has a fluctuating limit based on recent purchase activity, personal assets, and income (I guess that means it's "reset" rather than "preset"). Trouble is, the company refuses to tell you what it is, even when pestered. So this "advantage" can turn into an embarrassing liability if you ever try to charge more in a month than Amex thinks you should. (Amex calls such behavior "an out-of-pattern spend.")

• Members have access to a worldwide network of travel-service offices, which can arrange personal and business travel and cash checks.

The service can book you a flight and a hotel, just like any travel agent.

• Some of the perks of membership are undeniably nice. The long list includes Buyer's Assurance warranty extension, Purchase Protection theft and accident "insurance," Car Rental Loss and Damage Insurance, travel accident insurance, emergency cash, Be My Guest certificates (which allow you to "host" a guest when you're not there by allowing his or her meal, plus tax and tip, to be charged to your account), and the Global Assist Hotline (medical and legal referrals worldwide 24 hours a day, pretrip information on weather, exchange rates, innoculations, customs, and so on). Although many of these services were pioneered by Amex, most have been pretty much matched by Visa and MasterCard gold-card programs (and even by Citibank's regular-card program). You can get the same for less by looking elsewhere. (Be My Guest, though, remains an Amex exclusive.)

MOVING UP TO GOLD

The Amex gold card, which costs $75 per year, provides some additional goodies. People can live without them, but they might make the card just the thing for you. The perks include club membership privileges at 90 private dining, country, and athletic clubs; a year-end summary of charges, broken down by month and category; Gold Card Events, which provides members with "exclusive or preferential" seating at certain theatrical, cultural, and sporting events; and Envoy, a more personalized 24-hour-a-day travel service, which can secure theater tickets in New York or London, among other things.

GOING PLATINUM

For some people, the $300-a-year Amex Platinum card, the nation's most expensive card, may be the best consumer value. No kidding.

When Amex introduced the card in 1984, it was little more than an egregious status ploy—another item in an insufferable Wall Streeter's perfect wardrobe and a vivid example of what Thorstein Veblen called "invidious comparison" ("My credit line's bigger than yours").

But in the late eighties, after a few hundred thousand white-collar people were laid off following the stock-market crash, Amex realized that some American consumers had lost their taste for glitz without value. (At the very least, it was now chic to *say* you were into value rather than status.) So the company has been adding features you can't find elsewhere and emphasizing the right reasons for getting the card.

What might they be? A much higher credit line—up to $100,000 —for starters. And free traveler's checks (although you'd have to use $30,000 worth each year to offset the $300 annual fee).

But the card can save you $160 a year if you're a member of the Northwest Airlines World Club ($110 per year) and the Hertz #1 Club ($50 per year): with the Platinum card, membership is free. The Hertz perk gives you everything but a chauffeur. At twenty-five airports in the United States, it lets you bypass both the riffraff counter and the express counter. Your preprinted agreement is attached to your car. Depending on the weather, either the heat or the air conditioning will already be turned on.

The card's Worldwide Personal Assistance is like having access to a round-the-clock concierge with global reach—very nice, if you can ever use that sort of thing. In addition to retrieving lost items from around the world or arranging for translators, babysitters, and computer rentals, the service can accomplish more exotic tasks. It located and purchased a Del Grange saddle in a French shop and shipped it to an American rider. It suggested and arranged a romantic gift for newlyweds in Spain. It had a cooked turkey delivered to a family in Salzburg, Austria, on Thanksgiving.

You also get free room upgrades, complimentary continental breakfasts, and late checkout at 120 leading hotels and resorts. At many of these same hotels, you may also receive "preferred welcome"—which usually translates into a large basket of fruit and an extraordinary display of toadying by the assistant manager. Both can be quite enjoyable. (Note: Use your corporate discount, and the upgrade privileges are void.)

At 120 top restaurants in the United States and Canada, Amex reserves one table at lunch and dinner exclusively for Platinum-card holders, which ostensibly means you have a better chance of getting a last-minute table at a posh place. Call a toll-free number and an Amex employee will discuss the cuisine, cost, and critical reputation of a particular restaurant.

Under the By Invitation Only program, cardholders can meet World Cup skiers, attend a private forum with *New Republic* editors (without, presumably, *New Republic* senior editor Michael Lewis), and have special access to gallery openings, screenings, and various celebrity events.

Wherever you are, the card's Personalized Travel Service can deal with unusual travel needs. "One of our paralegals once had her airplane ticket stolen in Panama City," says Robert L. Tucker, a New York trademark and international licensing lawyer. "Platinum Travel arranged everything very smoothly." The service also provides free emergency evacuation if you get sick while traveling.

Tucker, who often travels abroad on business, can't imagine using any other card. "First, I want the card's higher credit limit, because I never want to be in a situation where I can't buy a ticket to anywhere in the world," he says. "I also find the card is the quickest and easiest way to find out the phone number or fax number of a hotel in, say, Seoul."

And what about status? "It doesn't mean much here," says Tucker, "but in Europe people are often impressed because the card is almost nonexistent there."

CONCLUSION

For most of us, however, all these perks aren't valuable enough. Still, there may be a few reasons to acquire a regular American Express card. If you like getting mail—lots of mail—nothing can match it. (The endless stream of direct-mail pitches from Amex generates annual revenues of over $700 million for the company, making it the country's fifth-leading direct-mail merchandiser. *You* may not be buying, but someone certainly is.)

Getting the card may also be a good idea if you're determined not to carry a balance from month to month and suspect you lack the discipline to pay in full. This doesn't make a lot of sense to me, although I know people who swear by the approach. If that describes you, at least be honest about how you're using the card. Recognize that you're paying $55 a year for a bit of will power you might be able to acquire for free. (Despite the annual fee, some credit experts and financial planners consider the card an excellent money-management tool, precisely because people feel they have to pay off their monthly balance, no matter what.)

So why do I still have my green card? Well, I write off the annual fee as a business expense, part of my never-ending research on the subject of personal finance. Does this explanation satisfy me? Not really. I may get rid of the card next year.

If, after reading this chapter, you're not sure why you have yours, then try an experiment. Drop the card for a year. See what happens. Find out if the world suddenly treats you with less respect. Put the $55 in your DSF kitty, or spend it frivolously.

And if life without the card is simply unbearable, renew your membership. I think they'll let you back in the club.

10

THE STRANGE—
AND SOMETIMES WONDERFUL—
WORLD OF CREDIT-CARD PERKS

$ A few years ago, a man who had just purchased an expensive watch brought a prostitute up to his hotel room. Some time after the woman departed, the man discovered that she had stolen his watch. Luckily, he had acquired the watch with a credit card—one of the many cards promising compensation if an item is damaged or stolen within 90 days of purchase. So he filed a claim, dutifully mentioning the hooker. The card issuer, perhaps reasoning that no one would make up such a story, reimbursed the man for his loss.

Recently, another man was whooshing down a Colorado ski slope when the toupee he had just purchased flew off his head. The hairpiece was ruined. But it had been acquired with a Visa gold card, so this man filed a claim as well. After receiving his money, he sent Visa an extraordinarily warm thank-you letter.

Premium cards can pay off. Although it's not always easy to collect on a claim, as we shall see, the cards do provide many potentially attractive enhancements. But will your new toupee ever actually take flight while you're visiting Vail? And will you ever have your newly purchased watch swiped by a newly purchased friend? In short, do you really need a gold card?

FOOL'S GOLD?

Most people don't. Certainly, you shouldn't have one because you think it's a status symbol. There are now *50 million* gold cards in America. Everybody's got 'em. The death knell for any status grab was sounded in March 1990, when AT&T introduced its Universal card, which was available only in the gilded form, and for free, no less.

Nor is it necessarily logical to pay extra money for a gold card simply because you want a higher line of credit. True, gold cards start with higher limits—$5,000 is typical—but there's no actual credit cap on standard cards. If you can get a $5,000 line on a gold card, you can get one on a standard card as well—eventually. You can have your limit raised by fairly large increments several times a year. How? Just call the card's toll-free number and ask.

But what about all those enhancements? Surely they must be worth something. Well, the president of Bankcard Holders of America, Elgie Holstein, estimates that only 3 percent of all gold-card holders ever profit from an enhancement. An industry survey revealed that MasterCard users take advantage of the Purchase Assurance feature less than once in every 10,000 purchases.

PERKS GALORE

For millions of people, especially frequent travelers, cards loaded with enhancements can be extremely valuable tools. Among the key benefits provided by all premium cards are the following:

Car rental insurance. If you don't own a car but occasionally rent one, this is reason enough to have a gold card. When you rent with a gold card, the collision damage waiver (CDW)—now often called the loss damage waiver (LDW)—is automatically covered. In the event of an accident, the CDW, which usually costs about $12, and sometimes $15, per day, covers the deductible. These days, the deductible is often thousands of dollars, so going naked can be risky. (Note: Rent a car for 15 consecutive days or more and you lose this perk.)

If you have car insurance, you don't need the CDW; your policy will cover the deductible. Even so, a gold card may provide you with some extra peace of mind at the rental counter if you, like many others, automatically get nervous whenever you decline any insurance coverage. (Note: If you're renting in New York, Illinois, or Maryland, there's no need to worry about anything; those states have banned the CDW altogether.)

Purchase insurance. Your purchases are insured against theft, fire, or accidental damage, and breakage for 90 days after purchase, for up to $1,000 per occurrence. This sounds better than it really is. Yes, awful things do happen to consumer goods, but seldom within the first 90 days of ownership. Besides, this is secondary coverage; it only applies after your other policies (homeowner's, auto, etc.) have paid off.

(Warning: The coverage does not include anything stolen from a car or any jewelry, cameras, or video-recording equipment placed in checked baggage. See page 114 for other exceptions.)

Extended warranties. This feature doubles the manufacturer's warranty period, up to a maximum of one additional year. Be sure to save your credit-card receipt and all warranty information.

Medical assistance. When you're traveling more than 100 miles from home, premium-card issuers will help you get medical assistance, prescription information, and most kinds of emergency help—including emergency evacuation. In every instance, you or your health-insurance provider will pick up the tab.

Legal assistance. Think *Midnight Express*. If you're traveling and need a local lawyer, card issuers will provide referrals or the names of appropriate contacts at consulates and embassies.

Emergency road assistance. Perhaps this, more than any other benefit, illustrates that premium-card perks are primarily marketing tools and advertising gimmicks rather than services real customers might actually use someday. Consumers absolutely love this promised perk. Imagine: You break down on the highway, call a toll-free number, and, presto, the fix-it crew arrives. (As it happens, many consumers also think that they won't have to pay for the repair work, but the fine print indicates otherwise.) "Very few people will ever use this," says Holstein. "Besides, it's probably more valuable to belong to AAA or a gasoline-company road club, anyway." (In 1992 AT&T eliminated its emergency road assistance feature.)

Emergency card replacement. If you ever lose all your credit cards, cash, and traveler's checks while traveling, this benefit could be very helpful. Within 48 hours, the card issuer will provide you with a replacement card and emergency cash (the maximum amount is either the difference between your current balance and your credit limit or $5,000, whichever is less). Because it's unlikely that a couple will ever lose all their cash, checks, and plastic simultaneously, this perk is more valuable for people who travel alone. (Some standard cards, such as Citibank's, also provide this benefit.)

STILL MORE PERKS

Some premium cards provide other benefits as well. You probably haven't heard of many of the banks offering these extras, but don't let that worry you. Remember, it's the banks you haven't heard of that usually have the best deals, and every institution listed below offers gold cards with low rates and fees. Besides, there's no indication that smaller institutions stint on service. In fact, the opposite is often true.

Additional perks include the following:

Free credit-card registration. This lets you avoid the annoyance of notifying creditors when your cards are lost or stolen. Not worth paying for, but nice if you can get it free. Offered by the Bank of Hawaii, Bay Bank of Waltham (Massachusetts), First American Bank of Virginia, the Bank of New York, First Union Bank, and others.

Car rental discounts. The Bank of Hawaii, Bay Bank, the Bank of New York, Wachovia, NationsBank, and others.

Travel discounts. Chemical Bank, NationsBank, USAA Federal, and others.

Discount buying service. The Bank of New York, USAA Federal, Citibank, and others.

Free traveler's checks. First Virginia Bank and Amex Platinum.

Free merchandise. The more you spend, the more "bonus bucks" you earn, all redeemable for free goods. Fleet Bank New Hampshire; some standard cards, such as Citibank's, offer their own version.

Year-end summary of charges. Chemical Bank, USAA Federal, and Amex Gold.

Price protection. Chemical Bank gold-card carriers get Price Assurance, a benefit pioneered by Arizona's Valley National Bank and later popularized by Citibank (for its standard cards). If you buy an item with your Chemical gold card and within 60 days see it advertised at a lower price, you can pocket the difference—up to $250. You have to save your original receipt and the printed ad, and send them to Chemical within 10 days of the ad's appearance. There's a $1,000 annual cap on how much you can save. Exempt items include aircraft, watercraft, vehicles, meals, tickets of any kind (planes, trains, etc.), collectibles, antiques, food, fuel, animals, plants, jewelry purchased outside the United States, custom dental appliances, or anything purchased for business purposes. Going-out-of-business sales and closeout sales are also exempt. Citibank's Price Protection terms are virtually identical.

This can be a nice perk if you have the time, energy, and discipline to utilize it.

Here's how to contact the issuers mentioned in this chapter:
American Express—800 843-2273
Bay Bank—800 221-3393
Bank of Hawaii—808 543-9611
Bank of New York—800 942-1977
Chemical Bank—800 722-4653
Citibank—800 843-0777
First American Bank—800 572-4004
First Union—800 359-3862 (in North Carolina, 704 374-6161)
Fleet Bank New Hampshire—800 537-3777 (in New Hampshire, 603 880-5000)
NationsBank—800 548-2959
USAA Federal—800 922-9092
Valley National Bank—800 862-2427
Wachovia—800 842-3262 (in Georgia, 404 841-7641)

CASHING IN

If you're the type who's never had the time to switch to a lower-rate credit card even though you always meant to, then don't assume you'll take advantage of premium-card enhancements simply because they are there. Cashing in on an enhancement isn't the hardest thing you'll ever do—but it can be a bit difficult.

Actually, if you read the premium-card brochures too carefully, you might never file a claim at all. What the brochures promise with one hand they seem to take away with the other. In just the first two paragraphs of the 1991 Gold MasterCard "Guide to Benefits," the word "however" is used four times, and the dispiriting phrases "we cannot be held responsible," "situations arise that are beyond our control," and "despite our best efforts" each appear twice. (This is what lawyers call good writing.) I don't recall hearing those words in any MasterCard commercials. (However, if I am wrong, I cannot be held responsible.)

Yes, there *are* many fine-print exceptions. Your Purchase Assurance windfall goes out the window if the loss is caused by vermin, war, civil hostilities of any kind, public officials acting in a confiscatory capacity, normal wear and tear, radioactive contamination, or acts of God (flood, hurricane, earthquake). A theft is covered only if a police report is filed within 36 hours of the incident.

"You also have to jump through a fair number of hoops to get your money," says RAM Research president Robert McKinley. You may have to get certification letters from your insurance companies indicating that you're not otherwise covered. Occasionally, you'll have to send the damaged item to the credit-card issuer as well—at your expense—before any compensation is authorized.

GOLD-CARD ALTERNATIVES

You don't necessarily have to get a premium card to get premium features. Citibank's classic (i.e., standard) Visa and MasterCard, which carry annual fees of $20, offer many of the same benefits. The no-fee standard card from Abbott Bank (800 999-6977) offers virtually all of them and is a terrific deal.

The regular green American Express card ($55 per year) matches almost all of them, with the exception of emergency road assistance. In addition, if you use Amex to charge a trip, you automatically get $100,000 in life insurance (there are nice dismemberment benefits, too). See chapter 9 for more on the pros and cons of this card.

CONCLUSION

If, after all this, you're still uncertain about the value of credit-card perks, don't worry. A nearly foolproof solution does exist. Get a gold card with no annual fee (see the list in chapter 8).

11

AFFINITY CARDS: ELVIS, BASS ANGLING, FREQUENT FLYING, AND OTHER DELIGHTS

$ When affinity cards were introduced more than a decade ago, some thought they might eventually dominate the credit-card landscape. After all, the cards seemed to provide users with the best of all worlds: an interest-rate break *and* the chance to carry plastic with special personal appeal.

Certainly the cards were diverse enough, with plastic proffered by organizations such as the National Education Association, the Foundation for North American Wild Sheep, the Boston Celtics, the Environmental Defense Fund, the Society for the Preservation and Encouragement of Barber Shop Quartet Singing in America, the Elvis Presley Memorial Foundation, the Foundation for AIDS Research, Breyer's ice cream, Nikon cameras, and Young Astronauts of Utah. You could carry cards from Defenders of Wildlife or the National Rifle Association—or both, if you like to keep people guessing.

It has gradually become clear, however, that for most consumers affinity cards are neither fish nor fowl (except for the cards offered by Bass Anglers and Ducks Unlimited, which most emphatically are). Most cardholders can find a better deal elsewhere. Affinity-card interest rates are now about one or two percentage points below the national average, which is nice, but nowhere near rock bottom. Their annual fees tend to be slightly higher than average, as well.

Furthermore, cardholders who use affinity cards because they want to give money to a cause might be shocked at the paltriness of their

115

actual contribution. Affinity groups usually get .5 percent of a card-holder's annual charge volume but may receive only a few dollars of the annual fee. The typical affinity card earns the sponsoring group $10 to $20 per year.

In fact, some charities offering affinity cards have come to loathe them. Instead of constituting an exciting new source of funds, the cards can become a drain. Many consumers figure that since they're already shelling out money for the card, they no longer have to make an annual contribution to the organization. If you care about both the cause and your wallet, the optimal approach is to get the cheapest credit card you can find and write a separate check to your favorite charity. (In case you're wondering, the IRS has ruled that affinity-card annual fees are not charitable contributions, so you can't deduct them. If you use the card for business purposes, though, you may be able to deduct the fee as a business expense.)

I GAVE AT THE OFFICE

The most popular affinity cards are offered by labor unions and professional associations, among them the National Education Association (the largest, with 6 million cardholders), the AFL-CIO, the American Bar Association, and the American Medical Association.

The National Education Association has one of the better affinity deals around. Regular and gold cards have a 15.9-percent interest rate and a $9 annual fee. In addition, the cards have a cute gimmick; they allow members to skip payments in June, July, and August (when educator income is sometimes lower). Considering how underpaid educators are in general, it's nice they get at least a little break on their credit cards (although, of course, finance charges keep accumulating).

Some deals are even better. With a standard Union MasterCard from Amalgamated Bank of Chicago (800 365-6464) you get an 11-percent rate and no annual fee. An AFL-CIO Union Privilege card offered by the Bank of New York (202 336-5460) has an 11-percent rate and no fee, but no grace period.

AIRLINE CARDS

Every major airline offers an affinity card, which delivers one frequent-flier mile for every dollar charged. (The American Express card and

Diners Club have similar programs, as discussed in chapter 9.) But if you're not a big spender, or if you carry a balance from month to month, think twice before climbing aboard.

The annual fees ($25 to $100) and interest rates (up to 19.8 percent) can be sky-high, although some excellent deals are available. Since the value of a frequent-flier mile is roughly one to two cents, you should probably spend at least $5,000 a year on the card—and use all your miles—to recoup the annual fee.

For some frequent spenders, the cards are ideal. "When I spend too much at Saks with my American Airlines card," says one friend, "at least it's a comfort to know that I'm helping to pay for my next vacation." The logic isn't perfect here—in fact, it's downright dangerous—but you get the idea.

Some megaconsumers capitalized on the United Airlines program so well that the airline changed the rules. In mid-1991, United and First Chicago, which issues the carrier's affinity card, announced that 1.5 percent of their cardholders were charging more than $50,000 a year—25 times the annual average. Parents were charging college tuition. Doctors were using the cards to buy medical supplies for their offices.

Under the new rules for First Chicago's United Mileage Plus First card, users cannot charge more than $10,000 in any 25-day period or $50,000 in an entire year. First Chicago eased the pain of the new rules somewhat by reducing the annual fee from $75 to $60, but the variable interest rate remained fairly high, at prime plus 9.9 percent.

NationsBank has imposed similar restrictions for its USAir card. But determined cardholders may be able to circumvent such limits by taking out an additional card for a spouse or a child.

Some airlines, though, are still trying to find new ways to hand out free miles. For every $10 you keep on deposit in the American Airlines money-market fund, you get one frequent-flier mile. The fund has very competitive rates but a minimum balance requirement of $10,000.

MORE THAN ONE WAY TO GET A MILE

Most frequent-flier cards permit links with long-distance phone companies, thus providing an easy way to accumulate 50, 100, or 200 additional miles every month—possibly more, if you have your own business or a lot of far-flung friends.

If you're really determined to rack up the miles, you might consider charging:

- home- or auto-loan payments (GMAC accepts car-loan payments via credit card, as do some banks)
- your state and property taxes
- a car (some desperate dealers will acquiesce)

But how do you charge a $20,000 car when your credit limit is $5,000? It can be done, says Randy Petersen, editor and publisher of *InsideFlyer*, the Colorado Springs–based newsletter for frequent fliers. Line up your auto loan and have the financial institution wire the money to your credit-card account. In some cases, this will raise your effective credit limit and permit you to charge the car. It's a quick and relatively painless way to earn a free trip. If you try to do this with the Chase TWA card before getting prior approval, however, the issuer will suspect fraud and close the account. So call ahead to make reservations. With advance warning, many card issuers will let you boost your credit limit via a money transfer—if your excuse sounds legitimate (an extended business trip or a round-the-world honeymoon, perhaps).

Warning: Finding a dealer who'll accept plastic won't be easy. After all, on a $20,000 car, the 2-percent merchant discount fee would cost the dealer $400.

ELVIS AND THE CELTICS

And what of those cards catering to a more specialized audience? Well, some have been absolute flops, among them the Gone with the Wind, Classic Chevy, Breyer's ice cream, and Foundation for AIDS Research cards. Major successes include cards for sports teams with particularly rabid fans (and, perhaps not coincidentally, tremendous winning traditions), such as the Boston Celtics and the University of Kentucky Wildcats basketball team.

The Elvis card still lives, although it hasn't been a big hit. If you want to carry a black credit card featuring Elvis in a dinner jacket, you still can. Ten thousand people—65 percent of them women—do. The standard Elvis MasterCard, offered by the Leader Federal Bank of Memphis, has an annual fee of $36 and a 17.8-percent interest rate.

The main beneficiary of the proceeds is the Elvis Presley Memorial Foundation, which uses much of its income to provide music scholarships.

Who would carry such a card? "We don't think the users are really the hardcore Elvis fans," says Brad Champlin, executive vice-president at Leader Federal. "Cardholders are just trying to express an aspect of their personality."

Those seeking to project a tonier image could opt instead for a series of cards offered to people whose ancestors might have come over on the *Mayflower*. Actually, you can get cards in the Crest series even if your ancestors made landfall at Ellis Island or were convicted felons who helped Oglethorpe settle Georgia—as long as your family name suggests a more ancient or refined pedigree. Each card has your family crest, while the membership package includes a scroll with information on your family heritage. Finally, you get discounts on catalogue items such as clothing, household goods, and books. The annual fee for a regular Crest Visa or MasterCard is $20; a gold card is $40. The interest rate averages 17.9 percent.

It might make sense to acquire one of these tiny niche cards as a conversation piece or because it has a very specific benefit that makes it right for you. Some automobile cards (including Saab and Volkswagen) offer discounts on auto parts, which may be useful if your Peugeot is a *citron*. The *Sports Illustrated* card provides discounts from sporting-good manufacturers and retailers, but not free copies of the magazine. Carry the Bass Angler's card, though, and you do get a free subscription to *Bass Master* magazine.

Beware of benefits that may not be quite what they seem. The proud holder of a Citibank NFL Visa card can get a "free" $37.45 tote bag with the logo of his or her favorite NFL team just by making $10,000 in credit-card purchases. Such a spending spree would be more "profitable" with an airline or cash-back bonus card.

Of course, when you carry a card that touches something close to your heart, precise financial considerations may not be the determining factor. Flashing a credit card from the Sierra Club, the Child Welfare League, or Vietnam Veterans of America can have its own incalculable value. And besides, if you're going to get ripped off on the interest rate and the annual fee, wouldn't you rather get snookered for a good cause?

THE MONEY FLOW

When groups sponsor affinity cards, they can earn money in many different ways. Among the possibilities are:

- receiving a portion of the total charge volume (.25 percent to .5 percent)
- taking a fee (typically, 25 cents) for every card transaction (this is a good deal for sponsors and is the approach favored by UNICEF and the Special Olympics)
- getting a cut of the annual fee
- accepting a one-time bonus for each cardholder who signs up (generally $1 to $5)

12

KIDS AND CREDIT

$In the summer of 1989, the Young Americans Bank of Denver shocked a lot of people by offering kiddie MasterCards, with an initial credit limit of $100, to anyone 12 and older who had a parent as a co-signer.

Critics wailed about unnecessary temptation, the corruption of the innocent, and lender depravity. A few worried that promoters would soon try to introduce youngsters to some of the world's other notorious evils, like drugs, alcohol, and politics. If so many parents have shown an inability to handle credit cards, they argued, why would anyone want to give them to kids? Was it merely coincidental, some wondered, that establishments where kids hang out—such as Arby's, McDonald's, Popeye's, and some movie theater chains—were starting to accept plastic?

Yes, the pro-spending symbolism of kiddie credit cards is initially troubling—no one claims the kids *need* them in case of an emergency at the mall—but, over time, the cards could be extremely beneficial. They're liberating. They help take the consumer-debt issue out of the closet.

And if parents find the cards frightening, that's fine, too. Talk about the fear. Tell children precisely what's so scary about the cute little plastic things. Talk about the horrible mistakes some people have made. Mention the Midwestern college student with $100,000 in credit-card debts. (I know of at least one.) Perhaps even acknowledge that you might have handled your credit cards differently if you could relive your life.

121

As a learning tool, a credit card may have great value. The cards can help teach kids about credit while you, the parent, are still nominally in control of their lives. You can look at their monthly statements and discuss how they're spending the money. And what if they screw up and stick you with a $100 bill for green hair dye and Alice in Chains or M. C. Brains CDs? Well, that should be a fairly cheap price to pay for some essential financial education. Better a $100 mistake in junior high than a $1,000 lulu in college.

Parents can help determine how effective this experiment with plastic will be. What will you say credit cards are for? Is their purpose to add $20 or $40 in finance charges to the cost of a $20 meal? Or are they for emergencies, convenience, profiting from the float, and occasionally buying on time because you just don't have enough cash right now? Think of this as an opportunity to discuss the borrowing "facts of life."

YOUNGER CHILDREN

To the long list of subjects American schools don't teach well, add money management. Some school administrators assume the topic is being thoroughly discussed at home. What do you think?

Steven Sanders, a partner in Philadelphia-based Hunt and Sanders Financial Advisors and national spokesperson for Money Matters for Young Adults (a program sponsored by Citibank), thinks parents generally underestimate kids' ability to understand money—and debt.

"If you allow a child to borrow against his allowance, be sure to charge him interest," says Sanders. Otherwise, you're giving him a false idea about how the world really works. And don't be too benevolent about the interest rate. Sanders suggests charging what a local bank would for an unsecured personal loan. (A few points too stiff, I think.) Whatever the rate, work out a repayment schedule and have the child stick to it.

When can children really grasp the borrowing concept? Probably by age 10 or 11. Just don't oblige them too often. If they become experts at the art of owing but never comprehend delayed gratification, you haven't entirely succeeded.

OLDER CHILDREN

Let's assume you didn't get a kiddie credit card for your child. In that case, what sort of plastic rite of passage makes sense? Although a student about to head off to college may clamor for a card in his or her name, the best way to start may be with an additional card linked to the parents' account. "There should probably be strict rules and regulations about its use," Sanders says. His suggested approved transactions? Emergencies, books, train or plane tickets, and perhaps recreation charges (with a clear monthly limit).

Here's how the president of a small Midwestern bank handled the issue. When his two children went to college, he gave them Visa cards linked to his account. The rule: The cards were to be used only for "meaningful purposes," which he described in bankerly detail. When an early bill revealed some large clothing purchases by his daughter, the father said, "We have to talk." That sort of misstep was not repeated. (As the child gets older, he or she should be responsible for reimbursing the parents for a rising percentage of such expenses.)

And if the child breaks the rules again? Don't be afraid to revoke the card, just as a real-world credit grantor would.

When should a child graduate to a card in his or her own name? Many financial planners think the junior year of college is a reasonable target. Even then, however, they suggest that card use be monitored at least casually. (That doesn't mean peeking at your child's mail, of course. Try a conversational approach, if that avenue is open.)

THE FAMILY'S FINANCES

When major family spending choices are discussed, consider letting high school–age children in on the decision-making process. They don't necessarily deserve a vote, but it may help them later to see how adults cope with the idea of limits and trade-offs.

Don't clam up if times get rough. Credit counselors suggest that parents should be honest with children about their financial problems. Kids understand a lot of what is going on anyway. And they can profit from your experience—even from your mistakes—if you tell them exactly how you got into trouble.

It's natural to try to hide the bad news from the kids. But one credit counselor feels so strongly that children should know when their parents have hit a financial crisis that he will reject potential clients who insist that the kids be kept in the dark.

RESOURCES

For more information, the Federal Reserve Bank of New York publishes a series of comic-style booklets designed to teach kids about personal finance and economics. The free publications include *The Story of Consumer Credit* (also available in Spanish), *The Story of Money*, *The Story of Inflation*, *Once Upon a Dime*, *The Story of Banks and Thrifts*, *The Story of Checks and Electronic Payments*, *The Story of Foreign Trade and Exchange* (the perfect gift), *Too Much, Too Little* (about the origins of the Federal Reserve system), and *Alan Greenspan: Behind the Charisma* (just kidding).

To order, write to the Federal Reserve Bank of New York, Public Information Department, 33 Liberty Street, New York, NY 10045, or call 212 720-6134.

Other resources that discuss saving and investing (but not necessarily borrowing) include:

"You and Money," a free kit from Fidelity Investments for fourth
    to sixth graders (800 544-6666)

Zillions, a bimonthly kids' magazine, published by Consumers
    Union (P.O. Box 53016, Boulder, CO 80322; $16 per year)

Children and Money: A Parents' Guide, by Grace W. Weinstein (Sig-
    net, $4.50)

Teach Your Child the Value of Money, by Harold and Sandy Moe
    (Harsand Press, $7.95; 800 451-0643)

How to Teach Children about Money (Young Americans Bank, $15,
    311 Steele Street, Denver, CO 80206; 303 394-4357)

Money Skills (Young Americans Bank, $10)

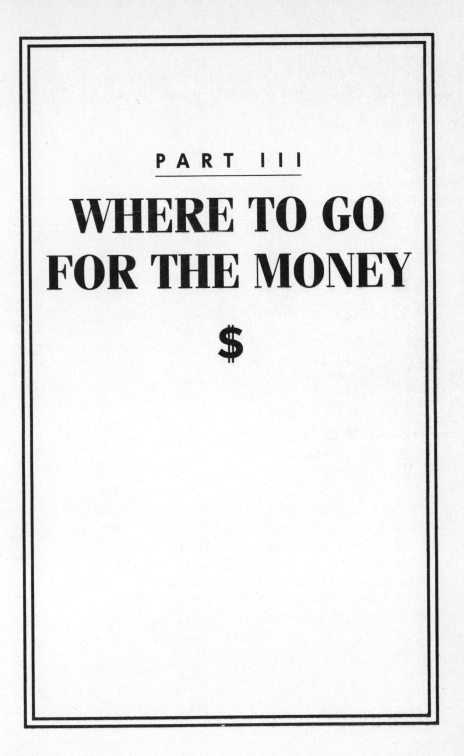

PART III

WHERE TO GO FOR THE MONEY

$

13

LOAN OPTIONS FROM A TO Z

"Holy shit. Now we've got to find seventeen billion dollars."
—Ross Johnson, CEO of RJR Nabisco, after deciding to attempt a $75-dollar-a-share leveraged buyout of the company (quoted in Bryan Burrough and John Helyar, *Barbarians at the Gate: The Fall of RJR Nabisco*)

$ Ross Johnson had it easier than most consumers. The best thing about needing $17 billion in a hurry is that there really aren't that many places to look. You just round up the usual suspects.

Consumers, on the other hand, have an almost overwhelming array of borrowing options—many of which they unfortunately neglect. So people get into borrowing ruts. And year after year, they spend billions more on finance charges than they should.

You can be different. In this chapter, I'll analyze almost every conceivable consumer borrowing option. Please don't try them all; you could get hurt. The intent is to be educational and provocative. I write about pawnshops and loan sharks not because they're tempting options for the savvy borrower but because they've been a part of the lending scene for hundreds of years. Long ago, pawnshops and loan sharks dominated the consumer lending business. (If Antonio had had access to a home-equity loan or overdraft checking privileges, *The Merchant of Venice* would have been a very different play.) Today, you can get money almost anywhere. This is either good news or bad news. It depends where you go—and when.

LOAN OPTIONS CHART

Type of Loan	Source	Rate	Should be Used For	Pros	Cons
* Retirement plans	Employer	6%–8%, 7.3% national avg.	House, tuition, emergency, debt consolidation	Great rates, with interest payments going into own account	Usually must be repaid in five years; if you change jobs, must repay immediately or face stiff penalty
Checking account overdraft privileges	Banks, S&Ls, credit unions	16%–22%	Emergencies	Easy access	Expensive, access too easy, fosters credit-card mentality
* Life insurance	Life insurance policy	5%–9.5%	Virtually anything	Low rates, flexibility	Borrowing can affect investment performance of policy, potentially diminishes death benefit
* Home-equity line of credit	Banks, S&Ls, credit unions, brokers	6%–9.5%, 7.7% national avg.	Big-ticket items, debt consolidation	Great rates, tax-deductibility	Huge temptation not to repay promptly, variable-rate risk
* Home-equity loan	Banks, S&Ls, credit unions, brokers	8%–10.5%, and up	Big-ticket items	Fixed rate eliminates rate risk, must repay according to 10-to-25-year schedule	Could be a budget-buster, result in loss of home
Secured loan	Banks, S&Ls, credit unions	5%–13%	Handling short-term needs, improving credit rating	Can allow savings to remain intact	When secured by savings, interest-rate spread works against borrower, resulting in reverse arbitrage
Unsecured personal loan	Banks, S&Ls, credit unions	12%–18%, 16% national avg. at banks and S&Ls	Emergencies	For some, rate may be better than credit cards and other sources	For many, better deals are often available
* Margin loan	Brokers, some banks	4.5%–7.5%	Tuition, debt consolidation, big-ticket items	Great rates, flexible, secured by investments	Risky if used improperly, could encourage unfortunate speculation
IRA	Banks, brokers	No interest	Short-term needs, bridge loan	One of the few places you can get 60-day, interest-free use of a large sum	Enormous, sometimes overwhelming temptation not to repay, with stiff penalties if borrower does not repay
Automobile loans	Banks, S&Ls, credit unions, auto-finance companies	9.1% avg.	Vehicle	Credit-union rates terrific	Home-equity funds a better, cheaper choice

* Denotes the more attractive borrowing options
  (Note: Quoted rates were in effect when the prime rate was 6%.)

BANKS AND SAVINGS-AND-LOANS

As a rule, banks and S&Ls tend to charge more for loans than credit unions do. Yet they frequently offer more borrowing options—and, in many cases, significant price breaks to established customers.

So do yourself a favor. Become an established customer, particularly at a relatively small bank or a small branch of a big bank, where you have a better chance of getting to know the people in charge. Profit from the fact that one of the hottest buzzwords in the industry is "relationship banking." Bankers love to talk about relationships. And, unlike anyone who has ever dated, bankers assume that all relationships are good.

Increasingly, banks are offering preferred rates on loans and savings to people they know. That means people who have accounts with the bank (accounts that are enormous and long-standing are preferable, but not essential) or existing loans there. For the rest of the decade, you'll be rewarded for consolidating business at one or two institutions. Customers who haul their savings from place to place chasing an eighth- or a quarter-point interest-rate differential on a CD will discover that this may be a losing strategy if they ever want to borrow a considerable amount of money.

Similarly, if you have a business account you might get a break on a personal loan at that bank—either on the pricing or the ratios required or both.

You may also be able to get a cheaper loan rate if you arrange for monthly payments to be automatically debited from one of your accounts.

And, yes, it does help if the manager of your local branch has, over the years, grown to respect you, or at least respect your money. Branch managers are almost always permitted to recommend loans for special handling or special pricing.

In the future, such tiered pricing will also be extended to certain borrowers the bank doesn't know particularly well. "You'll see more tiering based on sophisticated risk assessment," says S. A. Ibrahim of Chemical Bank. "Making loans at a bank will be less of a go/no go decision."

That is, the banks will start behaving more like auto-finance companies, which offer customers different rates (Ford Motor Credit has five tiers, GMAC four, and Chrysler twelve) depending on their credit-worthiness. Translation: A flawless credit report will be even more valuable in the nineties than it was before.

When might a bank be the right place to go?

For some people, bank loans might be a good alternative to credit cards. Get out of the habit of putting most major expenses—such as furniture, a new wardrobe, a big tax bill, or a dream vacation—on plastic. Consider establishing an unsecured line of credit at your bank or taking out an unsecured personal loan for one to five years (if you anticipate it will take that long to repay it). To pay that tax bill, you might get a loan for a period as short as three months. Like many short-term bank loans, this would often be renewable, with its rate adjusted if an index, such as the prime rate, has changed.

Rates average 16 percent nationally, according to Bank Rate Monitor, but may be lower where you live. There is usually no set-up charge. Be sure to request a simple-interest loan rather than a Rule of 78s or installment loan. Check the APR carefully.

The key is to get the borrowing option lined up a bit *before* you'll actually need it, so you're not caught short and forced to charge a four-figure sum on a 19.8-percent credit card. On a one-year, $3,000 loan you could save $120 or more by borrowing from a bank. If the payback period is five years, you could save almost $400.

But can you qualify? If a bank will offer you overdraft checking at 16 percent to 22 percent (see below), it will probably also approve you for a personal loan at a much more favorable rate.

A bank's best customers can get large personal loans at prime plus one. Usually these folks opt for home-equity lines instead, paying the same rate, or a little more, and deducting the interest cost.

CREDIT UNIONS

Despite having 61 million members, credit unions remain one of the country's most underutilized financial resources. They're terrific for saving (with returns consistently better than commercial banks and S&Ls) and even better for borrowing (with rates often one-half to four points lower than banks and S&Ls). Unsecured loan rates at credit unions average 13.5 percent, 2.5 percentage points lower than the national bank and S&L average. Currently, credit unions have $143 billion in outstanding loans; they should have much more. Before we address that issue, though, let's tackle a more basic one.

WHAT IS A CREDIT UNION?

A credit union is a not-for-profit cooperative owned and operated by its members. Many of the larger credit unions offer most of the important services of banks and S&Ls—savings accounts, checking accounts (called "share draft" accounts, they normally have very low fees and balance requirements), credit cards, payroll deductions, direct deposits, loans, and so on. On the other hand, smaller credit unions, which may offer only savings accounts and share draft accounts, often won't be able to handle all your banking needs.

The world's first credit union was founded in Germany over 130 years ago. Its purpose was to permit workers and farmers to pool their money and make loans to one another. In 1909, the first credit union in the United States was established in Manchester, New Hampshire.

One of the key organizers of the U.S. credit-union movement was Edward A. Filene, the visionary Boston merchant who invented the idea of the "bargain basement." Ultimately, Filene, a true believer, spent more than $1 million of his own money to spread the credit-union gospel.

ARE THEY SAFE?

A reasonable question, after the New Year's Day 1991 debacle involving many Rhode Island credit unions. The short answer, though, is a resounding "yes."

Approximately 95 percent of all credit unions are federally insured, just like commercial banks. In fact, on a percentage basis, the amount of reserves held by the federally backed credit-union insurance fund is about double the level of the federal fund for banks. So if you're not worried about dealing with Wells Fargo, Norwest, and Banc One, there's no reason to worry about a federally insured credit union.

But what if it's insured by a state fund, similar to Rhode Island's? While it's possible that a Rhode Island replay will occur, it's unlikely. Rhode Island's system collapsed because its members made some extraordinarily risky, S&L-type loans, exactly the kind generally avoided by other credit unions.

WHY DON'T MORE PEOPLE BORROW FROM CREDIT UNIONS?
Because they don't know how favorable the terms can be. And, perhaps more frequently, because they don't even know they're eligible to join a credit union.

Credit-union executives estimate that 60 percent to 70 percent of all adults could join—roughly double the number who already have. Millions of people wrongly assume that if their employer or place of worship doesn't have a credit union, then they're simply flat out of luck.

Actually, you may be eligible to join a credit union if:

• A member of your immediate family belongs to one.

• You live in the right neighborhood. Many credit unions—such as the Lower East Side Peoples Federal Credit Union in New York (212 529-8197) and the Delancey Street Federal Credit Union in San Francisco (415 546-7144)—have been organized on a community or zip-code basis.

• You belong to the right group—ethnic, religious, or otherwise. At the moment, there are credit unions for Lithuanians, Ukrainians, Hispanics (the Hispanic Credit Union in Houston, 713 928-8054), Koreans who live in and around Philadelphia, Hmong (the Hmong American Federal Credit Union in St. Paul, Minnesota, 612 487-3466), women (the San Antonio Women's Credit Union, 512 494-0353, and the Women's SouthWest Federal Credit Union in Dallas, 214 351-5180), feminists (the California Feminist Federal Credit Union in San Diego, 619 280-1922), gay people who live in Dallas (the Dallas Gay and Lesbian Alliance Credit Union, 214 528-4233), and the blind (the Blind of Minnesota Credit Union in Minneapolis, 612 824-6862, is one of perhaps ten throughout the country).

• You're a veteran. The Navy Federal Credit Union, with 1.1 million members and $5 billion in assets, is the nation's largest. Other branches of the armed services have their own associations.

• You work in the movies (the Universal City Studios Credit Union, 818 777-1295, is one of several serving the movie industry).

• You work in California agriculture (the Citrus and Avocado Employees Federal Credit Union in Ventura, 805 656-6747).

• You're a student at, or graduate of, Barnard College, Columbia University, Fordham University, Georgetown University, Georgia Tech, Howard University, Ohio University, the University of California at Berkeley, the University of Connecticut, the University of Illinois, the University of Louisville, the University of Massachusetts, the University of North Carolina, the University of Pennsylvania, and Virginia Tech, among many others.

For the names of credit unions that might accept you, call the Credit Union National Association (800 356-9655, ext. 4045) and ask for the phone number of your state credit-union association. The state folks will try to find some club willing to have you as a member.

OTHER FACTS ABOUT CREDIT UNIONS YOU SHOULD KNOW

- Credit unions are never allowed to charge prepayment penalties.
- Often, you can borrow a much smaller amount—sometimes as little as $50 or $100—at a credit union than at a competing bank. Many banks don't want to be bothered for less than $2,000.
- You must have a savings or share draft account at a credit union to be eligible for a loan.
- Default rates on credit-union loans average .4 percent, versus 1.5 percent to 2.5 percent for banks and S&Ls.
- Credit unions also handle credit insurance in a more enlightened way. As I discuss in chapter 21, credit insurance is typically an overpriced and unnecessary consumer product. It's also a major profit center for lenders. When offered by nonprofits such as credit unions, however, the insurance makes more sense.

Most credit union loans include low-cost or "free" credit life and disability insurance. Nothing's ever really "free," of course; your interest rate would be slightly lower if you could somehow decline the insurance. But for over fifty years, the idealistic philosophy of U.S. credit unions has been: "The debt shall die with the debtor."

Granted, such idealism hits you in your wallet. If you're already well insured and borrow from a credit union where every loan comes bundled with credit insurance, you're really paying for something you don't need. Even so, the credit-union deal may be unbeatable.

RETIREMENT PLANS

"Retirement savings plans are one of the most neglected borrowing options in the country," says Richard Friedman, a vice-president with the Employee Benefits Group of the Ayco Corporation, an Albany, New York, financial planning and consulting firm.

About two-thirds of all medium-sized and large companies permit such loans from 401(k), profit-sharing, or thrift plans, with the number growing steadily. Many tax-exempt, charitable, and educational organizations that administer 403(b) plans for their employees permit such borrowing as well, as do many state, county, and municipal employee union 457 plans. Federal employees may borrow from their thrift savings plans. The same rules generally apply to all borrowers.

The loans make sense for debt consolidation, home improvement, vehicle purchases, and tuition, although they're not as desirable as a home-equity loan (because interest paid on retirement-plan borrowing is seldom tax-deductible).

ADVANTAGES

The loans have many advantages, among them:

• Low rates—often prime or prime plus 1 (the national average is prime plus 1.3 percent).

• Quick access to your money, often within two or three days.

• Minimal paperwork.

• No credit check (a real plus if your ratios are temporarily out-of-whack and you can't get a loan at a reasonable rate anywhere else).

• Simple repayment via payroll deduction.

• Up-front fees are rare (sometimes a $25 charge is levied).

• And, perhaps most significant, the loan might improve your plan's investment return, since you're really paying interest to yourself. Let's say you've chosen to invest your retirement savings in a Guaranteed Interest Contract (GIC), as 60 percent to 70 percent of all plan participants have done. Your GIC yields 8 percent. If that's the prime rate and you're borrowing at prime plus 1, then you've improved your financial performance by 1 percent. Not a lot, but it sure beats losing money.

DISADVANTAGES

Among the disadvantages are:

• Instead of improving your financial return, you might considerably undermine it. What if you are in equities and the market rises 26 percent one year, but half of your account is earning only prime plus

1 because you've borrowed against it? No disaster, but your retirement picture won't look quite so pretty.

What happens if you've spread your plan assets over several different investment options? Some plans let you select which asset you'd like to borrow against; the vast majority simply prorate the debt. (Some rare plans absorb the market risk entirely. That is, you borrow from the entire organization's account rather than your own individual plan. In such cases, your personal investment return is completely unaffected by your decision to take out a loan.)

• Short repayment term. These loans must be repaid in 5 years, with payments made at least quarterly. (The money is usually deducted from your paycheck.) The repayment period can expand only if you borrow to buy or improve a primary residence; then the term can be stretched to 10 to 30 years. No problem for a car loan, but this might not be ideal in the case of tuition or similar financial hardships.

• If you leave the organization, you'll probably have to repay the loan immediately. If you can't, you'll have to pay tax on the amount you borrowed, plus a 10-percent penalty if you're not yet 59½ years old. (Note: You're exempt from the 10-percent penalty if you take early retirement after age 55.) So before borrowing, ask yourself if your job is secure (well, as secure as jobs get these days) and if you could repay the debt quickly if necessary.

Given all this, whether borrowing from a retirement plan seems like a prudent alternative or a ludicrous high-wire act will depend on your financial circumstances, job outlook, and temperament.

OTHER CONSIDERATIONS
Withdrawals. Some people wrongly think they can access retirement plans only via withdrawals. This is an expensive mistake, since you have to pay regular tax plus the 10-percent penalty, when applicable. Borrowing is much cheaper—if you can meet the payments. Besides, withdrawals may be restricted to specific "hardship" situations: e.g., medical bills that exceed 7.5 percent of adjusted gross income, imminent foreclosure, tuition bills, the downpayment on a new home and, at some companies, the birth of a child. According to the IRS, "hardship" withdrawals can be made without penalty if your medical bills exceed 7.5 percent of adjusted gross income or if you become totally and permanently disabled. In both cases, you have to *borrow*

the maximum from your plan before you make a withdrawal. (Similarly, some plan sponsors will not allow a withdrawal for other purposes—tuition, downpayment, foreclosure avoidance—until you've borrowed the maximum allowable amount.)

Deductibility. The odds are about 50-to-1 that interest on your loan won't be deductible, but ask your tax adviser anyway. The interest is never deductible if the money is borrowed from your own contributions or your employer's pretax contributions. With after-tax contributions, you may be able to take the deduction if you use the money for investments (and have net taxable income to show for it) or if you use it to buy a primary residence and the residence is used as collateral for the loan. That is, the plan puts a lien on your house, so, in essence, you're getting a first mortgage and a second mortgage at the same time. Few plans will do this, however.

THE RULES

• You can borrow up to 50 percent of the assets in your 401(k), 403(b), 457, profit-sharing, or thrift plan, but no more than $50,000. If your plan account contains less than $20,000, you may be able to borrow $10,000 if the loan is adequately secured.

• Some plans limit you to one or two loans at a time, so check the rules before you borrow. You may not be able to tap the account as often as you'd like.

• If rates have dropped since you borrowed from your account, you can sometimes refinance the loan with your own plan—if you haven't exhausted your borrowing power.

• Self-employed people cannot borrow from their retirement plans. Hands off that SEP (Simplified Employee Pension) or IRA, and don't hit up that Keogh unless you're an employee. (For borrowing purposes, owner-employees do *not* qualify as employees.)

IRAS

As I just said, you can't borrow from an IRA. Not ever. But you can have interest-free use of your IRA funds for one 60-day period each year, when and if you roll the money over into another investment. So, in effect, you can make a bridge loan to yourself if you're ever temporarily strapped.

To state the obvious: This is both a cheap and a potentially dangerous strategy. You've got to be sure you'll be able to replace the money in time, or else you'll pay income tax plus the 10-percent penalty.

EMPLOYER LOANS

Usually this is an ad hoc benefit. It's offered by relatively few companies on a formal basis.

But if you're faced with sudden hardship, particularly high medical bills for a spouse or child, many employers will volunteer to help. If they don't, there's no harm in asking. Although you don't have to be a senior VP to qualify, it helps if you've been there awhile and if they like you. Rates on such loans are usually great—prime or lower—and the repayment terms can be flexible.

Warning: Make sure the loan is properly documented, or the IRS may consider the money as extra income.

MARGIN LOANS

Margin loans deserve more respect and should be used by more people. Alas, they also have a well-deserved image problem.

What exactly is a margin loan? It's a loan from a brokerage firm— or occasionally a bank—collateralized by the securities in your account (stocks, bonds, mutual funds, Treasury bills). Historically, the problems have occurred when investors use such borrowing to increase their leverage—that is, to speculate—in financial markets. When markets decline rapidly, speculators who have bought on margin suffer grievously. They get margin calls, which require them to add more cash to their account or else have some of their positions liquidated.

Researchers have found that buyers who use margin generally have worse track records than investors who don't. A study at Parker/ Hunter, a Pittsburgh brokerage firm, partly attributed this to the "psychological pressure" of owing money. Furthermore, the amount of margin buying invariably peaks in the euphoric period right before a market crash, as it did in the autumns of 1929 and 1987.

Case closed? Hardly. A margin loan can be a fine idea if you use it to reduce net borrowing costs rather than to increase leverage in the securities markets.

For one thing, the rates are terrific—significantly lower than credit cards or new-car loans, and often lower than home-equity rates (the range is 4.5 percent to 7.5 percent). The rates are pegged to the broker call rate—what brokerages pay to borrow.

At most brokers and banks making margin loans, the more you borrow or the bigger your account, the lower the rate. Heavy hitters who borrow more than $100,000 at Fidelity Investments' Spartan brokerage (800 544-5115) or at the Boston-based Brown & Co. (800 225-6707) can get margin-loan rates of 4.5 percent—half a percentage point below the broker call rate. For big and small fish alike, the rates can be highly negotiable—if you ask.

Repayment couldn't be simpler, which for some borrowers is part of the problem with margin loans. You don't have to "pay" anything. The interest accumulates in your account, and you can settle up when you sell the collateral, or repay whenever you want. Most lenders do not charge any fees. And you can get the money fast—generally within a week, and sometimes within a day.

For anyone who either can't use a home as collateral or chooses not to, margin loans could be an appropriate second choice, especially for the oft-abused self-employed, who, as indicated above, can't borrow from their retirement accounts. Such loans could reasonably be used to consolidate higher-interest debt or pay for tuition or home improvements. A margin account might be the ideal source for anyone in need of a bridge loan.

Interest on a margin loan may even be deductible. Here's how. If you borrow to pay for tuition, you can't deduct the interest. But if you sell some assets to pay the bills and then take out a margin loan to replenish those assets, you are allowed to deduct all interest on the margin loan up to the amount of your investment income each year—in interest, dividends, and capital gains. If the interest paid is greater than the investment income, the excess interest can be carried forward and deducted in later years when you have offsetting investment income (from, say, selling the stock you bought).

The interest will be deductible only if you pay it monthly. Let it accumulate in the account and you lose the deduction. (You can never deduct the interest if you borrow to buy tax-exempt securities.)

But what about the risk? Well, don't borrow to the hilt. Although you *can* borrow up to 50 percent of the value of eligible stocks, convertible bonds, and many mutual funds (if they're held by the broker or bank); up to 75 percent of the value of listed corporate bonds; up to 85 percent of the value of municipal bonds; and up to 95 percent of the value of Treasury securities, *don't*. Set lower limits so you can sleep at night and avoid potentially rash investment decisions. Allow some margin for error.

When we think of margin loans, many of us assume that individual stocks will serve as the collateral, because that's what we've read about. Such borrowing may seem less terrifying, though, when backed by mutual funds. In the near future, more people will probably begin borrowing against their funds. As of now, securities laws require that such lending be done by a broker or a bank, not by a mutual-fund company. But you can transfer assets from Fidelity, Vanguard, Dreyfus, Twentieth Century, Janus, or other mutual-fund company to a broker or bank and use them as collateral if you like.

LIFE INSURANCE

Can a borrowing option be both underutilized and overhyped? Absolutely. Consider loans against life-insurance policies.

Like so many people today, insurance agents love to talk about win-win situations. If you die, for example, your heirs win—obviously. (Granted, agents occasionally soft-pedal this type of triumph.)

Should you linger longer, then you really win, because you've established a savings plan that can be accessed cheaply and strategically whenever you wish. You can always borrow against those savings without much red tape.

Some people, agents may tell you, are borrowing against their policies at rates as low as 4.5 percent, then paying for tuition or making a fortune in mutual funds or whatever. Unfortunately, many of these tales concern whole-life policies written before the second Nixon administration. It's hard to buy one of those today. In fact, it's impossible.

Nowadays, the cost of borrowing against new policies is typically 7.5 percent, or a variable rate such as prime plus 1, but that's usually not the real cost. A life-insurance loan may or may not be one of your cheapest borrowing alternatives.

THE REAL COST

Why? With insurance loans, you're borrowing against the cash value in the policy. That's the collateral. Almost invariably, this collateral —the portion of the cash value you've borrowed against—will grow more slowly when a loan is outstanding. Ask your agent how *much* more slowly, then do the following simple calculation.

If your cash value would have grown at 8 percent but instead will increase at only 5.5 percent during the term of the loan, you have to consider that lost 2.5 percent (8 percent minus 5.5 percent) as part of your borrowing cost. Add that 2.5 percent to the nominal interest rate you're paying (let's say it's 7 percent) to get the real interest rate, in this case 9.5 percent. Clearly, that's still a pretty good deal, although you may be able to do better.

With many whole-life policies, the decline in cash-value appreciation is likely to be 1 percent to 1.5 percent, so the true borrowing cost would be a very attractive 8 percent to 8.5 percent. Many universal-life policies would have about the same net borrowing cost. (With universal life, you have another option—a tax-free withdrawal of some of the money you paid in. At most, you'd probably pay a $25 fee for the transaction and avoid all interest charges. But will you leave enough in the till to keep your policy in force? Ask your agent.)

With variable-life policies, which offer you many investing options, including stock and bond mutual funds, borrowing is more of a crap-shoot. You haven't a clue going in just what the real cost will be. Borrow against growth-stock funds during a good year and you'll be shocked at the opportunity cost (the difference between what your stocks would have returned—say, 25 percent—and the return you actually did earn—perhaps 5 percent). Add that 20 percent to the 7 percent nominal interest rate and you've got a real interest cost of 27 percent.

New whole-life, universal-life, and variable-life policy holders don't have the opportunity to make that kind of gaffe. With such policies, it takes three to five years to have enough cash value to make borrowing a reasonable option.

With a single-premium life policy, on the other hand, you'd have much less of a wait, and there are no opportunity costs. How does it work? You make a one-time payment to buy the insurance, then cash value accumulates exactly as in a whole-life policy. You can usually borrow against the increase in cash value at any time, paying the same rate for the loan that the cash value is earning. Some agents call this an interest-free loan—which, of course, it isn't, since you'll have to pay back more than you took out. But it is a better loan deal nonetheless.

THE DEATH BENEFIT

The amount borrowed is always subtracted from the death benefit. So if you borrow $10,000 from a $100,000 policy and are then hit by an 18-wheeler, your heirs will collect only $90,000.

The "missing" $10,000 doesn't—or, certainly, shouldn't—just disappear. Theoretically, it should benefit those you leave behind. Borrowing to consolidate debts, make home improvements, or pay tuition bills shouldn't be embarrassing or terrifying. The money is not vanishing. Quite the contrary; it's probably working harder than if it had remained cocooned in the policy. If the true cost of the loan is extremely high, however, it would be a mistake to borrow this way.

THE PROS AND CONS

Among the advantages of life insurance loans are:

- Low rates (make sure they're *real*).
- Quick access (typically, within a week).
- No credit check.
- No fees (usually).
- The ability to borrow up to 90 percent of cash value.

The disadvantages:

- It's tempting not to repay the loan, which would reduce the death benefit.
- You can't tap most new policies. Often, there's hardly anything to borrow against in the early years because of high up-front costs.
- In most cases, outstanding loans become taxable withdrawals if you cash in your policy, just like any other non-death-benefit distribution.
- If your premiums were originally calculated so that earnings on your cash would eventually take care of part of the cost of the insurance, watch out. If you borrow heavily and, therefore, your cash buildup lags behind expectations, you may be liable for additional premiums later on—or else face the risk of having your policy lapse.

OTHER CONSIDERATIONS:

• You can pay interest on the loan with periodic checks if you like, although most people don't. Instead, the interest compounds in the account and is subtracted from the cash value.

• You can't borrow against single-premium deferred annuities, although you can usually make a limited number of withdrawals at little or no cost.

OVERDRAFT PRIVILEGES

These "privileges"—actually, lines of credit linked to your checking account, savings account, or home-equity line—can be as expensive as the worst credit cards (16 percent to 22 percent). They can be either great stress-reducers or potential budget-busters. It's up to you.

Among the virtues of such credit lines:

• No more worrying about bouncing a check, wondering if the money's there or not, trying to decide whether it's worth it to call the bank or check the ATM to find out if a deposit has cleared.

• You may pay much less in interest than you would in bounced-check fees. Writing rubber checks is a very expensive habit, often costing $10 to $20 a pop. Bounced-check fees are a huge profit center for banks, since processing each transgression costs only 20 to 60 cents.

• The privileges couldn't be simpler to exercise. Just write a check or make a withdrawal with your ATM card.

There are some real negatives, however. Among them:

• In the wrong hands, such "privileges" can be as dangerous as credit cards. When some people no longer have to worry about bouncing a check, they also stop worrying about what is or isn't in their checking account.

• Some users start to see the credit line as *their* money rather than money that belongs to an institution and can be accessed only at considerable expense.

• Some institutions charge an annual or monthly fee for the service, or a per-loan surcharge in addition to interest.

• Many lenders require you to mail in a separate check for the overdraft loan, so you can't pay off the loan simply by making a deposit. Writing the check costs time and money (a 29-cent stamp plus a check, which may cost 35 cents, as well as some needless aggravation).

• Some lenders compel you to borrow more than you actually need by permitting overdrafts only in hundred-dollar increments. For example, you're overdrawn by $250.19, and the bank says, "Call it $300."

FINANCE COMPANIES

Historically, a finance company is an entity that lends money to individuals or institutions but takes in no deposits. In practice, finance companies do much of their business with customers who have slightly tarnished, badly damaged, or utterly imploded credit ratings.

For good credit risks, these outfits, which frequently charge at least 1 percent more for any loan than a bank or S&L would, have only one advantage: more liberal standards on home-equity lines and loans. Many companies, such as Beneficial Finance, will lend up to 85 percent of the home's value, less the existing mortgage, as opposed to a 75-percent average for banks, S&Ls, and credit unions.

How expensive would this money be? Home-equity loan rates at the largest companies typically range from 10 percent to 14 percent, (*with* 2 to 5 points for good measure), then go much higher for bad credit risks. Unsecured debt-consolidation loans could start as high as 18 percent.

Finance companies specialize in customers who would have trouble qualifying for loans at a typical bank. Often, bad credit is no problem, unless it's really really bad. What's unacceptable? "Someone who has had three or four repossessions, went bankrupt two years ago, and is still having trouble paying bills on time," says Lowell Swanson, president of United Finance Company of Portland, Oregon. (Large national companies are likely to have somewhat tougher standards.)

Some finance-company borrowers *could* strike a much better deal elsewhere. "A lot of people pay us 25 percent who could get a loan at a bank for 18 percent," says Swanson. "They don't want to go through all the red tape or run into someone they know at the bank who might think they're in trouble. That would make them feel ashamed."

On a $3,000, 2-year loan, this "strategy" might cost the borrower $200 or more. Anyone who accepts this trade-off *should* feel ashamed.

For people with halfway decent credit, there are two other powerful reasons for staying away. Since finance company clients tend, as a group, to be greater credit risks, many credit-scoring systems have a bias against anyone who has ever dealt with a finance company. The computers won't worry about the facts of your personal payment history. By taking money from a lender specializing in higher risks, you've virtually signed a confession that *you* are a high risk.

In addition, many finance-company borrowers receive Rule of 78s loans, which become much more expensive if you want to prepay (see chapter 16 for details).

A very good credit risk might consider using a finance company if he or she needs a sizable sum in a tremendous hurry. Some finance companies can give you cash a half hour after you fill out the application.

Late fees represent a major profit center for finance companies. United Finance, which has only $35 million in outstanding loans, collected a remarkable $800,000 in late fees in 1991. Some people may pay late twenty-four times over the course of a 24-month loan, consistently missing the deadline by a few weeks. (There is a way off this bizarre merry-go-round: borrow an amount equal to one month's payment, get ahead of the game, and avoid those late charges for the life of the loan.)

SECOND-MORTGAGE LENDERS
WHO ADVERTISE A LOT ON TV

Some heavy advertisers may tell you on the phone or in person that they offer second-mortgage loans at prime or close to it. Technically, this may occasionally be true, but once all the points and fees are factored in, or once the teaser rate expires, the rate will shoot up. Others don't play such games; their rates simply start out high.

Shop at The Money Store and you'll probably end up paying 10 percent to 12 percent for your home-equity money, plus two points. If you have very good credit, you could beat that rate at a credit union or bank and avoid the points. (Of course, if you had great credit, you'd probably feel weird about getting a loan at a place called The Money Store, anyway.) Money Store loans have LTV caps of 65 percent.

Champion Mortgage and other lenders who avidly solicit customers with serious credit problems—bankruptcies, liens, judgments—may charge rates of 14 percent, 18 percent, or higher.

HARD-MONEY LENDERS

Hard-money lenders often charge rates consumers will find hard to swallow. They focus almost exclusively on a customer's collateral (usually a home) rather than income or creditworthiness, charging home-equity rates ranging from 18 percent to 36 percent (once the often-hefty points have been factored in). These lenders tend to be experts in foreclosure. Many are perfectly legitimate, if not necessarily compassionate, lenders.

Hard-money types are likely to contact customers via direct mail. Some may charge 6 or 10 or even 20 points on a second mortgage. Kathleen Keest, a staff attorney with the National Consumer Law Center in Boston, tells of one lender who charged a woman 40 points!

BORROWING AGAINST SAVINGS

Say you have a CD earning 5 percent and the bank will let you borrow at 9 percent if you pledge the CD as collateral. To encourage you to do this, some bankers will attempt to convince you that the "real" interest rate you're paying is 4 percent. This is a fiction; 4 percent is merely the spread between your savings and borrowing rates.

Your "real" interest rate is 9 percent. That's what you'll be paying out of pocket. Whether it's a good deal or not is a complex question.

Such secured loans are terrific for people with meager or shaky credit histories. But they're only occasionally appropriate for more sophisticated borrowers. The rate banks charge for loans secured by savings is often two to four percentage points higher than the rate paid on the savings.

Back to that CD. When should you "break" it (cash it in) and use the proceeds to buy something like a car? The answer will partly depend on the interest you're earning and what the loan would cost. Calculate the cost of paying the early-withdrawal penalty (typically 3 months' interest for a CD maturing in one year or less, and 6 months' interest for one with a longer term) and forgoing the additional interest you would earn if you kept the CD intact. Then compare that with the cost of the loan. (If the interest is deductible, be sure to compare the after-tax costs of the two alternatives.)

• If the loan is cheaper, you've been blessed with a no-brainer. You take the loan.

• If the loan is slightly more expensive, there's a decent, although by no means conclusive, argument for paying that small premium. Your savings will remain intact, and you won't have to worry each month about replenishing the kitty—or giving in to temptation and not replenishing it, as the case may be.

• To make the after-tax calculation accurate, realize that there's a small bonus for CD-breakers: the early-withdrawal penalty is deductible on next year's 1040.

(Note: The same calculations can be used with any savings or investment vehicle.)

LOAN BROKERS

Bad idea. (See chapter 21 for a more extensive discussion.)

MAIL-ORDER LOANS FROM INSTITUTIONS YOU'VE NEVER HEARD OF

Another bad option. (See chapter 21.)

PAWNSHOPS

Of late, pawnshops have become much more popular. Pawnshop operators say this is because they have made their operations more modern, sophisticated, and attractive, with some shops now resembling brightly lit catalogue showrooms. ("Pawnshops Shed Their Dingy Image," trumpeted a 1991 headline in *The New York Times*.) Those who study the health of the economy might offer other explanations.

Whatever the case, there has been progress of a sort. For example, five pawnshop chains—Cash America Investments, Ezcorp, Express Cash International, First Cash, and U.S. Pawn—have gone public since the late eighties. Still, most customers don't patronize the nation's 10,000 pawnshops because of the ambiance. They usually go because even finance companies won't give them money.

Pawnbroker interest rates are regulated by individual states—although the word "regulated" might seem a tad strong when you consider what the rates are. New York, for instance, has the toughest law; pawnbrokers there may charge no more than 3-percent interest per month. Georgia has the peachiest terms for pawnshop operators—25 percent a month for some loans, or 300 percent per year.

Pawnbrokers typically lend one-quarter to one-half of what they think an item is worth. Most smaller operators hope you'll never pay off the loan, so they can then sell the pawned item at a profit. The publicly traded chains generally prefer that you pay the interest and redeem the object, then come back a few months later and repeat the process.

Auto pawning is the industry's latest wrinkle. Collateral Lender of Beverly Hills is filled with Porsches and Rolls-Royces that have been hocked by their owners. Autopawn USA, located in the Denver suburb of Aurora, invites car owners to drive on in and walk on out with a wallet full of cash. Owner S. Brad Carey is so convinced he's discovered one of the country's great new growth industries that's he's begun selling kits so others can set up auto-pawn dealerships.

Autopawn USA's interest rate is about 10 percent a month. In Florida, state investigators have found some dealers charging customers as much as 1,000 percent a year.

(Note: Some nonprofit institutions operate "pawnshops" called Remedial Loan Societies, which generally charge much more humane interest rates.)

LOAN SHARKS

Can you do even worse than pawnbrokers? Of course, if you go see the folks best known for their untraditional collection methods. The New York Police Department tells me that the going loan shark lending rate is 1.5 percent to 3 percent per week—or an average of prime plus 111 per year—a nice spread if you can get it. Special promotional rates may be available in your town, however.

For borrowers, there is at least one bright side to this financial arrangement. Such lenders seldom report delinquencies to credit bureaus.

14

A DEBT IN THE FAMILY

The holy passion of friendship is of so sweet and steady and loyal and enduring a nature that it will last through a whole lifetime, if not asked to lend money.   —Mark Twain, *Pudd'nhead Wilson*

Acquaintance, n. A person whom we know well enough to borrow from, but not well enough to lend to. . . .
                         —Ambrose Bierce, *The Devil's Dictionary*

$ The good news about borrowing from a bank, or even a finance company, is that the unpleasantness you have to endure is predictable. Generally, the humiliations are minor, and they're likely to be fleeting. Best of all, a banker will probably never suggest that you would have been a miserable failure without his beneficence—even if this happens to be true.

Borrowing from family members and friends, on the other hand, often represents a treacherous journey into the unknown. When things go wrong, they can go *very* wrong. Paying back all the money on time and with interest is no guarantee that problems won't arise.

But let's not be naive here. Millions of people ask their loved ones for a loan every year. Many realize the potential downside. They know that what they're doing is a bad idea *in theory*; they just figure that it will work out in practice. Maybe the theory only applies to other people.

Of course, for many people there are few obvious alternatives. Financial planners say intrafamily borrowing has probably increased in the last decade—the Fed doesn't keep tabs on such things—because the growth in personal income has lagged behind inflation.

So we borrow from Mom, Dad, Aunt Penelope, and Uncle Waldo. While such borrowing may not do a whole lot for family harmony, it's at least good to know that it does benefit the economy. Without these temporary—or presumably temporary—asset transfers, the housing market might crumble. (The National Association of Realtors reports that 32 percent of first time home buyers receive loans or gifts from relatives or friends. And that figure, which takes only down-payment money into account, is undoubtedly low; it doesn't include those secret bank account–padding loans so many people get in order to qualify for financing.)

Given that typical first-time home buyers have to come up with $13,000 in cash to cover closing costs and a 10-percent down payment on a $90,000 house, it's no surprise that they start looking around for assistance. Some experts actually think the practice should be more prevalent than it is.

"In America, the family is probably the most overlooked resource most people have access to," says George E. L. Barbee, executive director of client services for Price Waterhouse in New York City. "When a good relationship exists, you can structure a win/win deal that gives the borrower a lower interest rate and the lender a higher return. Repayments are more flexible, and you avoid the hassle of dealing with a bank. Besides, why not take the bank's interest-rate spread—and the closing costs—and keep all that money in the family?"

Financially, the logic is impeccable. But one reason problems often occur is that the process is not institutionalized in our culture. Whereas some immigrant Asian groups have successfully established "launching funds" for the young, which enable them to purchase businesses and homes with cash accumulated by their elders, the average American family handles all this on an ad hoc basis. There are no rules. No one knows what to expect.

In fact, it's frequently not clear if loans to loved ones will eventually become gifts, whether voluntary or de facto. Financial planners suggest that 50 percent of all loans between family members are never repaid; with friends, the figure may be 75 percent or higher.

BUT YOU NEED THE MONEY

For the sake of argument, let's assume all borrowers will repay the loan. Two traps await them, nonetheless. First, borrowers don't recognize that the financial transaction is likely to trigger powerful emotions and affect the relationship between the parties. (Money, a marvelously symbolic substance, can easily represent love, control, or independence.)

Second, a lot of people don't think the deal through. They neglect to take the kind of precautions that can often minimize negative fallout.

BORROWING TROUBLE

Forget for just a moment that loans from family and friends are usually terrific financial deals. Let's look instead at the psychological and emotional costs. Consider these stories.

Like many parents who lend money for a down payment, Jim Knowlton* had a distinct view of geography. It was as easy, he felt, to find a nice house close by as it was to find one far away. Jim, it turns out, was so considerate that he went and found the house for his daughter Jane and son-in-law Steve. Remarkably, it was located only 30 minutes away from his Southern California home.

The problem was that daughter Jane also knew what *she* wanted— a much larger house an hour away. But Jane waffled, wilted, and ultimately succumbed. She knew her father meant well, and she believed he knew more about real estate than she did. And, after all, it *was* his money.

The decision was a disaster. Jane and Steve quickly grew to resent the new house, which always felt cramped. Family tension has increased so much that even though father and daughter are closer geographically, they now see each other much less often than before.

At least Beth Mickelson,* a 30-year-old Arkansas teacher, likes the house her parents helped her buy five years ago, when they lent her $20,000 for a down payment. At many family gatherings since then, however, her father has reminded her that she couldn't have purchased the house without his help.

He tells Beth constantly that he was responsible for her getting off the ground. The situation has become ugly. To him, the loan proves that she's just a child who couldn't handle things by herself. If paying back the money would help, she'd do it, but it wouldn't matter at this point, because she can never undo the transaction. Beth's been *helped*. People told her there might be strings attached, but in her case, the strings are ropes.

When Lesley Goldberg*, 32, a free-spending New York City ad agency executive, borrowed $20,000 from her mother to pay off credit-card bills, her mother's behavior abruptly changed. She didn't lecture Lesley about profligacy. Instead, she became increasingly demanding, requesting many more favors and command performances. She became unbearably *mothering*. Her new attitude seemed to be, "I gave you the money, now behave yourself." The two didn't fight about money per se—just about filial duty, ingratitude, indifference, you never call/you never write, and so on. Lesley now feels defensive around her mother much of the time.

Three years ago, Jeff Sticht* borrowed $25,000 from his brother Sam to help start a custom printing business. The business flopped. The money is gone.

Jeff's brother, whose needs for cash have increased since he made the loan, is demanding repayment. But Jeff simply doesn't have any money. In fact, he's contemplating filing for personal bankruptcy.

Though Jeff has sworn he will repay every penny with interest as soon as he can, the two brothers no longer speak to each other. "I don't think the damage to the relationship will ever be repaired, no matter when the money is repaid," says Jeff.

It may be easiest to understand the problems involved in borrowing from family and friends by focusing on one of the riskiest types of loans—start-up capital for a new business venture. In such cases, failure is more likely than success, so the stakes are higher from the outset. Furthermore, there are innumerable opportunities for criticizing the wisdom with which the money is deployed. There are always so many decisions to make: Should you expand, retrench, diversify, cut prices, try direct mail? When you use Mom and Dad's money to buy a new chintz sofa, on the other hand, they'll probably only deplore your taste a few times before moving on to another topic.

In a study of love and lending, *Inc.* magazine concluded that intra-family business loans should be avoided all the time, without any exceptions, period.

Why such an absolute prohibition? Because where the money comes from is likely to have a detrimental impact on management decisions. An entrepreneur might be overly cautious with his parents' money; if he lost it, he might lose a part of himself—the part that so deeply wants approval and respect. So, seeking approval, he may overlook opportunities.

Business is tough enough without constantly second-guessing yourself, wondering how Mom and Dad might view your latest marketing plan. For many business people, it's hard to feel fully in command before the parental debt is discharged. "Until you pay them off, you can't have a sense of autonomy," one entrepreneur told *Inc*. "There is a kind of emotional collateral."

It's an evocative phrase. What do you really *owe* the lender? I think *Inc*. overstates the case—I know several entrepreneurs who've successfully used parents as bankers—but it raises the right issues. Money is often beside the point. Starting a business is a very grown-up thing; borrowing from your parents is not—at least, not in our culture. How can the two activities be reconciled? What kind of price will you pay for attempting to do so?

If you're considering borrowing money from your family or friends, think about it carefully. The key questions you should ask are: Does it make sense for *me*? What could go wrong? If I'm late repaying the money, will the lender be understanding, or will he or she ask me about it all the time? Is is worth risking the relationship?

HOW TO DO IT RIGHT

1. Carefully consider all the alternatives—banks, credit unions, credit cards, delayed gratification, or an austerity plan. "Some people have a tendency to turn to family and friends much too quickly," says San Francisco financial planner Lawrence Krause. "It's the easy way out."

In truth, that's an awful misconception: long-term, it's seldom the easiest way. View it as a last resort, and you'll probably end up happier.

2. Do the math. Yes, the loan with love attached will almost definitely be the cheapest, but do the math anyway. See exactly how much you're saving over the least expensive loan you can obtain through mainstream commercial channels. Write down the difference on a sheet

of paper and stare at it for a while. Is it $100? $500? $2,000? Weigh the savings against the risk. Think of the extra money as a one-time premium payment for relationship insurance. As I've said elsewhere, the cheapest loan is not necessarily the best loan.

3. Take a clear-eyed look at the health of your relationship with the lender. Many who've borrowed from loved ones and lived to regret it feel especially bad because they think *they should have known*. It's a fair bet that a person who puts you down for who you are and for how you live your life won't suddenly become more understanding when you borrow money. Rather, he or she will now have another reason for believing that you don't manage your affairs as you should.

But even with a good relationship, it pays to take out the microscope. Examine both your motives and the motives of the lender. Does the loan represent something else to you—a sign of approval, a gesture of love, a much-deserved payback for past injustices? In asking for a loan, are you really hoping to get a gift instead? (If so, be very careful. You may get what you ask for and resent it nonetheless.)

Look for the hidden agendas so common on both sides. Who, for instance, *wants* to lend money? People who are generous and benevolent, sure; but also people who are controlling, manipulative, needy, and excessively impressed with their own success. And let's not forget parents who want to be more involved in their children's lives, who may not be quite ready to let go.

4. Once you have a handle on the emotional present, consider the future. How will you feel after you get the loan? Will you suffer borrower's remorse—that vivid feeling of self-doubt and inadequacy that results from asking for a "handout"? Will the feeling be ephemeral, or will it linger until you repay the debt? The lender-borrower relationship is not charactrerized by equality. ("The borrower is servant to the lender"—Proverbs 22:7.) The very act of borrowing may lead to a dramatic power shift, which can be very upsetting to a person trying to establish his independence. Being prepared helps, up to a point.

Borrowing shouldn't feel shameful, but sometimes it does. When it does, you may well end up resenting the lender. In addition, if you feel guilty about taking the money, you may begin seeing shadows. That is, you may assume that the lender is always thinking about you and the debt, even when he doesn't mention it at all.

Of course, the lender may actually resent *you* for asking. When asked, most family members—especially parents—will lend you money, no matter what they really think. It's a test of love, and they don't want to fail.

5. Assess the financial health of the lender. Can he or she manage financially if you default? Will circumstances make an already pressured situation unbearably oppressive?

6. Handle the transaction as an arm's-length business deal, preferably one that benefits both parties. (Splitting the difference on the interest rate—choosing a rate midway between what the lender is earning on savings and what the borrower might pay at a bank—makes sense financially and emotionally. That way, the borrower feels less beholden, the lender less exploited.)

Put everything in writing. Consider having a lawyer draw up a promissory note, or buy a blank note form in a stationery or business-supply store. Yes, this might be uncomfortable, but it has several benefits.

The written record adds a certain solemnity to the transaction. It also reminds the borrower that repayment is expected. Later on, if the borrower has trouble making the payments, it's much healthier for the relationship if he can blame an inanimate piece of paper rather than a loved one who is "unreasonably" dunning him for money.

Be clear about the terms. Will the loan be amortized? Will it be payable on demand, or will the money be due on a specific date?

7. Make sure both sides are really comfortable with the details. If the loan is for a business start-up, the lender has a right to expect a higher rate to offset the risk. Similarly, for a long-term loan, you might want to adjust the interest rate on a monthly, quarterly, or yearly basis, so the lender doesn't feel cheated if rates rise sharply.

Realize, too, that a financially successful deal can harm a relationship as much as, if not more than, an out-and-out fiasco. Things can get really tricky, because you're dealing with subjective concerns rather than objective business standards. For example, a venture capitalist will, by definition, share in the good fortune of anyone he backs. A bank that made a loan to the same entrepreneur won't share the profits—unless, that is, it has negotiated an equity kicker. In either case, the apportionment is well defined.

But what about a friend whose $20,000 loan helped plant the seed for, say, Apple Computer, or a relative who provided down-payment money for a house that tripled in value? Is repayment and a thank-you note sufficient?

Realize that a runaway success can cause hard feelings if it is not shared. Addressing such issues in writing doesn't always make everything better. People's circumstances change. A degree of success that seemed purely theoretical at one point looks very different once it's real.

Bankers and venture capitalists never expect more than their duly contracted pound of flesh. A friend or relative, however, may want something more. That doesn't mean you have to give, but it's unwise not to consider the possibility before making the deal.

8. When drawing up the loan agreement, discuss the worst-case scenario, especially if the loan is for a new business. What will happen if you can't repay? Is there any collateral you could offer that would ease the sting of a default?

Some lenders are too polite to bring up such things, much as they might want to. So, borrower, it's probably your job.

Default won't be a pretty prospect no matter what you do. Still, you wouldn't believe how often a charged situation is worsened because the idea of default was never discussed. In such cases, when the worst does happen, the lender may feel profoundly abused. Was he hoodwinked, or were his interests simply ignored from the outset? Since, presumably, you're borrowing the money in good faith, don't underestimate the importance of making that clear to the lender every step of the way.

9. Don't do anything to erode the lender's trust. If repayment suddenly becomes a problem, be honest about it. Never promise a payment you'll be unable to make unless your boss gives you a surprise 52-percent raise. Explain the problem, and, if necessary, renegotiate the payment schedule or request a one-time extended grace period.

Again, when there's a problem, it's always vital to let the creditor know exactly where things stand *as soon as possible*. Remember, you're never talking only about money; there's a human being on the other end of the transaction. A friend or relative, in particular, needs to know that you've given some thought to his well-being and his financial concerns.

10. Respect the delicate psychological balance of the debtor-creditor relationship. It is, for instance, entirely natural for a lender to be concerned about the way the borrower is spending his money. The announcement of an impending two-week trip to Hawaii won't be greeted with smiles.

That's one of the galling aspects of borrowing money from people with whom you are—at least for now—on speaking terms: you think they're looking over your shoulder, always assessing the scope and quality of your spending, gauging how your affairs are going. You're probably right. They're just minding their own business. It's only that now you've become *part* of their business.

This can take a toll on social relations. "The most mundane things, like the choice of a restaurant, can become complicated and awkward," says Olivia Mellan, a Washington, D.C., psychotherapist specializing in the psychology of money.

It is no pleasure to watch someone who owes you money dine well.

Those who lend money sometimes show an inordinate interest in the business affairs of the borrower. Or perhaps they show no special interest at all. It's hard to tell. And that's the point. Every question seems loaded. Furthermore, it's hard to know what the right answer is to a prosperity-related question. If business is good, where's my money? If business is bad, well, are you telling me that I'm never going to see my money again? The borrower can't win.

Don't be shocked if borrowers' syndrome strikes. "People who owe money to individuals rather than institutions often come to resent the lender and feel that he or she doesn't really need the money back," says Judy Barber, a San Francisco psychotherapist specializing in money issues.

The feeling may be most acute when you've borrowed from parents who are comfortable financially. After all, you assume you're going to get the money someday.

Such feelings are very common; they're also usually unfair. If you accept a low-interest loan from a wealthy person, try to be grateful. Don't torture yourself with dreams of a better deal or a magical borrower's amnesty.

CAN IT EVER WORK?

Of course, it can. Borrowing from Mom and Dad doesn't have to make you feel like a child or send you hurtling into therapy. "When I borrowed money from my parents to pay my taxes," says Denise, a 35-year-old Boston lawyer, "I matched the investment return they were getting. That way it didn't feel like a handout. I've worked very hard to feel independent; I didn't want to undermine that in any way.

Everything worked out fine. I paid the loan back a year and a half early."

Sometimes, entering into a financial transaction with someone you love—as risky as it may be—can produce nonfinancial benefits. "Money can offer you an opportunity to renegotiate your relationship with your parents," says Annette Lieberman, a New York psychotherapist and author of *Unbalanced Accounts: How Women Can Overcome Their Fear of Money*. "If you approach them not as a child but as a serious adult offering them a mutually advantageous deal, that can change the power dynamic. You can show them you're responsible about money."

Still, one financial planner in the Southwest will pass on that opportunity. "My father has offered me low-interest loans for years," she says, "but if I accepted, I would never feel that my success was totally mine. And he would keep reminding me of that. Once he offered me an 8-percent loan when the bank wanted 18 percent, but I decided that the loan from the bank was much cheaper."

TAX ISSUES

No matter which side of the transaction you're on, be aware that for tax purposes, a personal loan that goes sour may be only partly deductible—and sometimes it's not deductible at all. First, the good news. Bad *business* debts are completely deductible, so this might affect the way you want to structure a loan.

And if it's not for business? The IRS says you're allowed to write off $3,000 in nonbusiness debt in any one year if you can prove that you made a genuine attempt to recoup the money and you can show that there's really no chance of collection.

(Warning: Even when you can prove both points, the IRS will sometimes remain dubious if the loan is to a relative. A loan to a loved one may really be a gift, whether you know it or not.)

Below-market-interest-rate loans or loans that turn into gifts may raise gift-tax issues, although this doesn't happen very often. Under current law, one person can give another $10,000 a year without any tax consequences—thus, two parents can give one child $20,000 a year, and they can give the child and his or her spouse $40,000 a year.

As a matter of practice, there won't be tax consequences for the lender on any loan up to $100,000 if the borrower's investment income is less than $1,000. The IRS, it seems, will be placated if the borrower really is using the money to buy a home or in some other federally sanctioned manner. What the Feds clearly want to discourage is sleight-of-hand income shifting—when a child would use the parents' money to earn investment income that would be taxed at a lower rate.

How does the IRS define the market rate? Usually, it's approximately 1 percentage point below the prevailing rate for 30-year fixed-rate mortgages. The government announces the new Applicable Federal Interest Rates monthly. You can find them in *The Wall Street Journal* on or about the twentieth of each month (usually on the Credit Markets page) or in the monthly *Internal Revenue Bulletin*.

A BETTER WAY TO KEEP IT ALL IN THE FAMILY

Forget your parents. Consider borrowing from your kid.

Parents are allowed, for instance, to borrow from a child's trust account if the trustee approves, as he or she often will if a fair interest rate is set.

You may also be allowed to borrow from a child's Uniform Gifts to Minors Act account (if you can claim this somehow benefits the child) and you may certainly borrow from a child's regular savings account. Sometimes this might be a smart alternative to seeking a loan elsewhere, but only if there is no risk of your being unable to repay. Defaulting on a loan from a parent is bad, but there's a certain generational logic to it, and it's not the most heinous financial offense imaginable. But losing your kid's money? That's your kid's job, not yours.

15

HOME-EQUITY LOANS

$Ellen and Matt have a $25,000 home-equity line of credit—and they hate it. They've tapped the line for $5,000, mostly to pay off credit-card debt and cover medical costs for their two young children.

"We're only paying interest on the debt," says Ellen. "We haven't made a dent in the principal. We're afraid we're going to find a reason to borrow some of the $20,000 that's available. It's like this monster we're always staring at. Or it's a monster that's staring at us."

Ellen and Matt have a nearly perfect attitude toward home-equity loans (HELs). They're paranoid.

But not paralyzed. They figured out the Jekyll-and-Hyde quality of HELs, recognizing that they're both the best loans in America and also among the most insidious. A home-equity credit line, after all, offers virtually the same temptations as a dozen credit cards, although at a much lower and tax-advantaged interest rate. This means it can let you ruin your financial life more slowly and, from an accountant's perspective, more intelligently.

So we face a paradox: If you absolutely hate the idea of borrowing against the value of your home, you may be the ideal candidate for a home-equity loan.

THE HOME-EQUITY CULTURE

If you had told people in 1940 that Ronald Reagan, one of the stars of *Knute Rockne—All American*, would serve two terms as president of the United States in the 1980s, they would have laughed. If you had told them that second mortgages, then viewed as one of the major causes of human misery and financial ruin during the Depression, would one day be chic, they would have been too shocked to laugh.

Some strange things happened in America during the eighties.

Total second-mortgage debt on private residences has surpassed $300 billion, and it's still soaring. As you know, there's virtually no other game in town for a consumer seeking tax-deductible interest payments.

You can deduct the interest on second mortgages up to $100,000 as long as the loan doesn't exceed the original purchase price plus improvements. Deductibility is great, of course—but only up to a point. In isolation, deductibility is not the highest of fiscal virtues. Many consumers and quite a few bankers need to be reminded of that.

Two things are scary about home-equity borrowing. One is obvious: botch the job, and you could lose your home. (More on this in a moment, but not much more. After all, the delinquency rate on second mortgages is lower than it is on first mortgages.)

The second potential pitfall is more subtle and, for millions of people, far more dangerous. The real problem is that home-equity borrowing can encourage the growth of perma-debt. Worse, it can almost make you accept that state. Borrowing against your home can make perma-debt seem normal and painless.

Still, HELs are a marvelous tool when they are used appropriately—that is, when they reduce the overall cost of borrowing rather than increase it. If, for example, you had $10,000 in credit-card debt at 19.8 percent and paid off the debt with a home-equity line of credit that cost you about 5.58 percent after taxes (the nominal rate is 7.75, but for people in the 28-percent tax bracket the after-tax rate drops to roughly 5.58 percent), how much would you save? Well, it's important to recognize that there's no absolute answer. It all depends when you would have paid off the credit-card debt (doing that *could* take almost 24 years) and when you *will* pay off the home-equity line. What if you decided that, in either case, you'd discharge the debt in 10 years? Then you would save about $10,000 in interest by getting the credit line. Not a bad move. (Closing costs and annual fees would reduce the savings by $300 to $1,000.)

This example assumes that interest rates will remain flat. Of course, interest rates almost never remain flat. It also assumes that you'll pay off the home-equity debt religiously, without adding to it. This is definitely possible, but will you?

What if you took a somewhat different tack and used the same credit line to buy a car and pay it off over 30 years? (Whether they acknowledge it or not, many Americans are pursuing this strategy.) Here's how the numbers look.

Assume that same flat 5.58-percent after-tax rate for 30 years and a 4-year new-car loan rate of 8.5 percent. The cost of financing $15,000 for 4 years at 8.5 percent is $2,747. (I'm assuming you got a great rate at a credit union or bank.) At the much better after-tax rate of 5.58 percent, 30 years of finance charges would cost six times as much, or $17,054. Pay nothing but interest on the debt for the first 10 years—as many lenders encourage you to—and the total interest cost jumps to $18,849—seven times as much as the more expensive (from an annual-interest-rate perspective, at least) 4-year deal.

So you could end up paying $33,849 for a $15,000 car, or quite a bit more if the variable rate on your credit line jumps. When rates are low, the idea of transforming a cheap 4-year loan into a 30-year variable-rate loan is particularly unappealing.

HOW THE DEALS WORK

Home-equity deals come in two basic flavors. The plain vanilla version is the closed-end home-equity loan, which is really nothing more than a traditional second mortgage. It almost always has a fixed interest rate. The tutti-frutti variety is the open-end line of credit, which almost always sports a variable interest rate. It's the hot, sexy, and dangerous product—the one that sometimes gets even the savviest borrowers in trouble.

The products have some similarities. Both are cheap and easy to obtain from credit unions, commercial banks, S&Ls, mortgage banks, finance companies, major brokerage firms, or even General Motors Acceptance Corporation. Be sure not to overlook the brokers, who sometimes offer great rates, especially to existing customers.

The average credit line has a rate of prime plus 1.75 percent, with the typical second mortgage about 2 to 2.5 points higher. Not too long ago, someone contemplating a home-equity product had to do some real math to see if it was worth it. There were points and origination fees and hefty closing costs. No longer. Today, if you're thinking about this kind of loan, it's almost always worth it in purely financial terms—which isn't the same as saying it's a good idea. According to the Consumer Bankers Association, total fees and closing costs in 1991 averaged $486 for lines and $456 for loans. (If you use a lawyer or live in a state with a mortgage-recording tax, you'll pay more.)

Lenders will often waive almost all fees for existing customers, especially during periodic promotions. When the competition gets particularly savage, fee waivers are granted to new customers as well. So if you can wait for a deal, you might save $400 or more. It's a buyer's market. (Credit unions are less likely than banks to waive fees or run no-fee promotions.)

On average, institutions will lend up to 75 percent of the value of the home, minus any existing mortgage debt. If your home is worth $200,000 and you're carrying a $100,000 mortgage, you'll be able to borrow $50,000 ($200,000 × .75 = $150,000; $150,000 − $100,000 = $50,000). The LTVs (loan-to-value ratios) vary from region to region, however. In much of New England, LTVs of only 65 percent prevail. On the West Coast it's 75 percent, while in the Midwest, LTVs are typically 80–85 percent.

These days, you may be able to qualify for a credit line with an LTV of 100 percent. Key Federal Savings in Baltimore and Banc One in Cleveland are among those offering the feature, which costs about 2.75 points more than a standard LTV product. This loan makes it possible for homebuyers to get a credit line right after closing on a new home. So, in effect, they can begin equity stripping immediately, without that unpleasant and unnecessary *waiting* period. Naturally, the lenders contend that such deals allow good people to buy a lot of house and still have funds to furnish it. Precisely how much distress and chaos such offers will cause is hard to predict.

The 100-percent LTV deals are important symbolically. Home-equity lenders have become accustomed to such a low default rate that some may be willing to lend you more than you can really handle. They know you'll find a way to pay them *first* (or second, anyway). How you handle your other obligations really isn't their lookout.

Therefore, many lenders will let you stretch; they'll tolerate a gross debt-to-income ratio of 43 percent, and often more with special pleading. But don't ever confuse a creditor's concept of security with your own. When you borrow against your home, get in the habit of taking less than the maximum the lender is willing to give you. If you have to, you can always go back for more.

THE HOME-EQUITY CREDIT LINE

One bank-industry official sums up the distinction between lines and loans this way: The line is the "champagne" product, the loan more of a "six-pack." (Both can get you drunk.) Surveys show that line users are more sophisticated, better educated, and richer than those who take the loans. They've also lived in their homes longer.

The great virtues of a line include:

• *Flexibility*. You can draw down as much or as little of the line as you want and pay interest only on the amount you actually use.

• *Easy access*. You can tap the line by writing a check, or in some cases by using an ATM (the minimum transaction is usually $250 or $500).

• *Lower rates*. Since they were introduced in 1986, lines have been a much better financial deal than fixed-rate second mortgages. Their variable rates start out several points lower than the fixed-rate loans, and they've tended to fall from there. (Don't bank on this continuing, however; see the "negatives," below.)

Among the negatives:

• *Constant temptation*. A line represents easy money. It's there whenever you need it. Think of Matt and Ellen staring at the monster. It's one thing for debt to cause anxiety; that's pretty normal. But do you want to worry about *potential* debt? Some people, of course, know that for them the temptation isn't theoretical, that it will lead directly to calls to travel agents, decorators, tailors, and merchants of every description.

• *Leisurely repayment terms*. Lenders permit, and even encourage, protracted repayment schedules. Virtually every line offers the opportunity to transform a good loan into a clinker. It takes strong discipline to ignore such opportunities. (Strategies for overcoming this problem are discussed below.)

• *Variable rates*. This is a great feature when the prime rate is going south, but what happens if your monthly payments start heading north? As with ARMs, you have to confront the borrower's hated enemy, the worst-case scenario. How high is up? Monthly principal-and-interest payments on a 10-year, $30,000 line would be $360.03 at 7.75 percent, $371.96 at 8.5 percent, $396.45 at 10 percent, $430.41 at 12 percent, $484 at 15 percent, and $579.77 at 20 percent. (You can easily do your own approximate calculations by referring to the table in Appendix B. Or ask your lender.)

• *Annual fees*. Second mortgages don't have them, but credit lines often do. They range from $25 to $100, and the trend is clear: fees are spreading and rising. And they're not included in the lender's APR calculations. On a fully utilized $30,000 line at 7.75 percent, a $50 annual fee would produce a real APR of 7.91 percent. A $100 fee would make the APR 8.06 percent. (Note: Fees may be tax-deductible if you use the line for investment purposes.)

Here's how to do a fast APR approximation that includes annual fees. Multiply the average outstanding balance (in the example above, it's $30,000) by the stated interest rate (.0775). That comes to $2,325, which is the amount of interest you'd pay per year. Then divide the annual fee ($50) by $2,325, and you get .02, or 2 percent. Multiply the stated rate by 1.02 to arrive at the APR—in this case 7.91 percent.

OVERCOMING THE NEGATIVES

Each of these negatives can be minimized or overcome.

1. We all cope with temptation every day. The question to ask here is: How well have you handled financial temptation in the past? The bank does a credit check, but you should do a gut check before taking out a line. How well do you know yourself? How sure are you that you've shucked the bad spending or borrowing habits that have made the line of credit you're now considering so appealing or so essential?

Rule number one: Don't take out a bigger line than you need. That's one of the mistakes Matt and Ellen made, but it's not an irrevocable one. At any time, you can ask your lender to reduce your credit line. (And if you've been too conservative about estimating your borrowing needs, it can almost always be increased as well. In 1991, it cost an average of $246 to increase a credit line.)

2. Forget the lender's repayment schedule. You're going to make your own: otherwise, the line of credit will always be a mistake—*always*. If you use the line to buy a car, pay it off monthly as if it *were* a car. Pick a loan term of 2, 3, or 4 years—not 5, 6, or 7—and make

the appropriate monthly payments (use the table in Appendix B). Actually, you can custom-tailor your own loan terms. Maybe a 38-month car loan is perfect for you. (In this case, use a financial calculator or a software package, or call the lender's customer service department to determine the monthly payment.)

Make a commitment to yourself to pay off home improvements in 5, 6, or 7 years. With a debt-consolidation loan, make monthly payments at least as high as your combined minimum payments before consolidating. (Do that and you're guaranteed to come out ahead. Pay more than the minimums and you'll come out even further ahead.) Pay back education loans as fast as humanly possible without decimating your life-style. Whatever term you choose, pick a schedule and stick to it.

Many lenders will help by accepting electronic payments (monthly withdrawals from your checking or savings account). Some might give you a slight rate break for using this payment method.

True, your friends may be handling their lines more casually, which might give them a few extra bucks to spend now on impressive gewgaws. But they're going to be paying for those frills for a long time.

It's scary how many people are taking those 10-year interest-only payment offers seriously. Nationally, about 33 percent of all credit-line borrowers pay interest only, but at some banks the figure is close to 100 percent! "I think it's really stupid," says an official at a large New York City bank, where such lemminglike unanimity prevails. "I'd never do it. These people just figure they'll pay off the debt when they sell the house. They're still operating on the assumption that real-estate appreciation will take care of everything, although that may not be true."

3. To minimize carnage from rising rates, look for lenders who offer caps limiting rate increases during the life of the loan. Shop carefully and you may be able to find lifetime caps as low as 5 points. Your initial interest rate may be somewhat higher; it's the price you pay for rate protection.

For lines originated after 1987, however, lifetime caps average 19 percent, with some as high as 25 percent. If you got your line in 1986 or 1987, your lender probably doesn't have any annual or lifetime cap. Consider requesting that a cap be added to the agreement.

4. Shop around until you find a lender with a competitive rate and fees not much above $25 a year. When you're contemplating a $30,000

or $60,000 credit line, I know that a $25 or $50 annual-fee differential doesn't sound like a big hit. But keep the line for 20 years and you're talking about $500 or $1,000.

It will help, as well, to do the math on the trade-off between fees and rates, as discussed earlier.

WHEN TO USE LINES OF CREDIT

Credit lines are best when you'll be making payments over an extended period: for tuition, recurring medical costs, or perhaps a lengthy home-improvement project. They can be fine for buying cars and consolidating debts as well, as long as you recognize how risky their flexibility can be.

HOME-EQUITY LOANS (SECOND MORTGAGES)

Second mortgages are much simpler than lines of credit. They're for a set amount of money for a definite term (usually 5 to 15 years), almost always at a fixed rate.

You can get one with a variable rate, although most people who choose second mortgages over credit lines don't *want* to take a ride on the interest-rate roller coaster. They tend to prefer certainty.

Indeed, second mortgages are great for people who want to know exactly where they stand, who don't want any surprises from without (in the form of higher rates) or within (spasms of imprudence, for instance). If you doubt your own discipline or are nervous about the yawning open-endedness of a credit line, then a second mortgage is a logical alternative. A traditional second is just like a first mortgage.

There are some potential negatives, though.

• You'd better be right about the amount you borrowed, because you can't go back for more—unless you pay a whole new set of fees.

• If you hit any cash-flow problems, you don't have the flexibility of a credit line to fall back on. Refinancing the second mortgage or your first one is always an option, although a costly one. If you have any reason to think you might eventually be backed into such a corner, consider taking a credit line instead—or, more to the point, think about taking out a smaller loan or no loan at all.

WHEN TO CHOOSE A SECOND MORTGAGE

Second mortgages make the most sense when you face a substantial one-time payment rather than a series of expenditures. They work well for home improvements, debt consolidation, a one-shot medical expense, or start-up capital for a business.

WHAT TO WATCH OUT FOR

• Beware of teaser rates on credit lines. Be sure to read the fine print in any ad or brochure. Some loan rates may jump three points or more just three months into the life of the loan, regardless of what happens to the prime rate.

If you fall for one of these sleazy deals or if, for any reason, you have second thoughts about the wisdom of accepting the line, the 1988 Home Equity Loan Consumer Protection Act can save you. You may back out during a three-day cooling-off period after you apply—without losing your application fee.

• Many borrowers don't realize that if the lifetime interest-rate cap is ever reached, the lender has the right to shut down the credit line and halt additional withdrawals. A lender, however, may not demand accelerated repayment for this reason. (All contracts written after October 1, 1991, must put this restriction in writing.)

• When seeking a credit line, avoid weak S&Ls. If an institution is dissolved, credit lines could be canceled.

• If you don't itemize, or won't exceed the standard deduction (currently $6,000 for married couples filing jointly and $3,600 for single individuals) even after paying tax-deductible interest on a line or loan, don't worry about the deductibility issue. Pick the cheapest loan you can find.

• To initiate a second mortgage, both spouses must sign. Tapping a home-equity line, though, requires only one signature. In a rocky marriage, it may not be a good idea to maintain a huge open line of credit that one spouse can access in a moment of pique.

• If you don't have a loan or line yet but it seems like a logical, money-saving idea for you, be sure to clean up your credit report so you'll be able to qualify for a low interest rate. "If you have any delinquencies of 60 days or more in the last few years, we won't let you borrow against your home," says a New York bank lending officer.

• On your credit report, a $25,000 credit line is counted as a $25,000 debt, whether or not you've drawn down a cent. Open a large line and you may find you no longer qualify for that cheap credit card you've been coveting. So apply for the credit card first. (Home-equity lenders are less concerned about your unused plastic credit lines than they are with existing balances.)

• Lenders can freeze or reduce your credit line if the value of your property declines substantially or if your financial condition worsens. In a weak economy, lenders freeze lines faster when customers lose jobs, because it might take a while for them to find work again.

Lenders can hit you even harder than that. Most contracts have a "call clause," allowing them to demand complete repayment of the loan should the value of the collateral or the financial health of the borrower weaken significantly. Even if property values are stable or rising where you live, lenders can call the loan if you let your property become run-down. Such actions are rare, however.

• On pre-1989 loans, lenders are able to change terms—fees, interest-rate calculations, minimum monthly payments, and so on— at will.

• Don't take out a line or loan without having an additional savings or borrowing cushion. No matter what happens, you must keep making your home-equity payments. On this point, you have no flexibility.

• Whenever possible, avoid taking a line or loan for the maximum available amount. If real estate prices decline and the loan becomes undercollateralized, you may be asked to make additional payments.

• If points ever come back into vogue in the home-equity market, remember: comparing APRs can get tricky. Up-front points are not counted in the APR for credit lines (nor are annual fees), so the line may look cheaper than it really is. For second mortgages, points are factored into the APR.

• Don't borrow $50,000 if you can get by with $49,999. When the $50,000 threshold is crossed, many lenders require title insurance, which can add $50 or so to your tab. (Your lender may have a different threshold, so ask.)

• Make sure the fine print does not mention prepayment penalties. If it does, ask that the penalties be dropped.

WHAT ARE PEOPLE DOING WITH THEIR HOME-EQUITY MONEY?

According to the Consumer Bankers Association's 1992 Home Equity Loan Study, the primary reason for home-equity borrowing is now debt consolidation rather than home improvement.

Credit-line users reported their uses as follows:

Debt consolidation—36 percent	Business expense—4 percent
Home improvement—28 percent	Other—3 percent
Automobile—11 percent	Vacation—2 percent
Education—9 percent	Medical—2 percent
Investment—4 percent	Tax payment—1 percent

Second-mortgage use was fairly similar:

Debt consolidation—43 percent	Other (including medical and
Home improvement—29 percent	tax payments)—5 percent
Automobile—10 percent	Business expense—3 percent
Education—7 percent	Investments—2 percent
	Vacation—1 percent

In 1991, the average line of credit at commercial banks and S&Ls was $32,095; the average second mortgage was $20,445. The typical borrower had tapped 59.6 percent of his or her credit line.

CONCLUSION

One Philadelphia-area lender, the Germantown Savings Bank, was so unnerved about how its customers were using home-equity money that it took out a full-page ad in the *Philadelphia Inquirer*. It read, "Although you have always wanted to go on safari, ask yourself whether your home is worth a few snapshots of wild giraffes."

A bank trying to drive away business? Yes, and for all the right reasons. It makes little sense to borrow against your house to pay for things that are nonessential or nonproductive, such as a safari, a fur coat, or a car you can't really afford. Default on the car, and they don't send a repo man—they send a sheriff to hold a foreclosure sale.

While I don't think home-equity loans will lead to the moral, spiritual, and financial decline of America (that's been taken care of already), it's likely that in the next five or ten years we'll see many more families *paying* money when they sell their homes rather than receiving it. Some people will wake up and ask, "Where did all the equity go?"

DEBT CONSOLIDATION

You're swamped by credit-card bills. You're steamed about paying such outrageous interest rates, about throwing good money after bad. Which is better for you, a line or a loan?

Maybe neither.

Consolidating debts with a line or a loan won't work if you keep creating new debt with credit cards. It has a better chance of succeeding, some experts say, if you undergo credit counseling beforehand.

It may be worth noting that, according to the Consumer Bankers Association, most of the credit lines and second mortgages that lead to foreclosures were used for debt consolidation. (Home-improvement loans have the lowest default rate.)

If credit cards are hurting you, I'm not trying to scare you away from home-equity debt. Not unequivocally, anyway. It's just vital to realize that borrowing habits don't change overnight simply because you've been granted a wonderful new cheap, tax-advantaged form of debt.

SHOULD YOU BORROW AGAINST YOUR HOUSE EVEN IF YOU DON'T NEED THE MONEY RIGHT NOW?

Yes. It can be a very smart thing to do. But only for those who are sure they can handle temptation, or those who worry that they may soon need a lot of money and want to get it as cheaply and intelligently as they can.

As will be discussed in chapter 20, few things are more predictable than unpredictable expenditures. They will happen. Whether they come in the form of out-of-pocket medical expenses, a large tax bill, or unexpected home repairs, they will happen. Instead of using plastic, overdraft checking, or any other kind of extremely expensive borrowing, you can save money by lining up the cheapest source of credit in advance.

You may also be glad you have a line when you're looking to buy a new home and fear that you'll have trouble selling your current one quickly. In short, you'll probably end up needing a bridge loan in order to close on the new property. You'll have to pay points to get a formal bridge loan, and a higher interest rate as well.

Consider setting up a line of credit if things look shaky at work or if the economic outlook for your particular industry is so bleak that you might be laid off no matter how much they like you. Once you're out of a job, you'll have a tough time getting a loan—any loan—because you *need* the money. Sure, you can use credit cards for a while; but how long will they last, and what kind of rates will you have to pay?

But won't the lender freeze your line if you're out of work? Maybe not all of it. More important, though, there may be a lag between the time you know things have definitely worsened and when you're actually let go (or when your commission income declines). Tapping the line during that period makes perfect sense. You're not getting the money under false pretenses.

Or tap the line even earlier and put the money in a savings account. If you're already worried about work, you don't also want to be agitated about the liquidity of your credit line should you get bad news.

Can't lenders demand immediate repayment if they hear you're out of a job? Technically, yes, although this seldom happens if your payments remain prompt. And it's especially unlikely if you talk to the lender, on the phone or in person, about your job prospects.

WAIT FOR THE APPRAISAL—PLEASE

Don't ever start home improvements until the appraisal has been completed. You could wind up like the East Coast doctor who was so eager to transform his $1-million, 3,000-square-foot home into a 6,000-square-foot colossus that he had the place gutted right after prequalifying for his loan.

Then the appraiser showed up—and gasped.

When a major New York bank reviewed the subsequent appraisal—which was done, as appraisals usually are, on an as-is basis—it withdrew its loan agreement. (The bank was perfectly within its rights, since the loan was contingent upon an appraisal.) "We can't accept appraisals 'on the come,'" explained one of the bank's senior credit officers.

After an interlude of pure panic, the doctor finally found a lender who could grasp his vision for San Simeon East, and he received enough money to complete the renovations.

OTHER FACTS TO CONSIDER

- You can save a few hundred dollars by not hiring a lawyer. Hardly any home-equity borrowers use them these days.
- In some states and municipalities, expect to pay a mortgage-

recording tax as well. Wonder where it's highest? New York. On a
$50,000 line or loan in New York City, you'd pay a tax of $875.

• If you love home-equity borrowing and think that someday you
might move to Texas, think again. Texas has a lot of attractions, but
loans secured by a home aren't among them: it's the one state that
forbids the practice. "And it's a good thing, too," says Houston financial
planner Ross Richardson. "People can already get access to credit too
easily."

• Home-equity lenders can charge up to seventeen different types
of fees. Some lenders even charge you for *not* using your line of credit.
So shop carefully.

• The average credit-line customer accessed his or her account
eleven times in 1991 (not including payments).

• Believe it or not, it may take no more than 15 or 20 minutes to
close on a home-equity line or loan.

PART IV

SMART MOVES

$

16

A FORTUNE FROM
SMALL CHANGE:
THE JOY OF PREPAYING

$My friends Stan and Pearl don't get many of their thrills from finance, but I like them, anyway. So I was stunned when they, of all people, became euphoric about the idea of prepaying their mortgage. "Just by paying an extra $25 a month," Pearl whispered, "we can save thousands and thousands of dollars."

She's correct, of course. By prepaying $25 a month—a month's worth of loose change for many couples—on a $100,000, 30-year, 8-percent fixed-rate mortgage, Pearl and Stan could save $23,337 in interest charges and cut the term of their mortgage by 3 years and 6 months.

Prepayment is a wonderful, simple, can't-miss proposition—and there aren't many of those around. Prepaying the mortgage, says *Work and Family Life*, can help reduce stress. It is also a good way to save for college or fund a retirement. (One reason retirement is so difficult for some people is that they're still coping with sizable mortgage payments.) Having a paid-off mortgage is becoming a nineties-style status symbol.

But you don't have to own a home to profit. Prepaying works with almost every kind of debt, including credit-card debt.

A few examples should help illustrate the power of prepaying:

• On that $100,000, 30-year, 8-percent fixed-rate mortgage, pre-paying $50 a month saves $39,906 in interest and reduces the term by 6 years and 1 month.

• Prepay $100 a month and you'll save $62,456 and have the loan paid off 9 years and 10 months ahead of schedule.

• Make that $200 a month and you'll realize savings of $88,260 and have the home paid off 14 years and 3 months early—cutting the loan term almost in half.

One of the beautiful things about prepayment is that any approach works. You can be rigorous or haphazard, use computer analysis or astrology, and it will still be effective.

WHERE TO START

Unfortunately, most articles about prepayment strategies have focused almost exclusively on mortgage debt. Not only has this caused some renters to ignore a profitable strategy, but it has led some homeowners to prepay the wrong debt first.

Financially, it's not smart to prepay a mortgage, which is usually the cheapest debt you carry, if you have *any* debts with higher interest rates. (Besides, your mortgage interest is deductible; interest on your other debts probably is not.) The prepayment strategy, therefore, is especially powerful when it is applied to credit cards.

If you owe $2,000 on a 19.8-percent credit card and make only the minimum payments (assuming Citibank's 2.777-percent minimum), the debt would cost you $2,254.01 in interest and take 12 years and 2 months to pay off. But prepay just an additional $5 a month and you'll reduce the interest costs by $595.24 and be rid of the debt 41 months sooner.

Prepay $10 a month, and you'll cut the interest by $933.94 and the term by 63 months.

Make it $20 a month, and you'll save $1,310.83 and 87 months.

Boost that to $40 a month—just a little more than a dollar per day—and you'll save $1,646.03 and 109 months.

At $50 a month, you slash the interest by $1,736.64 and the term by 115 months.

And what if you can afford $75 more a month? That gets rid of the debt 10 years and 3 months ahead of schedule and saves you $1,874.94 in interest.

In purely financial terms, the optimal prepayment strategy is to focus first on the loan with the highest interst rate. Once that is paid off, work your way rung by rung down the interest-rate ladder.

Not everyone agrees. Some say this cold dollars-and-cents approach neglects the psychological component. They contend that it feels better to pay down all debts simultaneously. That way, you have a sense of running on all cylinders. And there's often a special kick from knowing that the mortgage, that enormous albatross, won't be around your neck for as long as you once thought.

Some people prefer to adjust their strategies every month, depending on how flush they feel. One upstate New York husband and wife, for example, prepay an extra $25 every month on their $75,000 mortgage. That's a given. Then they see what's left and prepay up to $200 on their other debts. They say the flexibility works for them.

WHERE DOES THE MONEY COME FROM?

At this point, you may be convinced that prepaying is a great idea— for other people. For those folks, that is, who have the cash to carry it off.

According to Marc Eisenson, author of *The Banker's Secret*, the prepayment bible, almost everyone who is even vaguely solvent has enough to begin a small prepayment program. One of Eisenson's favorite starting points is the bowl, jar, or drawer where people stash loose change.

Nanette and Phil Leonard have been following his advice for years, prepaying their $40,000 mortgage with pocket change. Each month their 10-year-old son, Bradley, puts the change into coin sleeves. (If there's more than $25, Bradley gets the excess.)

Nanette and Phil enjoy prepaying so much ("We love the idea that we won't be into the bank for as long," she says) that they recently added another $15 to their monthly prepayment. "Building equity faster gives you this terrific sense that you're getting somewhere," says Nanette.

One of the keys to prepaying happily is to use money you won't miss. If you're not in any debt trouble, consider using some of the money-saving techniques outlined in chapter 20 to establish a small prepayment fund. Reduce spending by just a dollar a day and you could save over $27,072 on a $100,000, 30-year, 8-percent fixed-rate mortgage.

After reading *The Banker's Secret*, Dave and Juliette Heim, who run a corporate hospitality company called Details Unlimited in Lake Placid, New York, each decided to cut their pack-a-day smoking habits in half. The $69 they save every month goes toward prepaying their $69,000, adjustable-rate mortgage. Cutting down on smoking could save them $62,400 and 129 monthly payments—almost 11 years' worth. (Of course, it may save something else as well.)

Dave Heim has become so intrigued by prepayment possibilities that his latest hobby is creating and analyzing various prepayment scenarios. For example:

• If you used the $5 a month you received from deposits on bottles and cans (assuming a monthly consumption of 100 sodas or beers) and applied it to a $50,000, 30-year, 8-percent fixed-rate mortgage, you'd save $5,217 in interest.

• Eliminate one $60 dinner a month, use the money to prepay a $100,000, 30-year, 9-percent fixed-rate mortgage, and you'll save 7 years and 5 months of payments, and $55,838. (On an 8-percent mortgage, you'd save 7 years and $45,319.)

As I hope these examples show, there may be more money available for prepaying than you initially realize. But please don't overdo it. Some people hate a specific lender, or all lenders, so much that they try to prepay more than they can afford. In such cases, the vitriol will often outlast the cash. Instead of scaling back when the inevitable crunch comes, some people decide to abandon the plan altogether.

THE NUMBERS TAKE CARE OF THEMSELVES

One of the nicest things about prepaying is that you don't have to worry about the math for a second. It's simple enough to explain in one sentence.

When you prepay, you are, in effect, making an investment with a guaranteed, risk-free, pretax annual return precisely equal to the interest rate of the loan. Period. Is your mortgage rate 9 percent? That means prepaying will give you a pretax return of 9 percent per year, compounded for the life of the mortgage.

MORE THAN YOU WANT TO KNOW

You don't need to know exactly how prepayment works to profit from it, but if you're curious, here goes. Every month, most lenders compute interest charges based on the existing balance of your loan. When you prepay $50 on an 8-percent mortgage, this stops the lender from collecting compound interest on the prepaid amount forever. Had you not prepaid the $50, you would have been charged an 8-percent rate on the money for perhaps as many as 360 months.

That's why the return on the money you prepay seems so astronomical—your fancy footwork allows you to dodge all that interest month after month after month. Prepay $50 once at the start of a $100,000, 8-percent fixed-rate mortgage and you'll save $493.18 over 30 years.

IS PREPAYMENT THE BEST "INVESTMENT" STRATEGY?

There's a big debate on this. The short answer is that for most people, prepaying offers a better return than their current investment portfolio.

For anyone holding an 8-percent mortgage, the simple financial question is: Can you find a dependable way to beat an 8-percent pretax return (the equivalent of a 5.76-percent after-tax return for someone in the 28-percent tax bracket)?

You can't earn 8 percent in a savings account, CD, or money-market fund. You might make 8 percent betting on bonds, or a lot more rolling the dice on a futures contract, but you certainly can't count on it.

Historically, there's only one place you have any right to expect such a return, and that's the stock market. Since 1926, the market's total return has averaged 10.4 percent a year according to Ibbotson Associates of Chicago.

Stocks are much safer than pork bellies—most of them, anyway—but, again, there's no guarantee. The only sure thing is that the market will take you on a wild ride on the way to generating that 10.4-percent return—if, indeed, that's what it does over the next 20 years.

The market is an excellent investment, but it has had some lousy 10-year periods. From 1930 to 1939, according to Ibbotson Associates, stocks returned exactly 0 percent per year. Consumer prices were declining 2 percent per year, however, so stocks actually kept investors ahead of inflation. But in the seventies they did not. From 1970 to 1979, stocks rose at a compounded annual rate of 5.9 percent, while inflation galloped along at a compounded annual rate of 7.4 percent.

Of course, some people who'd love to make 10 percent shun the market because it causes indigestion, anxiety, or dementia. They may be the perfect candidates for prepayment.

And even those who don't avoid the market may be logical candidates as well, since most equity investors don't put *all* their investment dollars into the stock market. They diversify. They invest in stock funds, bond funds, individual equities, savings accounts, T-bills, and money-market funds. By diversifying, they reduce their risk, but also their overall return. If the investment mix is heavily weighted toward stocks, over the years the blended return might beat prepaying a mortgage—but definitely not prepaying a credit card.

PREPAYMENT PENALTIES

Before starting a prepayment plan, check your loan agreement or call your lender to see if you're subject to any prepayment penalties. As the prepayment gospel spreads, though, the penalties are becoming much less common.

But if your loan agreement includes prepayment penalties, *don't give up*. These days, the penalties are often not enforced. Many lenders will waive them if you ask nicely or make oblique threats.

The penalties exist primarily to discourage the premature payment of the entire principal, not to thwart piecemeal prepayment techniques. That's why many penalties apply only to the first few years of the loan.

The penalties became popular many decades ago, when lenders charged borrowers almost nothing up front. So if a borrower could find a slightly cheaper rate across the street, the only thing to stop him from "refinancing" his loan with another bank was the prepayment penalty.

Today, many borrowers don't have to worry about prepayment penalties at all. They're not allowed on any FHA or VA loans, and according to the Mortgage Bankers Association, they're forbidden on mortgages in Alabama, Iowa, Maine, Minnesota, New Jersey, New Mexico, Pennsylvania (for loans made after January 30, 1974), and Vermont.

They are also illegal in Alaska (unless required on a federally insured loan), the District of Columbia (except in the first three years), Illinois (if the interest rate exceeds 8 percent—unless required by a federal agency), Kansas (except in the first six months), Mississippi (except in the first five years), Missouri (except in the first five years), North Carolina (unless the loan exceeds $100,000), Ohio (except in the first five years, for loans made after November 4, 1975), and South Carolina (unless the loan exceeds $100,000).

WHEN YOU SHOULDN'T PREPAY

• Some loans, especially Rule of 78s loans, are front-end loaded with interest charges. If you have one of these monstrosities—which are so unfair to consumers that they've been outlawed in seventeen states— don't think of prepaying. It's a losing strategy, and it becomes more disadvantageous the closer you get to the end of the term. Many installment loans use this method of calculating interest.

I could explain exactly how Rule of 78s loans work, but for most readers this would constitute cruel and unusual punishment. Suffice it to say that for a 12-month loan, the first month's payment would account for $12/78$ of the total interest charges, the second payment for $11/78$, the third for $10/78$, and so on. (Added together, the numbers 1 through 12 equal 78, which is why this method of calculating finance charges is also known as the sum of the digits.)

How much more expensive can this kind of loan be? According to the National Consumer Law Center, if you had a $10,000, 10-year loan at 12 percent and prepaid it at the wrong time, you could lose $384. If your deal was worse—say, $20,000 for 12 years at 18 percent—you could lose as much as $2,512 by prepaying.

With Rule of 78s loans, the numbers often don't mean what they seem to. If you have a 12-year, 14.5-percent Rule of 78s loan, you'd naturally be tempted to refinance at today's lower rates. But after 9 years, your loan is really carrying an interest rate of 9.19 percent for the remainder of the term. Don't refinance unless you can beat *that* deal.

• Don't prepay any low-cost loans, especially a mortgage, if you might need to borrow money in the next few years—for college, home improvement, or whatever. Your mortgage debt is almost always the cheapest, most hassle-free financing you can get (once you've got it, that is).

• Stop prepaying your 8-percent mortgage if savings rates rise sharply. If you can earn 8 percent or more risk-free, take it. Your return on investment will be equal to, or greater than, the prepayment option, and you'll have more flexibility. When savings rates fall again, go back to prepaying.

BUT WHAT ABOUT MY TAX DEDUCTION?

Some people don't want to prepay their mortgage because they find the idea of losing their mortgage-interest tax deduction galling or frightening. Why, they wonder, would anyone struggle and skimp to eliminate the only decent thing the government does for them?

Well, when it comes to our ardor for deductions, love is often blind. While it's true that if you're in the 28-percent tax bracket, prepaying an 8-percent mortgage generates an after-tax return of only 5.76 percent, the basic investment question remains unchanged. On an after-tax basis, can you beat it?

Author Eisenson tries to sway skeptics by pointing out that at first, the amount a homeowner can deduct is hardly affected by prepayment. A person in the 28-percent bracket who prepays $25 a month on a $100,000, 30-year, 8-percent fixed-rate mortgage *will* face a higher tax bill. It will rise by all of $3.15 in the first year of the prepayment plan. "Being liable for that extra $3.15 in taxes will ultimately give you deferred savings of $2,808.19, and I think that's a reasonable trade-off," says Eisenson.

As the years pass and your accelerated principal payments reduce your total interest costs, the "lost" deductions will grow—but only very slowly. The real tax kicker comes when the mortgage is fully paid and the deductions disappear entirely. Or do they?

Once your mortgage deduction vanishes, you may finally get to take advantage of the standard deduction available to all Americans. (As we went to press, it was $6,000 for a married couple filing jointly.) Even if you don't itemize, you can deduct $6,000 from your taxes. In effect, therefore, the first $6,000 in annual deductible mortgage interest isn't worth anything because you'd get to deduct that amount no matter what. Even renters get the deduction. (Of course, if your nonmortgage deductions already total more than $6,000, the mortgage-interest deduction is worth exactly what it appears to be.)

Those considering prepaying a mortgage should note that the standard deduction is adjusted upward every year for inflation.

But what about the possibility that the loss of the mortgage-interest deduction will, at some point, push you into a higher tax bracket? Yes, it's conceivable that this could happen, but it will rarely torpedo a sensible prepayment plan. Nonetheless, consult your accountant or financial adviser about possible tax consequences.

If you're still uncomfortable about losing any part of your deduction, that's another argument for prepaying your other, nondeductible debts first—especially those high-interest credit cards—and then tackling the mortgage.

A SLEW OF MORTGAGE-PREPAYMENT STRATEGIES

Once the nondeductible debts are out of the way, you may want to move on to the mortgage. Among the strategies you might select are:

The two-principal payment method. A simple way to cut the term of any loan in half. To execute the strategy, you need an amortization schedule. For a $100,000, 30-year, 8-percent fixed-rate mortgage, you would begin by sending in the regular monthly payment of $733.76 plus the principal amount for month number two ($67.55). The next month, you would send in the regular payment plus the principal amount for month number four ($68.45). And so on.

Since the amount of principal you pay each month rises throughout the term of an amortized loan, your monthly payments will gradually increase under this method. Be prepared. Your last payments will be real doozies.

Designer term prepayment plan. You can turn a $100,000, 30-year, 8-percent fixed-rate mortgage into a 15-year loan by prepaying a set amount—$221.89—every month for 15 years. In pure dollar terms, this is a better deal than the two-principal method. It will save you an extra $10,224.76 in interest because the amount you prepay each month in the early stages of the loan is considerably higher. The money would be working for you longer.

But suppose you can't afford to pay off the $100,000 loan so fast. Well, prepay $102.68 a month and you'll own the home outright in 20 years. What if you prefer, say, 22 years? Then prepay $72.41. Suppose 18 is your lucky number, and you think 18 years is the perfect duration for a mortgage? Then prepay $141.20. Just decide when you'd like to own the home debt-free and you can find a prepayment plan to achieve that goal.

So how do you figure out the right prepayment amount? Your friendly banker might tell you. Your friendly real estate agent would certainly tell you, if you remember to ask while you're shopping for a new home. Or you could get the information from Marc Eisenson (through his book, software, or hotline; see page 187). Many money-management software programs can do the work as well. Or you can get the number from an inexpensive, widely available mortgage-table book, such as Barron's *Mortgage Payments* ($5.95).

A warning: Clearly, both irregular and fixed prepayments can transform a 30-year mortgage into a 15-year deal, but both alternatives might involve unnecessary costs. Always remember that a synthetic 15-year mortgage is *not* the same as a standard 15-year mortgage. The flexibility you get by choosing the prepayment approach—retaining the ability to decide later that you want to alter your monthly payment yet again—comes at a price.

A real 15-year mortgage is always cheaper than a 30 that is gussied up to look like a 15. Typically, you get a .5-percent interest-rate break when you choose a 15-year mortgage up front. As wonderful as flexibility is, you should know precisely what it costs. Over the life of the two loans, the difference between the real 15-year fixed-rate $100,000 mortgage at 7.5 percent and a $100,000, 30-year, 8-percent fixed-rate mortgage that is transformed into a 15 via prepayment is $5,216, before taxes.

Regular prepayment. Pick a set amount you can comfortably prepay month after month. If it has to be small, so be it. Promise yourself that you'll always prepay this amount every month, without excuses.

Sporadic lump-sum payments. While specific goals are both admirable and highly useful, sometimes it's okay to prepay without either a goal or a plan. Some people prepay whenever they have a little more cash on hand than they expected—when, for instance, the stock market, the poker table, or the business world has treated them especially well.

Regular prepayment with a twist. A combination of the preceding two techniques. Your regular monthly prepayment remains stable *except* when you have a little extra cash on hand. Then you raise the payment by an appropriate amount.

Interim prepayment plan while pondering. Prepaying is a great idea if you find yourself on the fence about refinancing. Instead of behaving like Hamlet, *do something.* Prepay. (It's what Hamlet *should* have done.) If rates are falling but you think they'll fall still further, prepaying can ease the mental burden of your wait-and-see strategy. At least you'll know you're doing something right while agonizing over all your alternatives.

IF YOU PREPAY TOO AGGRESSIVELY

Warning: Prepaying too aggressively can lead to unfortunate tax consequences. Some people assume that it they significantly reduce their mortgage and then—oops—need to turn some of that equity into cash by refinancing, they won't be hit with anything worse than additional closing costs. Not necessarily. When you refinance, you cannot deduct all the interest or points if the new mortgage is larger than the original one (unless the increase is used to fund home improvements). A home-equity loan has the same restrictions.

Warning number two: If after prepaying diligently for several years you suddenly hit a rough patch and wish you could skip a mortgage payment, don't expect any favors from your lender. What's done is done. Your monthly obligation to pay in full and on time will never be affected by any payment approach.

The moral: Prepayment is a terrific idea, but don't ever take the benefits of your existing mortgage for granted.

BIWEEKLIES

Biweeklies are another variation on the prepayment theme. They've received a lot of attention lately—much of it misleading. Although most banks won't set up a biweekly program for you, quite a few companies say that they would be willing, for a hefty fee, to transform your mortgage into a biweekly.

In theory, a biweekly is an excellent prepayment option. You divide your monthly payment in half and pay that amount every two weeks.

This way, you'll make 26 half-payments a year—the equivalent of 13 full payments. That, obviously, is one more than you would normally make. Depending on your interest rate, this will slash the term of a 30-year mortgage to 18 to 22 years.

Unfortunately, however, most of us don't live "in theory." Now, for the problems.

• Even if you ask for a biweekly from the start, most banks won't give you one. (Only 6 percent to 7 percent will let you, according to HSH Associates.)

• Some of the banks that will do it hit you with a higher interest rate, wiping out much of the prepayment benefit.

• The set-up charge (often $500) and transaction fees extracted by those who convert your mortgage into a biweekly can eliminate much, or all, of what you could save with a far simpler approach.

• Often, consumers who think they have a biweekly really don't. To put it benignly, many of the high-pressure biweekly conversion operations don't deliver what they promise. Instead of sending your payments to the bank every two weeks, they make one or two additional lump-sum payments each year. All you get is a very expensive version of a lump-sum prepayment plan.

In their defense, the middlemen say that many people don't have the discipline to stick to a prepayment program. This is true enough in some cases, but if consumers knew what they were getting for their money, many would quickly discover heretofore hidden quantitites of resolve.

There's good news, though. You can set up a no-fee prepayment plan of your own that matches the term savings of a biweekly and comes very close to matching the dollar savings as well. Just divide your monthly mortgage payment by 12 and prepay that amount every month.

HOW TO PREPAY

With credit cards, simply pay more than the minimum. There's nothing extra to do, no humans to contact.

With other loans, though, it is probably wise to tell your lender—as a courtesy, if nothing else—that you plan to begin a prepayment program. The most cooperative lenders will actually print out a new amortization schedule to reflect your chosen prepayment strategy.

Ask the lender if you should send a separate check for each pre-payment or simply add the extra amount to the regular payment. If the lender prefers a separate check, ask what language should appear on it. For your own peace of mind, it's smart to enclose a short note stating that the extra check represents a prepayment on the principal of your loan. (Your prepayments should never cover interest charges, only principal.) Include your loan ID number on the front and back of the check.

Eisenson says it's a good idea to check with your lender a week or two after starting a prepayment program to make sure that your additional payment has been properly credited.

Note: Most computations in this chapter were made with the Banker's Secret Loan Software ($39.95) and Banker's Secret Credit Card Software ($25), both excellent packages. For $12.95, Marc Eisenson, author of *The Banker's Secret* ($14.95), and his partner, Nancy Castleman, will send a computer printout analyzing the savings of any prepayment strategy. Or, if you wish, they can tell you what amount to prepay each month so that your 8-percent, 30-year fixed-rate mortgage becomes a 23½–year mortgage. You can reach Eisenson and Castleman at 800 255-0899.

A TIP FOR GETTING STARTED

If you think prepaying sounds great but you keep putting it off, ask your lender (or your computer) to draw up a new amortization schedule based on a reasonable monthly prepayment figure. Sit down in a quiet place and compare your new amortization schedule with your old one. The contrast can be so dramatic—for one thing, the new schedule may be hundreds of lines shorter—that it may stop you from procrastinating any longer.

17

HOW TO SAVE MONEY—
AND TIME—
WHEN PAYING BILLS

$ Generally, playing the float is what companies do with *your* funds. For too many folks, "other people's money" refers to the stuff for which they're perpetually waiting. The other person's check is always in the mail. Once it materializes, you discover that it's drawn on an out-of-state institution, so it will spend a few extra days in financial limbo at your bank, like a tourist trapped during the monsoon season, waiting for things to clear.

Turning the tables can be enjoyable and mildly profitable.

FLOATING

Don't underestimate the power of the float. It forms the very essence of some businesses, such as the issuance of traveler's checks. American Express issues almost $25 billion in traveler's checks per year. Once customers pay for the checks, Amex has interest-free use of the money until a purchase is made. At 6 percent per year, two weeks' worth of interest on $25 billion comes to about $57 million. Amex won't comment on the exact amount (possibly because it's difficult to count that high).

You'll probably earn less than $57 million a year from the float, regardless of your diligence. But you might earn enough to make the process interesting.

AMERICAN EXPRESS

Despite my tirade about the American Express card, I realize it's quite possible that you still have one. Let's see what would happen if someone tried using the float against American Express.

While I don't recommend violating your cardholder agreement (which requires you to pay in full each month), here's what would occur if you did.

When customers pay every other month, Amex does not impose late fees or report the circumstance to credit bureaus. Not ever. (Amex will report you to credit bureaus only after it has canceled your card, which means you almost always have to be at least 90 days late.)

Amex *is* getting a little tougher on late payers, though. Before 1991, you could dawdle for at least 60 days, or two full billing cycles plus a week, before incurring a late fee. Now that's been cut back to 50 days, at which point a fee of $12 is imposed. If you're 60 days late, the fee is $20 or 2.5 percent of the amount delinquent, whichever is greater.

How much might an Amex floater make? If you charge an average of $1,000 per month, the difference between paying immediately or letting the bill sit for 40 days would net you $66.50 per year before taxes, if you were earning 5 percent on your money. That's almost enough, after taxes, to pay for the card's annual fee, or more than enough if you're able to deduct the fee as a business expense. (At 4 percent, you'd make $53.20.)

MORTGAGES

There are two different sets of rules here, one for consumers and another for people who run their own businesses. Although late fees are seldom assessed before the sixteenth of each month, some lenders will consider you "late" on the second of the month. For consumers, this isn't a problem. No late fee is required, and credit bureaus never find out. But the information is in the lender's files nonetheless.

For an entrepreneur who might someday seek a substantial loan, however, it's probably smart to avoid being labeled a late payer.

Ask your lender how its computer system works. Lenders such as Countrywide Funding are particularly lenient—you're late on the sixteenth, but not before. In fact, Countrywide executives with Country-wide mortgages typically pay by electronic funds transfer on the fifteenth of each month. If consumers schedule electronic payments, they may pay Countrywide on the twentieth of each month with no penalty.

How much can you save? Assuming you make a $1,000 monthly payment on the fifteenth instead of the first, you could save $20 a year before taxes, if your savings earned 4 percent.

(Note: Anyone contemplating automatic payments should ask if there's an additional charge. If so, that will cut into, or obliterate, the savings.)

UTILITIES, PHONE, CABLE TV
Bills from phone, utility, and cable TV companies can also be paid every other month, although, like American Express, some of these companies are imposing late penalties faster. Whereas you once could have paid every 60, 70, or 90 days without incurring a late charge, now some companies are slapping fines on floaters after only 50 days. Among the newly vigilant are New York Telephone, Manhattan Cable TV, and Paragon Cable.

This makes the game a lot less fun than it used to be. Still, it might be worth playing, especially if your monthly bills are well above average. If phone, cable TV, and utility bills come to $120 per month, paying 40 days late would net you all of $6.38 per year, pretax. With bills of $300 a month, however, the pretax savings would grow to $15.96.

OTHER CREDITORS
Without special moral justification, I'm not in favor of stringing along landlords, doctors, lawyers, accountants, hospitals, merchants, or tradespeople. Here I believe in the golden rule of bill paying—unless you've come to loathe the creditor so much that paying promptly would make you seethe.

THE ADVANTAGES

CHECK SAVINGS
If you don't have free checking, you probably pay 25 to 50 cents per check. Let's split the difference and call it 37.5 cents. Pay five bills a

year bimonthly instead of monthly and you'll use 30 fewer checks, for a savings of $11.25.

In reality, you do even better, since checks typically cost 4 to 6 cents apiece. Call it a nickel. That's another $1.50 per year.

POSTAGE SAVINGS

You can't forget postage. If you avoid using 30 stamps a year, that's another $8.70 in savings at current prices.

OTHER BENEFITS

Playing the float saves something at least as valuable as money. With fewer checks to write, stamps to lick, and envelopes to mail, you can also conserve time.

And while the game may not generate a lot of additional revenue, it can make you feel smart, which is always nice. It also might prove a healthy outlet for one's normal hostility toward creditors.

THE DISADVANTAGES

• Paying every two months might lead to a false sense of financial well-being. It could cause some people to spend as if they were debt-free, when, in fact, they're a month behind on many bills.

• Paying at your own pace might make you uncomfortable. If you worry a lot about whether your payment will arrive on time, such gamesmanship is just not worth it for you.

• If several payments do arrive late, much of what you save during the year will be lost. (But that doesn't mean you should worry about the impact on your credit rating. Phone, utility, and cable TV companies don't report to credit bureaus unless they get a judgment against you.)

PAYING YOUR BILLS

Saving money, though, may not be your major concern when you're paying bills. You might be more like Sally*, a compulsive bill payer I know.

When a bill arrives, Sally goes on instant bomb-squad-style alert. Her immediate goal: to get the bill paid and out of the house.

She rushes to her checkbook, writes a check, licks a stamp, and often walks the letter to the corner mailbox. Sally can't bear to be in anyone's debt for an extra moment. She needs to avoid guilt, a feeling of obligation. So she quickly washes her hands of the whole affair.

At least it's a system. And Sally does have a very good credit rating. You, however, may wish to do things differently.

SYSTEMS

When you have enough money on hand, there are only two wrong ways to pay your bills—sloppily or inefficiently. Anything else you do is fine, although after reading about some of the alternate approaches in this chapter, you may decide your system could use an upgrade.

There is no excuse for ever misplacing a bill. As soon as it arrives, either pay it or immediately put it in a "To Pay" file, drawer, or basket. It's fine to pay late strategically, as discussed in the next chapter, but not inadvertently. (Note: If you're in charge of paying the bills and you always "forget" about some of them, you risk damaging more than your credit rating: you're also sure to drive your companion up a wall if he or she finds out.)

Two possible approaches are to pay all bills on the same day each month or to pay one batch around the fifteenth and another on the thirtieth.

STRESS KILLS . . . CREDIT RATINGS

Many people neglect or misplace bills during times of severe stress. It's entirely human, yet ultimately it merely compounds the strain. Be aware that this could happen. Put a reminder on your calendar to pay what you owe so you avoid late fees and credit blemishes.

I know someone who moved across the country to care for her dying father for two and a half months. Allison's devotion was total, her attentions heroic. She did everything she could for her father.

But not for herself. Allison left her entire life behind in New York, including 80 days' worth of unpaid bills, which she spoke about periodically. She had not forgotten them. Allison could have asked a friend to forward the mail, but she didn't. Her plate was full as it was. She felt she simply couldn't deal with anything else.

For her sake, I wish she'd handled if differently. After her father's funeral, Allison returned home to a damaged credit rating. Down the road, she'll probably be able to explain away the black marks. In this case, the truth will help. Still, taking care of the bills promptly would have been smart—and it would have been something else as well. It might have been a welcome distraction from her sadness, terror, and grief.

TECHNO-PAYMENTS

Computer programs such as Checkfree (which can be used separately or in conjunction with Andrew Tobias's Managing Your Money or Quicken) and Prodigy's BillPay USA can take care of any recurring monthly payments. Once you key in the details, the programs hardly need you anymore. For unpredictable payments, you use a few additional keystrokes.

You can also pay bills faster without using a computer. Some banks, such as Citibank and Chase Manhattan, are now allowing customers to pay bills via telephone.

Several people I know consider these various electronic payment programs a godsend. A few have found they now enjoy paying bills.

(Note: The new systems are seldom cheap, but after the awkward start-up period, they can save you time.)

AUTOMATIC PAYMENTS

You don't need a computer or a telephone to make payments electronically. If you have any loans where you bank, the lender will usually be happy to debit your savings or checking account every month. Generally, there is no charge for the service. So you save time, you save postage, and you make a little extra room in your brain to think about more interesting matters.

And remember: automatic payment systems are terrific for guaranteeing loan-repayment discipline, particularly for home-equity lines of credit.

18

THE ART OF REFINANCING

$Refinancing may be the perfect financial move when you want to do any of the following:

• Reduce monthly payments when interest rates decline (and perhaps use the savings to pay down other debts that carry higher rates).

• Tap some of the equity in your home and do something productive or extraordinarily enjoyable with it.

• Consolidate existing debts (typically a first and a second mortgage, but conceivably any higher-interest-rate debt, including credit cards).

• Switch to a different type of mortgage (usually from an ARM to a fixed, but potentially vice versa).

Are there bad reasons to consider a refinancing (refi)?

• It may not be the cheapest or simplest loan for your purposes. What you really need may be a home-equity line or loan (see the "Cashing Out" section on page 199).

• Your particular circumstances may make it unlikely that you'll ever recoup the closing costs. (There are ways around this problem.)

• You're practicing equity stripping without a terribly compelling justification.

TIMING

First thing you do, forget the conventional wisdom. (If you don't know the conventional wisdom, you're already off to a good start.) The rule of thumb used to be that it didn't pay to refinance unless your new mortgage would have a rate at least two percentage points lower than your existing mortgage. The rule was almost *always* wrong, but it's especially wrong today, when many lenders are offering no-cost refinancings.

People who plan to be in their homes for a long time and yet doggedly wait for that magic 2-percent rate gap to appear could easily forfeit tens of thousands of dollars in lost savings. The real losers in the refinancing game are those who think and think about doing it, but never do.

THE MOVING ISSUE

What questions should you ask to determine how long you might remain in your home?

1. What are the odds that you or your spouse will be transferred?
2. Do you have any health problems that might cause you to move?
3. Are you planning to have children? (Is your home right for them?)
4. Are you planning to have more children? Are you sure there's enough room? What if you have twins?
5. What are the chances that your family income will rise or fall substantially in the next five years? Might that force you to move? Or, looking at the bright side, if you were making an extra $25,000 a year, would your home suddenly look like a hovel in your eyes?

If there's a very good chance that you'll move in a few years, you have three options (besides just doing nothing):

1. Refinance to an ARM, which can pay off in a year, and sometimes even sooner.
2. Look for no-points, low-closing-cost refi deals.
3. Strongly consider a no-cost refi deal, particularly if you might move in a year or two. A no-cost refi can pay off in less than 6 months. Why is it "free"? It's not, but all the costs are folded into the interest rate, which is, as you would expect, considerably higher than loans with up-front costs. (As we went to press, you could get a no-cost refi with a rate of 8.625 percent. Your only out-of-pocket expenses would be for an appraisal—$250 to $300—and a credit report—$18 to $40.)

Doing a no-cost refi almost always beats doing nothing. It becomes a mistake, though, if you do stay in the house a long time. (Countrywide Funding offers no-cost refis to existing customers, as do Citibank Mortgage, Sibley Mortgage, and many other lenders. So does the Bureau of Veterans Affairs.)

WHEN DO I BREAK EVEN?

Closing costs for refinancing are typically 3 percent to 6 percent of the amount borrowed.

According to HSH Associates, the following are the costs you might incur if you were to refinance a $100,000, 30-year, 10.25-percent fixed-rate mortgage and get a $100,000, 30-year 8-percent fixed-rate mortgage.

Points	$2,000
Application fee	350
Credit check	70
Your attorney	200
Lender's attorney	200
Title-search fee	50
Title-insurance fee	400
Appraisal fee	250
Inspections	350
Local fees (taxes, transfers)	1,000
Other costs	250
Total	$5,120

Since the previous mortgage had a monthly payment of $896 and the new one costs $734, the monthly savings come to $162. Many people would then divide $162 into $5,120 and arrive at the figure of 32 months as the time it would take to break even on this deal. But that number does not provide a completely accurate picture because it ignores the tax consequences. The old mortgage was more expensive, but it also threw off a bigger tax deduction.

It's probably wiser to reduce the monthly-savings figure by the refinancer's tax rate. If it's 28 percent, that takes $162 down to $117 on an after-tax basis. Dividing $5,120 by $117 yields a break-even target of 44 months. This is a fairly rough appoximation. (If the cost of the refinancing is lower, as it will be in many parts of the country, the payback period will be considerably shorter.)

For each point you're charged, the rate will drop by an eighth or a quarter percent. Paying more points—if you can do it—typically becomes a winning strategy after about 6 years. (Check the formulas in chapter 4 to see when going for the high-point loan might make sense.)

Refinancing *to* an ARM is relatively unusual, but it can be a shrewd move, especially if you find a deal that guarantees a break-even period of less than a year. Let's say you can switch a $100,000, 30-year fixed-rate mortgage at 10 percent to 4.625-percent ARM. If closing costs were $3,000, you'd be slightly ahead after only 12 months. That might be quick enough for almost anybody. (And unlike the no-cost refi, you'll probably be left with a better deal if you stay in the home somewhat longer than you had originally anticipated.)

PAYBACK SCOREBOARD

If you're paying $878 a month in principal and interest on a $100,000, 30-year, 10-percent fixed-rate mortgage, how long will it take you to realize a net savings with several different loans? (Assumptions: Not counting the points, closing costs total $1,000, except for the no-cost refi. Months to recoup takes taxes into account, with refinancer's rate pegged at 28 percent.)

30-year fixed at 8.125 percent with 2.5 points
New monthly payment: $743
Months to recoup costs: 36

30-year fixed at 7.875 percent with 4 points
New monthly payment: $725
Months to recoup costs: 46

1-year ARM at 4.625 percent with 2 points
New monthly payment: $514
Months to recoup costs: 12

No-cost refi at 8.625 percent with 0 points
New monthly payment: $778
Months to recoup costs: 5

CUTTING THE COSTS

• Refinancing with your existing lender can save you money in many ways. The lender may waive the appraisal, title-search, and possibly credit-check fees. It may also decide to update the title insurance instead of getting an entirely new policy. And there's a good chance that you'll get a better interest rate.

• When refinancing, ask the lender to order title insurance from the same company that was used before—and request a discount. You can save as much as 25 percent to 40 percent of the approximately $400 charge.

THE 30-YEAR VERSUS 15-YEAR REMATCH

A refi can be a way of *building* equity rather than stripping it away, and more people should view it in that light. Everyone loves lower monthly payments. If you're in a major debt bind, this may be your first priority—and a totally legitimate one.

But do you really *need* to reduce your monthly payments? At least don't do so before looking at the 30-year versus 15-year math once more—this time with a little twist. A 15-year mortgage, as you'll recall, costs about 25 percent or 30 percent more per month. But if rates are now approximately two and a quarter to three percentage points lower than your existing fixed rate, you'll be able to switch from a 30-year to a 15-year mortgage while keeping your monthly payments virtually unchanged.

The monthly payment on a $100,000, 30-year fixed-rate mortgage at 10.5 percent, for example, is $914.74. If you can get a $100,000, 15-year mortgage at 8 percent, you'd pay $955.65. Remember, though, the rates on a 15 are about 50 basis points (.5 percent) lower. If you could snag a rate of 7.5 percent, your monthly payments would fall to $927.02—just 40 cents a day, or $12.28 a month, more than the payment on the original mortgage.

This approach could save you well over $100,000 and let you pay off the mortgage in exactly half the time. If you have very young children, choosing the 15-year mortgage could mean that you own your home debt-free when they are in college. That would be a wonderful accomplishment.

Of course, you could have "saved" about $220 a month by getting another 30-year mortgage. Before deciding on a mortgage term, be absolutely honest about where that money would go and what it would do for your life or your investments. What would that $220 be worth? You know far better than I do. (It's much smarter to use that money to pay down more expensive debt rather than "prepay" the mortgage by taking out a new 15-year loan.)

Nonetheless, the people who always refinance into a new 30-year mortgage are going to get a nasty shock someday. They've hooked themselves to a perpetual-motion equity-stripping machine. They could near retirement with relatively little equity in their home.

This might be fine. Maybe they tapped the equity to pay for college, to fund other investments, to take some spectacular vacations (the kind they can't afford now), or to make a loan to brother-in-law Ethelred.

OTHER CONSIDERATIONS

• Under optimum conditions, a refi can be a way to switch from a 30-year to a 15-year mortgage relatively painlessly, without a jarring increase in monthly payments.

• If you decide to get another 30, however, consider establishing a prepayment plan to plow back some of your monthly savings into your mortgage.

• Naturally, you could ask your lender for advice on this issue. My friend Ted did this—and promptly regretted it. "I got three totally different answers from three different people," he reports. "I came away incredibly confused."

So what did he do? Well, I got to vote on this one, too, so now he has a 15-year mortgage with payments almost exactly equal to those he was making before.

CASHING OUT

A burning issue for the nineties: what's the best way to take cash out of your home? A cash-out refi or a home-equity loan?

• If you're doing the refi anyway, using it to take out cash makes some sense. You can avoid a second transaction and, assuming you're taking a fixed-rate mortgage, you can also avoid the risks inherent in a variable-rate home-equity line.

• You can't do a cash-out refi month after month, but you can tap a home-equity line over and over again, potentially to your detriment. The cash-out refi doesn't let you stick your hand back in the cookie jar. (But, a cynic might argue, if you've already taken all the cookies, this may not be an especially important point.)

• If the main purpose of the refinancing is not to capitalize on lower interest rates but just to get liquid, a home-equity line or loan is usually a much cheaper and simpler alternative.

Ultimately, you may want to sit down with a calculator or an accountant, depending on whose company you prefer, and see which approach works best on a cash-flow basis.

TAXES

• Unlike an original mortgage, points paid for a refinancing cannot be completely deducted in the year of the closing. The deductions must be spread out evenly over the life of the loan. There is an important exception: if you use part of the new loan for home improvements, you may immediately deduct the points attributed to that part of the loan. In such cases, it's smart to write a separate check to pay for the points.

Warning: If you try to deduct all the points during that first year, it's extremely likely that the IRS will notice. Deducting all the points on a refi is a very good way to trigger an audit.

• Will all your interest payments be deductible when you refinance? Not necessarily. For deductibility purposes a refi is sometimes treated just like a home-equity loan rather than a brand-new mortgage.

Suppose you have $50,000 left on your mortgage but you want to refinance for $175,000 to tap some of that equity appreciation. Here's how it works for a mortgage refinanced after October 14, 1987: If the new mortgage exceeds the outstanding balance of the original mortgage on the refinancing date by less than $100,000, the interest is fully deductible. But if the excess borrowed is greater than $100,000—and in our example it is—the amount over $100,000 ($25,000, in this case) is deductible only if it is used for home improvements.

• Watch out as well for the alternative minimum tax (AMT), which hits people who take more write-offs than the government thinks they should. Refis can jump up and bite you. If you get bagged by the AMT, you can't deduct the interest on the part of a refi that is considered home-equity debt. Example: If your mortgage balance is $100,000 and you refinance for $150,000, the interest on the $50,000 will not be deductible as long as you're AMT-bait. (No, you can't make the interest on that excess deductible by taking out a home-equity loan instead. Nice try, though.)

TIPS

• To simplify your shopping for a refi, ask the lender on the phone to calculate your new monthly payment and closing costs.

• If rates have fallen but you haven't refinanced because you have no money for closing costs, you have three choices: consider borrowing to pay for the closing costs, find a lender who will finance the closing costs, or tell your current lender that you're looking for a new mortgage elsewhere and ask for a better deal. You may be able to negotiate a lower rate.

WHAT NOT TO DO

• Don't wait *too* long. "I've seen people pay $400 a month too much month after month as they wait for rates to bottom," says David Davitch of American Financial Mortgage Corporation. "It's human nature. You want to be able to brag about your rate at a party on Saturday night."

But imagine someone with a $100,000 mortgage at 10.75 percent who could refinance at 8 percent but is determined to do it at 7.75 percent. This person is losing $199.72 a month hoping eventually to save an extra $17.34 a month. That's a ratio of 11.5-to-1. For every month this homeowner waits, he'll have to stay in the house 11 months and 15 days for his "patience" to pay off (and that's not counting how long it will take to amortize the closing costs).

• Don't forget to get rid of private mortgage insurance when you do a refi (if you haven't already). That alone can chop the equivalent of more than one-quarter of a percentage point off your rate.

• Refis are almost always done with a LTV of 80 percent. So where does that leave you if you made a small down payment to begin with? You're not eliminated from the refi game, but you will almost definitely have to come up with some cash to raise your down payment on the refi to 20 percent.

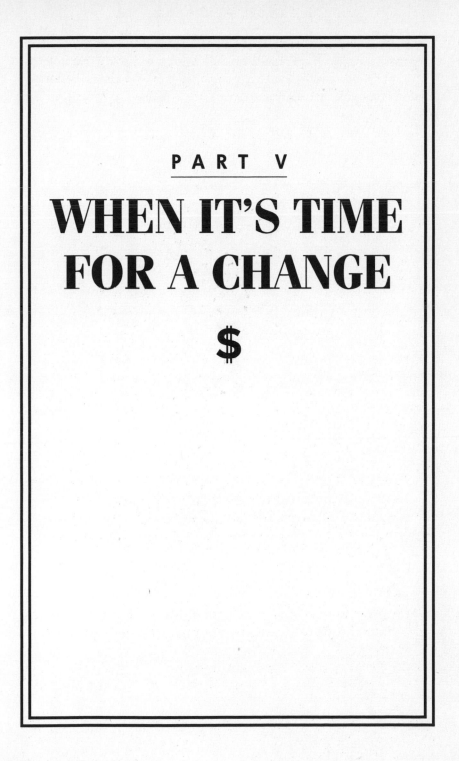

PART V

WHEN IT'S TIME FOR A CHANGE

$

19

DO YOU HAVE
TOO MUCH DEBT?

$ Tens of millions of Americans carry more debt than they should. Are you one of them?

Even if you answer no to every question on the quiz on page 208, you may still feel you owe too much. If you think that, you probably do.

Two of my friends, for instance, aren't in any financial danger. Still, their debts often make them uncomfortable. They feel they're on a financial treadmill; they're running as fast as they can without getting anywhere. Based on the numbers, they may or may not be "right"— but that's almost immaterial. They should probably begin a debt-downsizing program immediately (see chapter 20). It will give them the sense of control they yearn for and make them feel much better.

Most people, though, aren't worried enough. The average middle-class American is very skilled—perhaps too skilled—at consistently spending more than he or she makes and still managing to scrape by. The more you make, the more resources you have to sustain the illusion of prosperity.

Anyone reading *David Copperfield* today may be puzzled by Mr. Micawber's quaint view of personal balance sheets: "Annual income twenty pounds, annual expenditure nineteen nineteen six, result happiness. Annual income twenty pounds, annual expenditure twenty pounds ought and six, result misery." Having a losing year may be disastrous for baseball managers, but it no longer has such a simple impact on an individual's happiness—or personal freedom.

When it comes to running annual deficits, many of my friends are devout Keynesians. They think that something will eventually turn up to curtail the downward debt spiral—either the right lottery number or the kids' completion of college. Some legitimately believe that their best earning years are ahead of them—well, maybe one year, anyway—so they convince themselves that the current financial mess is temporary.

But Mr. Micawber's analysis isn't completely antiquated. Basically, he merely forgot to mention the time-lag factor, or what I call the "time value of (not having enough) money". Ignored or untended, debt burdens tend to worsen rather than improve. Ironically, in our turbo-charged culture, catastrophic financial upheavals now happen much more slowly—after all, up until the very end you still have instant electronic access to actual cash—but they most certainly do happen.

If, however, you can answer no to one question year after year, you will probably be able to avoid real trouble—barring a layoff or other unexpected calamity. The question is: Does more than 20 percent of your take-home pay go toward repaying nonmortgage debts? Add up all your monthly debt obligations—car payments, credit cards (be honest), installment loans, student loans, and so on—and then divide this total monthly debt payments by take-home pay. Lose the decimal point, and you have the percentage.

Between 1983 and 1989, the median percentage of take-home pay gobbled up by nonmortgage debt service grew substantially, according to the Federal Reserve Board. For the one-third of American families who used debt most aggressively, the percentage jumped from 15 percent to 21 percent. Small wonder so many people complain about being overburdened by debt.

Why is the 20-percent figure so important? "At that level, it's often hard to pay for necessities without going even deeper into debt," says Tom Hufford, executive director of Consumer Credit Counseling of Northeastern Indiana in Fort Wayne. "If you don't cap it at 20 percent, it can quickly move up to 30 percent or 40 percent. It will get worse unless you do something."

One of Hufford's clients, a successful salesman, first sought counseling because he had $80,000 in credit-card debt. But he left Hufford's office without formulating a plan for dealing with the problem. Too proud to admit how bad the situation was, he told himself he'd handle things by making more money.

But his commissions dropped again the next year. When the man returned to Hufford's office less than a year later, his credit-card debt totaled $150,000.

Moral: Just because you can continue to get away with it for a while longer doesn't mean you *should*. Eventually, you get cornered. You get squeezed. You take on more work, trying desperately to earn your way out of trouble. Whether that approach succeeds or not, your quality of life declines dramatically.

This grim scenario notwithstanding, there's no reason to panic because you respond affirmatively to too many questions. This doesn't necessarily mean you're heading for a financial crisis. But it should be a warning.

Actually, answering yes to one or more questions may provide you with a healthy shock. You may get a better idea about how much stress your debts cause. And that's part of the point. Mere survival—short-changing Peter just enough to keep Paul from taking you to court—is not the purpose here. You're supposed to enjoy your money.

THE DEBT QUIZ

1. Can you afford to pay only the minimum on your credit cards each month?
2. Do you ever take a cash advance on one card to make the minimum payment on another?
3. Are you at or over the limit on several credit cards?
4. Are you now charging items you used to buy with cash (such as food and toiletries)?
5. Do you ever buy things you don't really need just to meet the minimum-purchase requirement for using plastic?
6. Do you often worry that your credit card will be rejected?
7. Are you regularly tapping savings to pay your bills?
8. Have you been unable to accumulate any savings?
9. Are you eager to check your mail because someone may have sent you an offer for additional credit?
10. Do you dread looking at your mail?
11. Do you get annoyed when the calendar changes because the start of a new month signals the arrival of new bills?
12. Are you often assessed late-payment charges?
13. When you find a new source of credit, do you feel buoyant? Do you think, Well, that problem's taken care of?
14. Do you find that even though you took out a debt-consolidation loan, you're still running up new debts?
15. Have you recently been turned down for credit?
16. Have you begun working overtime to make ends meet?
17. Are you finding that two jobs aren't enough? Are you thinking of adding a third?
18. Do friends ever wonder how you do it—either how you manage to live so well or manage to keep so many balls in the air at once?
19. Are you increasingly using the "file and forget" system for unpaid bills?
20. Are you starting to borrow small amounts from friends?
21. Are you thinking of asking a good friend or family member for a large loan?
22. When offered a choice, do you always select the longest possible repayment term?
23. Do you borrow to pay predictable expenses such as insurance or taxes?
24. Do you put off medical or dental visits because you can't afford them?
25. Have you canceled any insurance policies to save money?
26. Do you often receive mail or telephone calls from creditors asking for money?
27. Have you grown accustomed to bouncing checks?
28. Have you "solved" this problem by routinely writing postdated checks?

29. Do money worries ever prevent you from having a good time—for example, from fully enjoying a vacation you "can't afford"?
30. Do you ever worry about money in the middle of the night?
31. Are you afraid of what your credit report says about you?
32. Would you be embarrassed if anybody knew the whole truth about your financial situation?
33. Do you have no idea how much you really owe?

• If you answered no to every question, terrific. You're not in trouble. But keep some of the questions in the back of your mind nonetheless. Should you feel the urge, or the necessity, to alter any aspect of your behavior, step back for a moment and quiz yourself about what's really going on. Are you meeting an unpredictable, one-time emergency? Or have you just learned a new bad habit?

• One yes response shouldn't cause heart palpitations, but it should put you on the alert. Perhaps it's time to become more vigilant. Try to transform that yes into a no over the next few months. It's a good sign if you can. If you can't, however, read the next paragraph.

• Several yes answers strongly suggest that the situation is either serious or at the very least unpleasant, and likely to become more so.

Debt, unfortunately, is a slippery slope. Once you start heading down, it can be hard to regain your momentum without some powerful intervention. Advice on how to fight back follows in chapter 20.

THE DEBTORS ANONYMOUS QUIZ

If you've ever wondered whether you might be a compulsive debtor, take the following quiz, which is reprinted (and adapted) with the permission of Debtors Anonymous. Debtors Anonymous says that most compulsive debtors will answer yes to at least eight of the fifteen questions.

1. Are your debts making your home life unhappy?
2. Does the pressure of your debts distract you from your daily work?
3. Are your debts affecting your reputation?
4. Do your debts cause you to think less of yourself?
5. Have you ever given false information in order to obtain credit?
6. Have you ever made unrealistic promises to creditors?
7. Does the pressure of your debts make you careless about the welfare of your family?
8. Do you ever fear that your employer, family, or friends will learn the extent of your total indebtedness?
9. When you are faced with a difficult financial situation, does the prospect of borrowing give you an inordinate feeling of relief?

10. Does the pressure of your debts cause you to have difficulty in sleeping?

11. Has the pressure of your debts ever caused you to consider getting drunk?

12. Have you ever borrowed money without giving adequate consideration to the rate of interest you'll have to pay?

13. Do you usually expect a negative response when you are subject to a credit investigation?

14. Have you ever developed a strict regimen for paying off your debts, only to break it under pressure?

15. Do you justify your debts by telling yourself that you are superior to "other" people, and when you get your "break" you'll be out of debt overnight?

If you answer yes to eight or more of these questions, consider contacting Debtors Anonymous (see Appendix A).

No matter how you scored, I hope both quizzes help you realize that debt can diminish your pleasure and deeply affect your life well before it does you grievous financial harm. Whether you're satisfied with your score or not, the next chapter will provide strategies for lowering your debt and easing your financial pressures.

20

DOWNSIZING YOUR DEBT:
THE ART OF OWING LESS

Interest works night and day, in fair weather and foul. It gnaws at a man's substance with invisible teeth.
                                                        —*Henry Ward Beecher*

$ Besides making you crazy in the present, too much debt can also imperil your future. Fred Waddell, a money-management specialist at Auburn University who trains credit counselors around the country, has a pet warning for overzealous debtors. "If your debt is out of hand, you may never be able to retire," he says. "One day, you may be like one of those 70-year-olds who wear those cute little hats while working behind the counter at McDonald's. You may *need* that job to survive."

Of course, trying to avoid becoming a burger slinger isn't the only reason to downsize your debt. Nor do you have to be one paycheck away from going under to realize the extraordinary psychological benefits of successfully shrinking your debt burden.

Kathie Anderson, a divorced 43-year-old Everett, Washington, business writer and mother of three, admitted to herself one day that her debts were taking a lot of the joy out of her life. They were wearing her down and changing the way she looked at the world.

"I used to look forward to opening my mail," she says. "But then I started dreading it. I was always being reminded that I was in debt, that I was wasting lots of money on interest payments."

Kathie's first debt-reduction move was controversial, but financially sound. She liquidated her $6,000 IRA and immediately retired almost all her credit-card debt (most of it at 19.8 percent). She also began prepaying her $44,000 mortgage, adding $50 to $100 a month to her regular $450 payment. If she pays only $95 more a month, she'll own the house outright in 15 years and save almost $45,000 in interest payments.

The payoff? Kathie says her debt-reduction plan has given her a tremendous feeling of "liberation." Indeed, it's very common for people in debt to feel imprisoned, to feel the walls closing in on them—to feel, as well, that they're not entitled to have any fun.

And a high debt load does invariably sap your ability to save for future pleasures. The good news is that your debt can be managed and your life can be put back on course. Your financial situation may *seem* overwhelming, but you can do a lot to change it.

The best news of all, though, is that by choosing to "invest" in your debt, you can realize returns that are unattainable for those not in hock. The only way to achieve a guaranteed tax-free return of 19.8 percent is to pay down the balance on a 19.8-percent credit card. (In pretax dollars, the return is even more impressive. If you're in the 28-percent tax bracket, you have to earn $27.50 to pay the interest on $100 of debt at 19.8 percent. And you have to do this every year.)

Again, you don't have to be in trouble to profit from debt reduction. Lots of people get in the habit of carrying large but affordable amounts of debt month after month, year after year. They feel less pain than they should because they don't ever do the numbers. This extra debt, which is generally used for questionable life-style enhancements (the latest electronic gadgetry, an extra dinner out every week), may not be something they think about much. It's simply there. They know they should deal with it someday, but they never do.

Well, the cost of carrying $5,000 in 19.8-percent credit-card debt for 40 years is $39,600 in interest alone. You could probably do something very nice with that money—if you had it.

You could do something even nicer with $100,000—the amount you could save in 21 years if you spent an extra $80 a month (that's just $2.67 a day) to reduce your debt load.

I'm assuming a blended interest rate of 13 percent on the debt. You might do better, or worse, but you would almost certainly whip any other investment option. Best of all, some of the $100,000 you'd save would represent after-tax dollars.

How can you get your hands on all this loot? The first step is to find out exactly where your money is going right now.

ANALYZE YOUR SPENDING HABITS

Most people *think* they have a pretty good idea about the different ways their money disappears each month, but few people really *know*. So don't be chagrined if the results of the exercise suggested below surprise you. The more surprised you are, the more opportunities you'll have to downsize your debt.

These days, the word "budget" is terribly unfashionable. Financial gurus have decided that it conjures up images of scarcity, deprivation, and joylessness ("I have a budget; other people have a life"), so they've substituted new terms, such as "spending plan" and "income-management system."

But what we're really talking about here is bigger than any of these terms: it's a blueprint for taking control of your life financially—and, to a large extent, emotionally as well.

What tools will you need? You can use a computer, a notebook, a legal pad, or an inexpensive budget book purchased in a stationery store. And you'll need something to handle the math—a calculator, an abacus, or a very bright 10-year-old. In short, whatever you have is good enough, which means that shopping for provisions is an unacceptable excuse for delaying a moment longer.

First, add up your total annual after-tax income from all sources.

Then estimate your annual expenses. Use any reminders that will help—your checkbook, expense file, and so on. The following list of categories should help you recall some of the items people commonly overlook.

Savings and Investments	Insurance
Life insurance	Maintenance/repairs
Retirement	Services/utilities
Other savings	Fuel, gas, electricity
	Lawn care/gardening
Housing	Water/sewer
Mortgage/rent	Garbage collection
Taxes	Telephone

Furniture
Cleaning supplies
Tools

Food
Groceries
Eating out
Snacks
School or work lunches

Transportation
Car payment
Gas and oil
Tires
Insurance
Maintenance/repairs
Registration
License
Bus/subway/taxis
Air/rail
Tolls
Parking

Health
Insurance
Medicine
Vitamins
Doctor/dentist
Therapy
Health club
Eyeglasses
Contact lens supplies
Lab tests
Hospital charges
Barber/beauty shop
Cosmetics
Personal care
Manicures/facials
Massages

Apparel
Clothing
Shoes
Shoe repair/shoeshine
Laundry
Dry cleaning

Professional
Union dues
Membership fees
Subscriptions

Education
Books
Supplies
Tuition/fees

Gifts
Church/synagogue
Charity
Birthdays/weddings
Holidays

Taxes
Income tax
Personal property tax

Recreation
Cable TV
Admissions and tickets (movies, theater, theme parks)
Games/hobbies
Lessons (music, dance, riding)
Newspapers/magazines
Sporting goods
Books
CDs/tapes/records
Videotapes
Videotape rental

Sports
Club memberships

Other
Alcohol
Cigarettes
Pets
Alimony/child support
Childcare/dependent care/
  babysitting
Software/hardware
Computer supplies
Home-office supplies

Debt repayment
Credit-card annual fees
Cash-advance fees
Late-payment charges/
  bounced-check fees
Rental agreements
Lottery tickets/gambling
  losses
Other insurance
Stamps/stationery
Legal services/accountant

Don't worry about getting the numbers right the first time. No one ever does. Just be sure that any ballpark estimates are generous rather than skimpy.

Now you have a rough idea of whether you're spending more than you earn. But you may not really know yet—and this is a crucial point. Unless you're a lot better with money than I am, these estimates will provide only the vaguest sense of how you're doing.

To get a much clearer fix, I strongly suggest you itemize every expenditure—down to the last nickel—for a month or two. *Really.* The task seems annoying (it *is*), but, I promise you, it is also extraordinarily powerful and rewarding.

It can almost be like a financial version of an out-of-body experience. You see yourself as a consumer in an entirely new way. And, if you're lucky, you quickly start to get a better sense of which dollars are well spent and which are frittered away. You notice, perhaps, that spending $60 to buy mediocre food for two in a restaurant doesn't look so good in hindsight, but that "splurging" for the latest hardcover by one of your favorite authors appears to be a bargain.

Getting precise about where the money goes may seem like needless nitpicking. Instead, it cuts through the vagueness and denial that shroud so many people's money-management techniques.

"You can't create a sensible financial plan without knowing exactly where the money goes," says Karen McCall, president of Financial Recovery, a San Anselmo, California, spending, credit, and debt-counseling service. "That would be like taking a trip without a map."

For almost everyone, a portion of the money winds up in some pretty strange places. One McCall client was stunned when she learned she spent $165 a month on cappuccino. That's a $1,980-a-year coffee-and-steamed-milk habit! No one with debt troubles would knowingly do such a thing, but people do it all the time.

Almost all of us have "hidden spending" habits with budget-breaking potential. Among the most common are eating out during the workday (brown-bagging lunch can easily save a person $25 to $50 a week), eating out at night, eating out on the weekend, long-distance calls, little-used health-club memberships, premium cable TV services (have you looked at your bill lately?), refreshments and snacks (soda, beer, coffee to go), parking (including tickets), bounced-check fees, and credit-card interest. Such spending is typically so high that credit counselors assume any family budget can be trimmed by 10 percent to 20 percent without enormous pain.

WHAT DO YOU OWE?

Millions of Americans are so afraid of their debts that they don't know how big they are. They assume that adding up the grim numbers would just make them feel more demoralized and hopeless. These feelings can be so strong that a large percentage of people actually overestimate their debts.

So that's one incentive to look at the real numbers. Another is that even if the facts are worse than you've imagined, knowing the truth will help. It certainly beats now knowing. ("The unexamined life," Socrates said, "is not worth living." The modern corollary: If you've got substantial debts, you can't afford to live an unexamined life.)

"Some of my clients look absolutely shocked when they add up their debts," says Ross Richardson, a Houston financial planner. "They're usually the people who get the most out of the exercise."

Next, look at your monthly nonmortgage debt payments. Most people who spend more than they earn or who never have anything left over for savings will look at this number and realize that if they didn't have all that debt to service they'd have more than enough to meet all their needs.

This should be inspiring. Yes, the debt is real, and it's not going away tomorrow. Nonetheless, it should be encouraging to see what your life might be like if the debt load were smaller. And if you follow a reasonable plan, it *will* get smaller.

If you haven't done so already, compute the percentage of take-home pay you devote to nonmortgage debt payments each month. Are you at or over the 20-percent limit?

If your financial decisions have a major impact on people you love, you need to talk to them before making a plan.

TIPS FOR COUPLES

Each of you should come up with a list of ideas about how to cut your spending, both individually and as a unit. (Warning: You may not have a clue as to why the other person considers certain "frills" sacrosanct. As long as you can make the numbers work, let your spouse or good friend buy all the manicures or socket wrenches he or she desires.)

Next, create a list of spending goals—for the next few months, few years, and few decades. Talk calmly about the trade-offs on the big items—cars, vacations, children, summer homes. If the two of you can communicate at all, you'll probably learn a lot about what your companion really values and what he or she hopes money can do. (You also may learn a lot about yourself. Everybody has fantasies about what they'd do with unlimited sums of money. Not enough people have reasonable goals about what they'd do with a little more money.)

But what if you can't come to an agreement? What if this budgeting attempt turns into a major domestic fiasco?

Before wondering about seeking love and companionship elsewhere, examine your assumptions about money. A good starting point, says Jeanne M. Hogarth, an assistant professor in the consumer economics and housing department at Cornell, is to determine which spending categories you fall into. (You may fit more than one.)

Spender Type 1
Spend only for what I need
Save for emergencies
Like to have money in my pocket
Shop around for the best deal

Spender Type 2
Nothing but the best for me
Expensive clothes are important
You've got to spend money to get ahead in life
Cheap stuff isn't worth much

Spender Type 3
Nobody ever has enough money
Credit is necessary
Buy the things you want, NOW
I deserve the nice things in life

Spender Type 4
Don't worry—the money will come from somewhere
Worrying about money never helps
Keeping track of spending can drive people crazy

Spender Type 5
Money can't buy happiness
You can have fun without spending money
Other things are more important than money

If the two of you are still having problems finding common ground, consider examining your deepest feelings about money and relationships. "If there's a serious conflict about the issue, it's certain that past influences are at work," says McCall.

What are your secret financial fears? Your major resentments? Why is it so important for you to have some money over which someone else has no control? (By the way, this is healthy and entirely normal —up to a point. It is one of the many feelings about money that can be communicated either constructively or in a thoroughly alienating way.)

There must be a lot of past influences around, given that money is the leading cause of marital fights in America. Experts say it's way ahead of sex in this regard.

TIPS FOR FAMILIES

Hold a family meeting to discuss how everyone can contribute to a debt-reduction plan. Ask the kids for ideas about what they can do.

Simply having the meeting will help your children. After all, they learn money-management skills from *you*.

Family meetings are often good safety valves for the stress that has been building up while the issue has not been discussed. The exchange of ideas may even be enjoyable.

It will be more fun if you take two specific steps, according to Flora Williams, an associate professor of consumer sciences and retailing at Purdue University. First, make it clear that any austerity plan is an interim measure. "Try it for two months, then make adjustments," says Williams. "Then tinker with it some more after another two months."

Second, decide what rewards the family—or individual members—will receive when the plan is carried out. Stick to the plan and the family gets to go to Aspen or Disney World.

If possible, try to maintain your sense of humor. "There are several ways to apportion family income," said Robert Benchley, "all of them unsatisfactory."

Perfect budgets don't exist. Good ones do.

CREATE A SPENDING PLAN

First, start with your goals. What do you want to accomplish? Pay down debt by $300 a month? Reduce debt by $300 a month and save an additional $100? Reduce nonmortgage debt payments to 20 percent of take-home pay? Eliminate all nonmortgage debt in three years?

Pick any goal you like, and remember, there are only two rules about setting debt-reduction goals:

1. The goals should be relevant. If bankruptcy is looming, next year's goal should not be to open an IRA.
2. The goals should be realistic. Make sure you can reach them—or, better yet, exceed them. Set yourself up to succeed, not to fail.

If a third rule exists, it is this: Whatever plan you create now will evolve. Things will get better. After eliminating some of those mediocre $60 dinners from your life, you may discover, for instance, that evenings spent outside the home are more essential than you had imagined. Fine. You just have to work at finding more creative and cheaper ways of spending them. Or become pickier about the restaurants in which you're willing to drop sixty bucks.

Now for the fun part. Take out your imaginary machete and begin hacking away at your discretionary expenses. You're clearing a path to the future.

It probably won't be a direct route, though. First see how the budget looks with across-the-board cuts. Then try the more subtle approaches. Cut some items by 5 percent, others by 20 percent. Eliminate some spending categories entirely. If you gave up that health-club membership (which now only helps exercise your guilt muscles, anyway), you could save hundreds of dollars year after year.

Your new spending plan should have enough slack so that you can give yourself occasional rewards for adhering to it. The rewards should be more significant, more personal, and more expensive than, say, buying a package of nongeneric toilet paper for a change. After all, the real goal of debt downsizing is to make your life more enjoyable and fulfilling.

Ideally, the new plan should address the issue of delayed gratification. That is, the plan shouldn't make you feel you'll never be able to buy a new car, new clothes, or new furniture, or to take a vacation away from Lake Erie. The process is much more pleasant if you know you're gradually saving up for that great desired thing, whatever it may be.

"Saving money to buy something you really want is half the fun," says Andrew Tobias. "Ultimately, you get much more pleasure from the things you save for than from those objects you buy on the spur of the moment and spend the next three years paying off."

STOP INCURRING NEW DEBT

Rule number one if you want to reduce old debt quickly: avoid new debt. This doesn't mean you have to slice up all your credit cards (although there are worse ideas; if you shop without plastic, you *will* spend less). What it does mean, at the very least, is that from here on in, you'll pay off all new charges in full when the bill comes—until you achieve your debt goal.

One way to make this happen is to enter all new charges in your checkbook, debiting the account each time. A more rigorous—albeit messier and more time-consuming—alternative: Place all your credit cards in a plastic bag or container filled with water and put them in the freezer. Then, says credit counselor Patricia Leonard of the New York City–based Budget & Credit Counseling Services, if you see something you simply must have, defrost a card. (Freezing a card will not affect its magnetic stripe or damage it in any way.)

WHAT DOES CREDIT REALLY COST?

Another way to dampen your urge to use new credit is to look at its true cost. For example, a $20 meal you charge could cost you $42.54 and take 12 years to pay off.

Or think of how long you'll have to work to pay for an item you charge. (Nothing takes *me* out of a buying mood faster.) Take a brand-new $17,000 car. Put 10 percent down and finance $15,300 for 5 years and its real cost is $20,756. That means you've got to earn about $30,000 before taxes to pay for the damn thing. Is it worth a year of work? Six months?

DEBT SHIFTING

Over time, one of the smartest and simplest ways to downsize your debt is to lower the interest on your loans. For one high-spending New York editor, this was the key step in his budget overhaul. With a $20,000 home-equity line, he liquidated $20,000 in credit-card debt —immediately reducing the interest he was paying by 10 percentage points. "It was one of the most important things my wife and I have ever done," he says.

Obviously you shouldn't wait to have $20,000 in high-interest debt before pursuing this strategy. Instead, use some of the techniques discussed elsewhere in this book:

- Get a cheaper credit card (chapter 8).
- Refinance your mortgage (chapter 18).
- Take out a home-equity loan or credit line (chapter 15).
- Consider all your cheaper borrowing options (chapter 13).

THE WRONG WAY TO BALANCE THE BUDGET

Do not attempt debt shifting unless you clearly understand the two ways in which the strategy can backfire.

1. You clean up credit-card balances with a new loan, and after a while you revert to your old ways with plastic. You run up new credit-card balances. This leaves you with new debt to service in addition to the old debt (which, though cheaper, hasn't disappeared).

2. You take out the wrong kind of debt-consolidation loan. Most of the consolidation loans advertised in newspapers and on TV or offered by finance companies typically give you the worst of both worlds—a higher rate (sometimes as steep as 30 percent) *and* a longer repayment term. True, your monthly payment may be lower, but over time your interest charges will be much, much greater—possibly two or three times as high.

"Bankers do not look at debt consolidation favorably," says financial planner Richardson, a former banker. "Their greatest fear is that people will just turn around and start charging all over again."

Debt-consolidation loans often cause more problems than they solve for other reasons. A study by Flora L. Williams, Kita L. Miller, and Mary Ellen Rider McRee of Purdue showed that in most cases consumers who take out debt-consolidation loans begin paying interest on debts that had previously been interest-free (such as bills from doctors, hospitals, and lawyers). In addition, the study found that getting a debt-consolidation loan was often the final step a family took before being overcome by financial disaster. That should tell you something.

A high-interest debt-consolidation loan is almost always the wrong solution—no matter what the problem. If you're really close to the edge and lack access to cheaper credit, it's usually smarter to negotiate a new payment schedule with creditors or immediately seek credit counseling.

An even more certain way to court disaster is to do business with a "debt pooling" service that can take as much as 35 percent of the loan amount as an up-front fee—and then charge interest on top of that. Anyone close to drowning before making this arrangement will find it hard to avoid going under afterward. (For-profit debt-consolidation firms are outlawed in many states.)

PREPAYMENT

When you regain your financial equilibrium—when it's clear that you're no longer spending more than you earn—turn to some of the prepayment strategies discussed in chapter 16. Start by using pocket change to save a small fortune in interest charges.

CONSIDER TAPPING YOUR SAVINGS

Millions of families shoulder high debt loads while also maintaining substantial savings or investment accounts. It may be okay to regard your savings as inviolate, but at least recognize that doing so has a price. Paying 18 percent interest on a credit card so you can keep earning 3 percent in a savings account is bad money management.

Yet it's not necessarily crazy. The key question is: What works for you? If you raided an account to pay down debt, would you use the money you save on interest costs to replenish the account? Financial planners have discovered that many people don't.

Debt *can* serve as a very effective, although extraordinarily expensive, tool to compel people to save. Planners who have clients with expensive tastes sometimes urge them to finance a $30,000 car rather than tap their savings and pay cash. The approach costs more, but the nest egg remains intact, as long as you can meet your payments.

THE EMERGENCY FUND

For some people, emergency funds are overrated. Possibly for most people. I know this is a radical idea, but it can be a mistake to carry high-interest debt while at the same time sitting on a 3- to 6-month emergency-fund cushion. After all, you can usually borrow to fund an emergency. Why pay the 18 percent interest and earn 3 percent while you're waiting for next year's emergency to happen?

For most people, though, I'd recommend a slightly less extreme approach, for two reasons:

1. It can be unnerving to have nothing in your savings account or emergency fund. Many people would feel exposed, naked, on the edge. Having savings, on the other hand, can provide a warm, glowing feeling. If this describes you, what you lose on the interest-rate spread may be money well spent.

2. Putting money in the bank or in an investment account often has a snowball effect. Remember when you were a kid how good it felt to watch your bank balance grow, even by a dime, a quarter, or a dollar?

And how it hurt to make a withdrawal because you knew it would take a long time to make up the "loss"?

"Saving money is one of the most addictive things there is," says Luther Gatling, president of New York's Budget and Credit Counseling Services. "Do a little, and you want to do more. It makes you feel as if you have a handle on your life."

So what do I recommend? Despite the risk that you might never put back the money, I'd still advise using most of your savings, perhaps as much as 90 percent, to pay down nonmortgage debt—if, that is, you can make a repayment deal with yourself and stick to it. When your targeted debts are taken care of, your monthly burden will be significantly smaller. Be sure some of that new "excess" goes right back into your savings or investment account.

But I'd keep the other 10 percent of savings where it is. And when you create a new spending plan, I'd try from the start to add to your savings every month. Because saving money *is* addictive, even when —for the moment, anyway—those savings are technically a losing proposition. With your debt life under control, saving will be a lot less expensive. It will then become the ultimate winning proposition.

STAYING ON COURSE

For some people, debt springs eternal. They spend months digging themselves out of a financial hole only to be blindsided by some "unexpected" expense. Then it's back into the abyss.

Such recidivism is avoidable. Unfortunately, many people go deeply into debt, and stay there, because they're perpetually surprised by expenses that are entirely predictable. Don't use home repairs, car repairs, minor medical and dental emergencies, holiday shopping, or insurance payments as an excuse for new borrowing.

Think like a Boy Scout. Be prepared to cover the consistent outflow. Leave some slack in the budget to take care of inevitable expenses.

If you have to take on new debt, make a deal with yourself to repay the money within a reasonable time. If the excuse is holiday shopping, make sure you pay off this year's bills before the next holiday season.

HINTS FOR MAKING YOUR PLAN WORK

• If you want to feel richer, make a graph of your declining non-mortgage debts and update it every month. This can be an inspiring visual reminder of your progress. It will show you what you've achieved thus far and help keep you focused on your goal. When your next bill comes, you'll be more likely to appreciate the lower balance rather than lamenting how much you still owe. (Some people prefer graphing their monthly finance charges instead of the total balance. The numbers are smaller, which is always nice.)

After seeing the graph slope downward month after month, you'll try extremely hard to maintain the southerly trend. An upward blip won't look pretty on your graph.

• Don't regard your tax refund as found money. It's not. Direct some or all of it toward debt payments.

Better still, increase the number of exemptions on your W-4 to boost your take-home pay and lower the refund. This way, you win twice. You reduce the amount of money you lend the government at no interest, and because you have earlier access to your money, you can cut your finance charges by paying your creditors sooner.

DEBT-FUND SAVINGS

Getting your debt under control can lead to some unexpected savings, as well. Stick to the plan, and money is more likely to stick to you. Eventually, you'll no longer spend money on cash advances, late fees, or bounced-check penalties. (This may mean hundreds of additional dollars to deposit in your debt fund.)

THE EASIEST SAVING STRATEGY

Just because saving is now sexy doesn't mean most people know how to do it. Here's a simple tip. Once you've slashed your debts to a comfortable level, try the pay-yourself-first system. It's the ideal way for most people to save. When you pay the bills each month, write the first check to yourself and invest it. Or eliminate the middleman—in this case, you—and have the money transferred automatically each month by your bank or employer.

NEW SPENDING STRATEGIES

• Try doing holiday and birthday shopping by mail. It's often easier to stick to your gift list—and stay out of trouble—when you avoid the stores.

• Consider making some gifts yourself.

• Set an absolute dollar limit on impulse purchases.

• Design weekly menus around coupons and foods on sale. Coupons alone could help you save as much as 15 percent to 20 percent on your grocery bill.

• Don't go food shopping when you're hungry.

• Go grocery shopping only once a week to reduce impulse buying and, if possible, leave the kids—those tiny ultra-consumers—at home.

• Try some generic products at the supermarket. Buy more store brands (some you'll like, some you won't). In 1988, *Consumer Reports* said that the average American family of four could save as much as $2,500 a year at the grocery store simply by shopping more carefully.

• Ask your doctor to prescribe generic drugs when possible.

• When an item you use all the time is offered at a very low price, buy in bulk.

• Get the same amount of insurance coverage for less. (For free information on cheap term life insurance, call SelectQuote [800 343-1985], InsuranceQuote [800 972-1104], or TermQuote [800 444-TERM]. If you live in New York, Massachusetts, or Connecticut, consider savings bank life insurance. For cheaper auto insurance, call GEICO (800 841-3000), a State Farm agent, or, if you're a present or former military officer, call USAA (800 531-8080).

• Don't pick up a check in a restaurant with a credit card and have co-workers or friends give you cash. On the surface, this transaction is an obvious wash. The problem is, the deal makes you feel artificially rich, and the cash is often spent before the credit-card bill arrives.

• Skimp on necessities to pay for luxuries. Drive the old clunker another year so you can afford a great vacation.

• Sell impulse purchases you never use—unless you feel they'll help ward off future profligacy. (More likely they're simply painful reminders of how you used to shop.)

• Decide that now is the time, finally, to call the Salvation Army or Goodwill and have them send a truck, and consider applying some or all of the tax deduction to debt reduction.

• Realize that time isn't always money. Spending more money to save time doesn't always work.

Some people I know make $120,000 a year, which would be $60 an hour, or a dollar a minute, if they worked 40 hours a week. (No one works only 40 hours a week anymore; however, let's stick with that dollar-a-minute figure, anyway.) Occasionally, these people tell themselves that since their time is worth a dollar a minute, anything that saves them 60 seconds could be worth a dollar. According to this calculus, a $5 cab ride that saves 10 minutes of walking is an outright bargain.

And it can be, especially if the time you save will translate directly into billable hours. For most people, though, time and money aren't always joined at the hip. Flaw number one: Your time isn't always worth your hourly rate, certainly not when you use the time you save to watch reruns of "Fantasy Island." Flaw number two: One of the new vices of the overstressed is to overpay for convenience. It's an easy habit to fall into, and a tough one to break. You can get addicted to takeout.

Spending a few hours a month to save money can be good for the soul. That doesn't mean a separate trip to a different store to save a nickel on a half-gallon of milk (although my grandmother used to do that, and she's now rich). What it does mean, however, is that becoming obsessive about how much time you save can cause your smart-shopper muscles to atrophy. Having the time for a nice vacation but lacking the money to go anywhere is not my idea of a good deal.

• How do you handle the kids, those creatures who often don't seem to understand the concept of limited resources? It's easier to say no to them if you blame "the budget," says Hogarth.

It's also easier to say no if you can convince them that they're not really deprived. Take them to a poor section of town to help them focus on what they have, not what they lack.

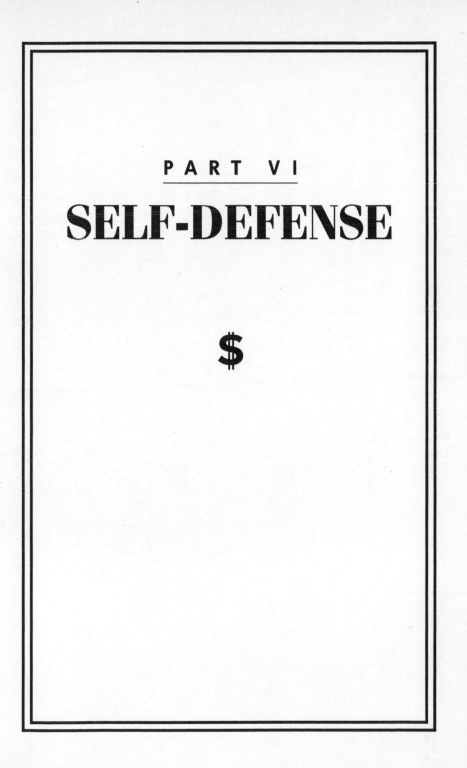

PART VI

SELF-DEFENSE

$

21

SCAMS, RIP-OFFS, AND OTHER ATROCITIES

$The stupidest $120 I ever squandered was lost in a run-of-the-mill debt scam, which I'll describe shortly. I'm not at all comforted by the knowledge that every year other borrowers lose billions to unscrupulous lenders, bogus middlemen, and bait-and-switch con artists.

People who need money are often vulnerable. The more intense the need, the greater the vulnerability. The worst lenders and the outright crooks know exactly whom to target. "In Massachusetts," says Jim Spencer, district representative for Congressman Joseph P. Kennedy III, "the most devious high-interest lenders go after people with big medical bills, women who have just been divorced, and those who live in neighborhoods that are redlined by the major banks."

If your borrowing needs are particularly acute, be especially cautious. And if they're not? Watch your wallet, anyway.

CREDIT INSURANCE

The nation's most common borrowing "scam" is usually totally legal, and it snares the needy and the well-heeled alike. Consumers spend $5 billion to $6 billion a year on credit insurance (which helps pay off a creditor if misfortune strikes), but what they buy is almost always overpriced and most likely unnecessary. A 1992 study by the National Insurance Consumer Organization and Consumer Federation of America found that credit life insurance, in particular, was the "nation's worst insurance ripoff."

Generally, credit insurance comes in three tempting varieties—life, disability, and unemployment. Many people are lured into buying the dreadful stuff because they assume it's like private mortgage insurance. It is not. Mortgage insurance is what many homeowners must pay until the equity in their homes reaches 20 percent of the loan amount outstanding (see chapter 4). Credit insurance, on the other hand, can sometimes be required as a condition for getting a loan, but it is usually optional, no matter what some high-pressure loan jockeys or car salespeople may tell you. (If you must have credit insurance, the lender must give you the option of buying the coverage on your own. Few do, however.)

In Alaska and Maryland, the insurance can be required only on real-property loans. In New Jersey, it cannot be sold on second mortgages.

If a lender says the insurance is required, threaten to look elsewhere for your financing. This may be either a bluff or a serious threat, depending on your mood. Consider asking potential lenders in advance whether they require the insurance. It can be a good negotiating point.

Even if the insurance was required when you got the loan, you can often have it dropped once you've paid off about 50 percent of your debt. Call your lender and ask.

Credit insurance is peddled by banks, finance companies, car dealers, and credit-card companies, among others. One of the reasons lenders love the policies is because *they* are the beneficiaries. The insurance guarantees that the lender will not lose anything if you die, become ill or disabled, or lose your job. What happens to your family, of course, is often beside the point.

Credit insurance is a raw deal for three primary reasons.

PRICE

Insurers and lenders overcharge consumers who buy credit insurance by well over $1 billion every year. According to the National Association of Insurance Commissioners, only 37 cents of every dollar spent on credit life insurance and 50 cents of every dollar spent on disability insurance is paid out in claims. By comparison, auto insurers pay out 60 to 80 cents of each dollar.

The credit insurance system has an inherent anticonsumer bias. In fact, it stimulates reverse competition. Lenders earn huge commissions for selling credit insurance—often more than 40 percent, and sometimes as much as 70 percent, of the premiums paid. They have learned to boost commission income by selecting insurers who charge the *highest* rates and thus pay the fattest commissions. So much for the splendor of the free market.

Still, the insurance may seem cheap when you buy it. Credit unemployment insurance, for example, will sometimes add only 5 percent to the cost of a loan and cover up to 10 months of unemployment, says the Consumer Credit Insurance Association, an industry trade group. (Many deals are far less generous.) That sounds reasonable enough, but watch how it plays out.

Let's say you have a $15,000, 48-month loan at 10 percent. Your monthly payment would be $380.44, or $399.91 if you took credit unemployment. (Warning: the lender may tell you your insurance rate equals 4 percent of the total loan payments, which, while technically true, might be misleading. If you finance the insurance—and lenders will fall all over themselves to help you do so, since it increases their profit while also making it more likely that you'll buy the stuff—you're actually adding *5 percent*, not 4 percent, to your total loan cost.)

That's an extra $934.76 over four years. So what happens if you win—that is, if you're involuntarily unemployed for 10 months? You would get $3,999.10 (10 times the monthly payment of $399.91, if the policy is retroactive), or a payout of roughly 4 to 1.

But in 1991 the average period of unemployment was 13.8 weeks, according to the Bureau of Labor Statistics, which means your insurance windfall might amount to only $1,199.73. That's virtually an even-money bet, the kind you'd make on a heavy favorite at the track. Is prolonged unemployment that likely for you? If so, consider taking the deal, as long as you realize that credit unemployment insurance usually has a payout ratio of 50 percent or less.

Credit-card issuers may seem to offer more enticing terms. Revolving-credit companies often bundle together credit life, disability, and unemployment insurance, typically for 60 cents a month for each $100 outstanding. A sweet, cheap, three-for-one deal?

Assume a balance of $2,500. That means you're paying $15 a month ($180 a year) for protection. If you die, the credit grantor gets the money, and your heirs are released from the $2,500 debt. (Your heirs may remember you less fondly if someone tells them that $180 a year could have purchased $125,000 worth of term life insurance for a 40-year-old male nonsmoker.)

You've got problems, however, if you're laid off or disabled. Most policies will cover only your minimum payment—usually about $70 a month on a $2,500 balance—for a fairly short time or up to a limited amount. Unless you expect to be laid off or disabled on virtually an annual basis—in which case you might consider choosing a more stable or less dangerous occupation—you'll realize a loss if you pay the $180 year after year.

In addition, the fine print on these insurance contracts may often bring distressing news. Many disability and unemployment policies don't begin to pay benefits until 31 days after you qualify. Since many disabilities last only a brief time, you may never see a penny. (Policies with retroactive benefits invariably cost more.)

REDUNDANCY

Insurance you don't need is always overpriced. And most people don't need any credit-insurance products.

If you work for a company with good benefits (or have had the presence of mind to marry someone who does), or if you have your own life and disability insurance, you can certainly forgo credit insurance. But what if you don't have enough insurance to cover your debts in case you die or become disabled? Instead of throwing away money on credit insurance, use the funds to buy policies that will offer you some real protection. (See page 226 for phone numbers of quote services specializing in cheap term insurance.)

FRAUD AND DUPLICITY

Many people buy credit insurance because they're falsely told that they can't get the loan without it or because they've been misled about its benefits. Millions more buy it unwittingly. One recent survey revealed that 30 percent of credit-insurance "customers" didn't know they had purchased the stuff. They never knew what hit them.

I understand their position. When I got a car loan in 1986, my bank gave me a dose of credit life without ever mentioning the matter. The insurance premium was folded into the monthly payment and buried in the fine print of the loan agreement.

Always read what you're signing. Then don't do what I did. I *did* read the loan agreement. And I did notice that the monthly payments were slightly higher than I had expected. I realized the bank was sneaking an extra $120 out of my pocket to pay for life insurance. But, I coolly reasoned, how significant was $120 when I was staring at a payment booklet commanding me to fork over more than $12,000? Talk about a drop in the bucket.

Actually, drop-in-the-bucket thinking wasn't my only justification for behaving like an idiot. Temporarily mistaking myself for someone who routinely billed $400 an hour, I concluded that calling the bank and mailing back the agreement wouldn't be worth the trouble. On top of that, I made a classic borrower's error. I worried that causing any fuss might somehow jeopardize my loan. Then, in one final attempt to make myself feel better about a transaction I knew I would live to regret, I tried to sell myself on a product I had not intended to buy, thinking of the virtues of extra protection (you can't be too careful) and the fact that it really wasn't so expensive (hah!).

What I never really faced were the facts: that I already had $300,000 worth of term life insurance and didn't really need an extra $12,000 at any price, *and* that the new coverage was almost four times as expensive as what I already had, so if I *did* need the extra $12,000 of coverage, I should have purchased it for $32 rather than $120.

I signed the loan agreement anyway and bought the credit life. I was busy. I was distracted. I was dumb.

I thought about canceling the insurance almost every month, but I didn't. Every month I had less reason to do so, for there was less money at stake to save. You can be smarter than I was. It's never too late to cancel credit insurance you don't need or want. Look over all your existing loan agreements. If, to your surprise, the insurance is in there, don't be embarrassed. Don't even waste any energy on being angry, although you have every right to be. Just make a call or write a letter and get rid of the damn thing. Add the savings to your debt-savings fund.

How can you avoid getting stuck with insurance you never asked for? Tell the lender you don't want it, then check the agreement to make sure your wishes have been honored. If you're getting the loan in person, bring a financial calculator with you. Why? To double-check that the monthly payment you're quoted does not include any extras and to keep the lender honest.

As the lender tries to hard-sell the insurance, never forget his powerful incentives for doing so. First, credit insurance is a guaranteed profit center. Second, it protects the lender from default should disaster befall you. As a banker once told financial planner Robert Klein of New York's Novos Planning Associates, "Without credit life, we'd be out of business."

Should anyone ever knowingly buy credit life insurance? Yes, if you're over 50 and in poor health, thus making standard life insurance either prohibitively expensive or impossible to get. And if you know that your heirs couldn't handle your debts if you die. Even then, you should be aware that the insurance may still be ridiculously expensive in some parts of the country.

State insurance regulations are notoriously lax in the South. In 1990, credit life policies in Louisiana paid out only 23 cents on the dollar. According to the National Association of Insurance Commissioners, residents of South Carolina, Oklahoma, Mississippi, and Alabama are also routinely gouged on credit insurance. The Northeast has the best deals, with the top payouts available in New York, Washington, D.C., Maine, Vermont, and Minnesota. The cost comparisons can be astonishing, with Louisiana residents paying more than four times as much as New Yorkers for the same coverage.

I hesitate to say this, but there is another time credit life makes sense: when you're terminally ill and have no ethics. You don't have to take a medical exam to get credit life. Usually, you don't even have to answer any questions (although insurance vendors may investigate your medical history before you're approved). So, if you're very sick yet still healthy enough to work (the insurers figure that if you're working, how sick could you be?), you could choose to leave your family with a valedictory present. Buy the expensive car, take the credit life, and your heirs will get the car free and clear. People run this scam on insurers all the time. (Some insurers estimate that 30 percent of their credit-life claims would fall into this category.)

But do I recommend it? Absolutely not. First, the idea is totally despicable. Do you really want to exit on this sort of larcenous note? Second, the claim might not be honored if you had to make any false statements to get the policy. Which might leave your heirs grieving about losing the Jaguar rather than losing you.

To conclude: Buy credit insurance only when it definitely makes sense for you, which will be rarely. If your traditional insurance is inadequate, use the money you would have spent on credit-insurance premiums to buy better types of insurance. Or, to get the best return on your money, use some or all of those credit-insurance dollars to pay down your existing debts. Or, finally, if you value the psychological comfort of an emergency fund, direct the dollars that way.

THE FIRST DEPOSIT NATIONAL BANK OF TILTON'S CAPITAL CASH ACCOUNT

One of my favorites, this legal, yet awful, deal epitomizes the worst in cash-advance direct-mail come-ons. The bank's envelope contains a nonnegotiable $3,000 "check" payable to you. Fill out a very brief application and you get a real check. Buried in the back of a brochure is the news that the loan will cost you 21.9 percent.

What logic would possibly compel you to accept this deal? Because, the bank's pitch letter earnestly notes, "The problem with personal loans is that too often the monthly payments you must make are just too high! You begin to wonder if it was worth taking out the loan in the first place."

To the bank's credit, the monthly payments are comparatively low—just 2 percent of your outstanding balance. And that's precisely the problem. High monthly payments help you get out of debt. Low monthly payments help keep you in debt virtually forever. In this case, you pay down the principal by 2 percent a month while interest accrues at 1.825 percent a month. So after making your first month's payment of $60, your new outstanding balance will be $2,994.75. The next month you'll pay $59.90, but you'll still owe $2,989.50. The month after that you'll pay $59.79 and owe $2,984.27. (Hmm, this is beginning to feel a bit like a bad mortgage.) You'll continue to owe a large amount after the fourth payment, the forty-fourth payment, and the eighty-eighth payment. Even after 231 payments, or 19 years and 3 months' worth, you'll still owe $2,001.69.

When will it ever end? Incredibly enough, it will take *77 years and 3 months* of minimum payments to get rid of this albatross. (It makes a standard mortgage look like a short-term loan.) If you never borrow another cent, the total finance charges on the $3,000 loan will be a staggering $24,734.58. The bank, aware that you may never be able to get off the merry-go-round no matter how long you live, sends you a batch of checks allowing you to replenish the loan at any time.

The pitch letter says, "Capital Cash could be the last loan you'll ever need!" It's really the last loan you'd ever want.

TAX-REFUND-ANTICIPATION LOANS

Want a quick way to make part of your tax refund disappear? Go for this legal rip-off offered by H&R Block and four major banks, among them Banc One and Mellon Bank.

The logic is beautiful. You've got money coming from the government. Wouldn't it be nice if you had access to that money now? Especially if you could pay just a flat, $29 fee?

Unfortunately, the $29 that Banc One would charge you for a $300 to $3,300 advance can translate into an astronomically high interest rate—far above what you'd pay for a credit-card cash advance or almost any other kind of loan. (Presumably, such loans are targeted, in part, at people who have no other borrowing alternatives.) Worse yet, the bank computes the loan's APR as if the debt would be outstanding for an entire year, which, under the circumstances, is unconscionable and extremely misleading. It generally takes six weeks to get a refund; since H&R Block is filing electronically, the average is closer to 18 days. To be kind, let's call it a month. In that case, the alleged 9.7-percent APR would really be an APR of 116 percent on a $300 loan.

Clearly, the flat-fee approach becomes more tempting if you're waiting for a big check. On a $1,800 refund, the $29 fee would translate into an APR of 19.3 percent for one month. The rate falls to 13.2 percent for six weeks, which turns out to be a better deal than you can get on most cash advances. If your refund is that large, and you need the money now, consider the deal. But you and your accountant should do something to try to diminish your refund next year.

LOAN-BROKER CONS

Be suspicious of loan brokers, or anyone who claims to have access to financing you can't tap yourself. Some loan brokers are undoubtedly honest, while others will remind you of used-car salespeople who couldn't handle the ethical demands of the auto-resale business.

The Iowa attorney general has issued a televised warning about loan brokers who promise financing to small-business owners and desperate consumers without any intention of ever delivering the money. Fraudulent loan brokers have been exposed in California, Texas, Florida, New Jersey, and elsewhere throughout the country. Often the con artists set up shop out-of-state, making it harder for consumers to press suits to recapture their money and for prosecutors to bring charges.

The advance-fee scheme is an old one. It becomes more popular whenever credit gets tight. One California man couldn't find a traditional lender willing to finance his purchase of a car wash, so he paid a $17,000 advance fee to Diamon International of Dallas, a loan broker. In return, he got a commitment letter for financing. Backed by that letter, he gave the seller $100,000 to secure the sale.

But Diamon International, which has since been shut down by the Dallas district attorney, never came up with a dime for the would-be borrower. The sale fell through. The California man lost about $125,000—his life savings.

Some smart swindlers now draw up fancy contracts promising that any advance fee will be refunded if the loan doesn't materialize. Don't be fooled. By the time you realize that the financing is nonexistent, the advance fee will probably be eaten up by expenses, most of them bogus.

What kind of due diligence will help protect you? Ask brokers which lenders they typically use—and verify them. Find out where the broker is based and then call the Better Business Bureau, state attorney general, and consumer-protection agency in that area. Consider having any advance fees placed in an escrow account.

After all, it's unfair to say that loan brokers never provide a service. When investigators looked at the records of one Florida loan broker, American Financial Connections, they found that the firm had opened files on, and presumably received fees from, twenty-five hundred people—and had successfully secured financing for five of them.

900 NUMBERS

Using 900 numbers to find out about credit cards, credit-repair services, or borrowing "opportunities" is almost always a bad idea. At best, these telephonic marvels will give you information that is overpriced and incomplete.

Some 900 numbers will refer you to another 900 number (an ex-

traordinarily expensive version of telephone tag), while others may put
you on hold or slowly and deliberately repeat parts of the message to
pump up your charges. Sometimes the services will charge very high
flat fees—up to $50—for thoroughly worthless information.

In an attempt to boost their credibility, debt telemarketers hired
sitcom dads Alan Thicke and the late Robert Reed as spokesmen and
offered guarantees to respondents (one pitch promised a $100 bill to
anyone turned down for credit). Don't be seduced.

Usually, credit-card telemarketers are really offering one of two
things: either a secured card, which can almost invariably be obtained
more economically elsewhere, or a sham card, which you can use only
to buy undesirable goods (often schlocky merchandise at list price)
from one particular catalogue—and we're not talking Sears or Spiegel.

In one scam, two Baltimore companies, First Capital Financial and
Midas Financial (nice touch), ran TV and newspaper ads stating that
consumers who called a special 900 number would receive gold cards
very much like those offered by American Express and MasterCard.
The number was indeed special (each call cost $49.95), but the cards
were not. They were standard catalogue-card ripoffs. (The FTC won
court orders freezing the assets of the two firms and ordering them to
halt such marketing activities.)

Sometimes these pitches come in the mail. A postcard from the
"Credit Notification Center" in Daytona Beach features a Visa logo
and, as if that weren't enough, the image of George Washington. It
offers an "Instant Credit Gold Charge Card from National Credit Savers" to those who call a 900 number.

The call yields a $1.95-a-minute recording that blathers on for 10
full minutes before finally making its point. You have to send another
$29.95 to get the card. It's not a Visa card, though; it's a National
Credit Gold Card, another catalogue exclusive. If you want a Visa card,
that will run you another $29.95. Of course, this is a secured card,
which means you'll have credit only if it is backed up by a bank deposit.

One of the many terrible attributes of catalogue cards is that their
issuers almost never report your transactions to credit bureaus, so using
one will deplete your resources without enhancing your credit rating.
Some catalogue cards come with particularly repugnant requirements.
If you want to get the $5,000 credit line promised by National Financial
Network, you first have to charge at least $1,000 worth of merchandise
from its catalogue. For most people, racking up $1,000 in new charges

is not necessarily the best way to begin extricating themselves from financial difficulties.

Secured cards can sometimes be very valuable and sensible things for people to have. But don't get them from a 900 number. See Chapter 26 or contact RAM Research or Bankcard Holders of America (see Appendix A). Unlike most telemarketing services, their lists will allow you to do some genuine comparison shopping to find the card that is best for you.

CREDIT-CARD BROKERS OR MIDDLEMEN

Dialing an 800 number isn't always a toll-free experience.

In recent years, shysters have sent millions of postcards to consumers promising credit cards with rates "as low as 11.88 percent." If you call the 800 number on the postcard, as I've done several times, a person will try to sell you an information package filled with data on low-rate and no-annual-fee credit cards. The cost of the information—which can be obtained from Bankcard Holders of America for $1.50—ranges from $70 to $200.

Obviously, this is a lousy deal; but it gets worse. Either on the postcard or on the phone, the middlemen usually guarantee that all applicants will be accepted by at least one of the banks to which they apply. This is a fabrication. The middlemen have no relationships with the banks in question. Even if they did, they couldn't guarantee that everyone would be accepted for anything other than a secured credit card.

In April 1991, Visa and MasterCard filed a $95-million lawsuit against a national telemarketing network that allegedly made such false guarantees to consumers. The attorneys general of Oregon and Colorado have also filed fraud charges against similar telemarketing outfits.

HOME-IMPROVEMENT
AND SECOND-MORTGAGE SCAMS

This is a combination scam. The con artists typically follow a reverse redlining policy, targeting only the poorest neighborhoods. They look for poor people who have paid-up or nearly paid-up mortgages and offer them "improvements" such as vinyl siding, new windows, or porch repairs.

Often, the renovations are never completed, but that's only a minor irritation next to the main event. The contractors direct their victims to lenders offering back-breaking second mortgages. (In an alternate version of the scam, the contractors have the owners sign a trust deed, which secures the home-improvement loan with their home. Even when the owners refuse to pay for shoddy or unfinished work, the contractor may be able to use the trust deed to force the sale of the house and, in the process, collect his payment. Note: The repair contract itself is often a loan application secured by the home.) In such scams, the interest rates range from 18 percent to 40 percent, with loan-origination fees sometimes as high as 20 percent to 40 percent.

Obviously, no one who did the math or carefully read the papers would ever consent to such a horrendous deal, but many borrowers, even some who are relatively sophisticated in other financial matters, suffer from the "sign here" syndrome. They don't really read every document placed before them. That can be a deadly mistake.

Lesson number two of this scam: Always be wary of anyone, such as a contractor, who offers easy access to financing. Package deals frequently involve kickbacks or other types of financial abuse. Remember that, at best, the person providing a service just wants to be paid. He or she is not concerned with your long-term financial needs or goals.

Lesson number three: Consider getting professional legal advice before signing any papers you don't completely understand.

BAIT-AND-SWITCH LOANS

Middlemen who promise rock-bottom rates for mortgage loans or refinancings don't always deliver. They may come up with the money. It's the interest rate that often causes a problem.

Take the case of James and Sharon Conti of East Wareham, Massachusetts. The Contis say that U.S. Funding Inc. of America, a Massachusetts mortgage company, promised them an 8-percent, 30-year mortgage with payments of $700 a month. Before the Contis could get that loan, though, they first had to sign a high-interest mortgage.

The terms: 15 years at 18 percent, which translated into monthly payments about twice as high as the Contis had originally been promised. "They said I would have to make only one monthly payment, and then I'd have the other loan," James Conti told *The Boston Globe*.

Accepting that fiction as fact, the Contis went ahead and financed their $95,000 home with the high-interest loan. But the 8 percent mortgage never materialized. Eventually the Contis fell behind on their payments, and the lender foreclosed. (In April 1992, fifteen people associated with U.S. Funding were indicted by a federal grand jury.)

What should have tipped off the Contis? First, the promise of what was at the time a below-market rate. If a financial offer seems too good to be true, it invariably is. The second red flag was the bogus notion that the Contis couldn't get the loan they wanted without first accepting a loan that would break them. Loans come with all sorts of conversion features, but no legitimate lender ever operates *this* way.

MORTGAGE-TRANSFER SCHEMES

These days, mortgages move around almost as often as people do. In fact, the odds are 3-to-1 that any mortgage will be sold at least once during its typical 7-year life span.

Aware of this trend, some crooks write letters telling people their mortgages have changed hands when this is not the case. The redirected payments are then pocketed by the con artists.

So how can you tell if your mortgage really has been sold? The servicer selling your mortgage should send you a formal "good-bye" letter 5 to 15 days before your next mortgage payment is due. It will tell you the name of the new servicer and give you information about whom to contact if you have any questions and tell you where to send your next payment. Shortly afterward, you should receive a similar "welcome" letter from the new servicer. If you don't get the "good-bye" letter, call your lender.

What else should you watch out for?

A MISCELLANY OF SLEAZE

• Credit-card issuers, such as the First National Bank of Omaha, who boast about not charging any annual fees because they levy *monthly* fees instead.

• 900 numbers that offer prizes as well as guaranteed credit cards.

National Credit Authority, a California outfit, dangles a $5,000 grand prize before applicants; the odds of ever collecting it, unfortunately, are 1 in 1,096,782.

• Companies that claim they can "erase bad credit" (see the section on credit repair in chapter 5). These firms can't wave a wand and make legitimate negative information disappear. Under the law, anything they can "erase," you can erase, too—on your own, without paying extravagant fees.

• Mortgage-reduction information kits. For $195 and up, door-to-door reps sell information to homeowners about how to lower mortgage costs via refinancing. Once again, the scam is that what the reps are marketing is easily available elsewhere at little or no cost.

• Mail-order loans. Some firms advertise in tabloids promising loans by mail with no questions asked, even if you have bad credit ("Bad Credit No Problem"). Respond to the ads, and you seem to get instant gratification; you're "preapproved" for a loan. All the companies ask is that you send in a check for several hundred dollars ($249 and $299 are common numbers) as an application or processing fee.

Often, that's the end of the transaction. They keep your check, and you never hear from them again. One Florida company, First Southeastern Corporation, apparently adhered to such stringent credit criteria that it cashed thousands of checks from "customers" without ever granting a single loan. Investigators call such operations "turn-down rooms."

In 1991, the nation's Better Business Bureaus received 300,000 consumer complaints and inquiries about such practices.

If you encounter any dubious credit-card pitches, you can blow the whistle by writing to the general counsel at Visa (P.O. Box 8999, San Francisco, CA 94128) or MasterCard (888 Seventh Avenue, New York, NY 10106). Misleading mail or phone offers for other financial products should be reported to the Direct Marketing Association (6 East 43rd Street, New York, NY 10017) or your state's attorney general.

If you have an extra minute, please consider alerting me as well (c/o Penguin Books, 375 Hudson Street, New York, NY 10014).

22

SAFEGUARDING YOURSELF
AGAINST CREDIT-CARD FRAUD

$ Credit-card fraud is a big business—the American Bankers Association says it exceeds $500 million annually, with much of the haul going to organized crime—and it victimizes tens of thousands of cardholders every year. The greatest potential harm to consumers isn't financial (under federal law, the maximum liability per card is $50, and this is often waived by card issuers in the event of fraud). The biggest threat is damage to one's credit record and the many frustrating hours it may take to undo it.

You can take steps to reduce the chance that you'll become a target. A few of the tips may startle you because they mean it's time to change some ingrained credit-card habits. Destroying your carbons is not enough.

All a crook needs to charge merchandise to your account is a stolen credit-card number. The thief can acquire a number from dishonest store clerks and bank employees, or by sorting through the trash to find discarded credit-card receipts. If the malefactor has both your number and your address, he may even be able to open a credit-card account in your name. One fast-growing identity-snatching scam, called account-takeover fraud, doesn't require a credit-card number at all. What's needed? Just enough information—such as your name, address, phone number, and social security number—to allow someone to impersonate you.

Therefore, whenever possible, zealously safeguard all credit-card numbers and personal information.

• Never give out your credit-card number except when you're making a purchase or booking a hotel. If you're paying by check, never write your credit-card number on the check for identification purposes—no matter what a store clerk says. No one can compel you to do so. Flashing your card as an ID is fine, as long as no one copies down the number. Just so you know, the request for a credit-card number has no financial basis. If your check bounces, a merchant can't charge your credit-card account.

(Occasionally, a merchant will refuse your check under such circumstances. If so, what can you do? Find out the name of the bank that handles the merchant's credit-card receivables and complain to Visa or MasterCard, or contact your state attorney general.)

Why shouldn't you put a credit-card number on a check? Many people will see your check as it goes through the clearing system; one of them might be a member of a number-stealing ring. Because of this, it is now illegal for a merchant to record a customer's credit-card number on a check in California, Delaware, Florida, Iowa, Kansas, Maryland, New Jersey, Virginia, and Washington.

But wait a minute. Don't some credit-card companies themselves ask you to write your account number on the checks you send them each month? Sure they do. But don't worry; your check will be cashed with or without the number.

• Avoid putting your address and phone number on credit slips. Most people are so accustomed to being asked that they hardly think about it, but this is a dangerous habit. Furthermore, the practice is forbidden by Visa and MasterCard, and it's even illegal for merchants in California, Maryland, New York, and Virginia to request such information.

In my hometown of New York City, where most laws are honored in the breach if at all, many merchants nonetheless persist in making the request. If your gentle refusal to acquiesce is met by resistance, you don't have to cause a fuss. Just use a time-honored expedient for financial transactions: lie. Write down a phony address and bogus number. If this violates your moral code, just pretend you're a doctor and scrawl something illegible instead.

• Never give your card number to any telemarketer unless you initiated the call. Be particularly wary of anyone who, after saying that you've won a prize or a trip, casually mentions that a credit-card number is needed for verification. It will be used only to verify that you're a dupe.

• Keep your credit card in view at all times during a transaction. This will discourage crooked clerks from making a second imprint. Financial planner Phyllis Wordhouse of Plymouth, Michigan, uses this approach even at gas stations. "I watch them put the card through the machine and have them give it back before I fill up," she says.

• Draw a line through the blank spaces on your credit-card receipt above the total so that the amount you owe can't be changed.

• Keep personal information private whenever you can. All some credit-card crooks need to apply for credit in your name is your name and social security number and a "new" address. Guard your social security number vigilantly. Be especially careful in states that use social security numbers on driver's licenses. Show your license for ID purposes if you must, but discourage the clerk from recording your license number.

• Before tossing direct-mail credit pitches in the trash, tear them into several pieces.

• Never put your credit-card number on a postcard or on the outside of an envelope.

• And, of course, destroy all your carbons. But take this precaution one step further. Don't keep credit-card receipts where a dishonest person might find them—in your glove compartment, in a coat hanging in a public place, or in your desk drawer at work.

• Consider asking credit bureaus to put a statement in your file instructing all lenders not to approve any application for credit unless you are personally contacted first. (You should know that there's a potential downside to this prophylactic measure: it can be a time-consuming nuisance when you need quick approval for a loan.)

• Beware of any consumer-protection product that promises to "insure" you against credit-card fraud. Since your maximum liability is so low—$50 per card—you're really already carrying enough insurance without paying a dime for it.

• Report lost or stolen cards immediately.

• When you get your monthly credit-card bills, open them immediately and check for any errors. You don't need to cross-check your receipts against each item. Eyeballing the numbers should be sufficient. (See chapter 23 for advice on how to dispute an item.)

23

YOUR CREDIT RIGHTS

$ Although not the most common causes of insanity, credit-card errors and billing disputes have driven some people bonkers. These poor victims might have avoided breakdowns if they had a clearer idea of where their credit rights began and where they ended.

The Fair Credit Billing Act requires lenders to correct errors promptly. Under the act, a billing error is defined as a charge for:

- something you didn't actually buy or a purchase made by anyone not authorized to use your account;
- an amount different from the purchase price or an item that is not properly identified on your bill;
- an item that you refused to accept on delivery or that was not delivered as promised.

These are the most common types of mistakes covered by the law. More unusual ones include an error in arithmetic, the failure to credit your account properly, and the failure to mail a statement to your current address (*if*, that is, the lender was notified of the address change at least 20 days before the end of the billing period).

Before you enter into the dispute process, be aware that if you're dissatisfied with the *quality* of the goods and services you've purchased, this does not constitute a billing error under the law.

I know that some people don't look at their monthly account statements promptly or carefully because the documents are depressing. It's not as if you're going to find a mistake in your favor, right? Well, errors do occur, and it usually takes only a few seconds to spot them. Besides, having the courage to go over your bills as soon as they arrive is good for your character; ignoring a bill is not.

Luckily, most of us can spot an error with just a quick glance. Nonetheless, it's essential to save all receipts, in case you ever do find a mistake (or meet with a reimbursable calamity according to the provisions of your credit card, as explained in chapter 10).

CORRECTING A MISTAKE

If you find an error in your bill or want an item clarified, you must do the following.

• Notify the credit-card issuer in writing, via registered mail, so that it receives the letter within 60 days of the bill's postmark date. Include photocopies of sales slips and any pertinent documents. Contacting the issuer by phone *does not* preserve your legal rights. (If you wait more than 60 days, you have to take the matter up with the merchant.)

• Send your letter to the address specified for such communications. (Note: It is almost always different from the address to which you send your monthly checks.)

• Provide the issuer with your name, address, and account number and give details about the error (when it occurred, how great the discrepancy is, and so on).

The card issuer then has 30 days to acknowledge your letter; it has 90 days either to fix the mistake or to explain why it believes the bill to be correct. While the investigation is continuing, you are legally allowed to withhold payment on the disputed item, as well as any related finance charges. (If your real dispute is with the merchant—perhaps about the quality of what you've purchased—notify the card issuer that you'll be withholding payment until the problem is cleared up. Realize, though, that you can't take back money you've paid. For example, if the amount in dispute is $200 and you've paid the card issuer $40, you can no longer withhold the entire $200.)

During the period of investigation, the card issuer cannot damage your credit rating by reporting your refusal to pay to a credit bureau. Nor can the creditor initiate any action against you to collect the money before it responds to your complaint.

Once the credit-card issuer has explained why it disagrees with you, it can then take steps to collect, and also report you to a credit bureau as delinquent. At this point, if you send another letter indicating your refusal to pay the card issuer, it must inform credit bureaus that the matter is under dispute. It must also tell you the name and address of anyone who has received information about your "delinquent" account. (When the dispute is finally settled, the card issuer must promptly report the outcome to all inquirers who have learned about it.)

If the issuer persists in claiming that you're wrong, and you're determined to fight, your target should probably become the merchant who reported the erroneous information.

When the issue concerns defective goods or services, you have an advantage if you've used a store credit card rather than a bank or T&E card. In this case, as long as you've made a genuine effort to resolve the problem with the merchant, you may withhold full payment without penalty, if you notify the merchant about your claim in writing.

If you made the charge on a card not issued by the store, your right to withhold payment is limited to purchases greater than $50 made in your home state or within 100 miles of your home address.

Finally, if the store doesn't somehow compensate you for the defective goods or services, you can stand by your refusal to pay. Even if the store eventually sues you for the money, which is unlikely, the inadequacy of the goods and services will constitute a valid defense.

REFUNDS

If your account has a credit balance of more than $1 and you want to get your hands on that money, write a letter to the creditor requesting a refund. It then has seven business days to cut you a check.

GRACE PERIODS

When you have a card with an interest-free grace period, the creditor must mail your statement at least 14 days before it is due, so that you are able to pay the bill without incurring a finance charge. (Twenty years ago, some credit-card issuers were known for timing their mailings so statements would arrive a day or two before the due date, thus making it impossible for a customer to mail back a payment fast enough to avoid the finance charge. This scam was legal then; it's not now.)

IF A CREDITOR DOESN'T COMPLY

If a creditor violates the law regarding billing errors, it forfeits the first $50 in merchandise or finance charges—even when it turns out that the creditor is right and you are wrong. In addition, you always have the right to sue the creditor for damages and twice the amount of finance charges between $100 and $1,000, plus court costs and attorney's fees.

DON'T SIGN AWAY YOUR LEGAL RIGHTS

All the rights discussed in this chapter are wonderful things to have, which is why some credit grantors are occasionally eager to wrest them from you. Always read any finance agreement carefully to make sure you aren't unwittingly surrendering anything you may need later. Some standard furniture company finance agreements, for instance, include a clause stating that in the event of a collection action or repossession, the consumer waives all rights to a defense. A good deal for the furniture company; a lousy one for the consumer. Whenever you find dangerous language such as this, demand that it be crossed out.

WHAT CREDITORS HAVE TO TELL YOU

Thirty years ago, it sometimes took a lot of work to find out the annual percentage rate of a loan. APR disclosure was not required by law until 1968. Until September 1, 1989, it was also quite possible to get a credit card without having a clue as to just how onerous the terms were.

Today, it's easy to find out. On mail solicitations, credit- and charge-card issuers must disclose (prominently, and in a table) all of the following information: the interest rate (and whether it's variable or fixed), the annual fee, the grace period, the balance calculation method, and all additional charges (late fees, over-the-limit fees, cash-advance costs, and bounced-check fees).

Unfortunately, the Fair Credit and Charge Card Disclosure Act is more lenient about disclosures made in other types of solicitations, such as applications contained in newspapers, magazines, and catalogues. The issuer may disclose all the information discussed above; more likely, it will provide a toll-free number that you can call to get the facts.

HOW TO COMPLAIN
ABOUT YOUR FINANCIAL INSTITUTION

If you've been egregiously abused by your financial institution, you'll probably want to complain. If you play golf with a senior officer of the bank, by all means complain to him or her. Otherwise, try dealing with a loan officer you know or with some senior officer who has the power to help you. Should these approaches fail, here's how to contact the appropriate regulatory authorities in Washington.

National Bank. The word "national" will appear in the bank's name or the initials "N.A." after its name.
  Comptroller of the Currency
  Consumer Affairs Division
  490 L'Enfant Plaza, S.W.
  Washington, DC 20219

State-chartered bank that is a member of the Federal Reserve System. Signs will grace its windows or lobby stating that the bank is a member of the Federal Reserve System and that all deposits are FDIC-insured.
  Federal Reserve System
  Division of Consumer and Community Affairs
  20th and Constitution Ave., N.W.
  Washington, DC 20551
You can also write to the Federal Reserve Bank with jurisdiction over federal banks in your area.

State-chartered FDIC-insured bank that is not a member of the Federal Reserve System.
  Federal Deposit Insurance Corporation
  Office of Bank Customer Affairs
  Washington, DC 20429

Federally chartered or federally insured savings-and-loan association. The name of the S&L will usually include the word "Federal" or the initials "F.A." A sign will say that deposits are insured by the FSLIC.

Federal Home Loan Bank Board
Office of Community Investment
1700 G St., N.W.
Washington, DC 20552

Federal savings bank. Usually the name of the S&L will include the word "Federal" or the initials "F.S.B."
Federal Home Loan Bank Board
Office of Community Investment
1700 G St., N.W.
Washington, DC 20552

State-chartered FSLIC-insured institution. No "Federal," "F.A.," or "F.S.B." appears in the S&L's name.
Federal Home Loan Bank Board
Office of Community Investment
1700 G St., N.W.
Washington, DC 20552

State-chartered banks or savings institutions without Federal Deposit Insurance. For violations of state laws, contact your state banking department (it's listed under state offices in your phone book). If you want to make a federal case out of it, write to:
Federal Trade Commission
Washington, DC 20580

Federally chartered credit union. The term "Federal Credit Union" appears in the name of the institution.
National Credit Union Administration
1776 G St., N.W.
Washington, DC 20456

State-chartered credit union. Write to the agency that regulates credit unions in your state or to the FTC.

Don't automatically rely on card-issuer employees for an accurate assessment of your consumer rights. For whatever reason, they sometimes make mistakes. "We see evidence every week that some of the biggest banks in the country—Chase Manhattan, Citibank, First Chicago, etc.—misstate the rules," says Elgie Holstein, head of Bankcard Holders of America. "They often ask for unwarranted documentation and put the burden of proof on the consumer when it should be on the merchant."

THE RIGHT TO BE LEFT ALONE

Borrowers who are worried about their privacy or concerned about the capacity of their mailbox can have their names deleted from lists sold by American Express, Citibank, TRW, and Trans Union. To get off the lists, write to:

American Express Cardmember Mailing List Services
P.O. Box 53710
Phoenix, AZ 85072-3710

Citibank
P.O. Box 6018
Sioux Falls, SD 57117-6018

TRW Marketing Services
Attention: Mail Preference
600 City Parkway West
Orange, CA 92668

Trans Union Corp.
Consumer Relations Department
TransMark Division
555 West Adams
Chicago, IL 60661

PART VII

MONEY TROUBLES

$

24

CRUNCHTIME: WHAT HAPPENS WHEN YOU CAN'T PAY?

$ Sometimes, you can't pay.
Maybe you're having a temporary cash-flow problem. Or perhaps you've suffered a serious loss of income or been jolted by emergency expenses (medical, legal, etc.). Or maybe years and years of juggling obligations have finally caught up with you.

For the purposes of this chapter, the reason matters only slightly. Creditors will be more sympathetic if your payment problem results from the serious illness of a child rather than an overfondness for Giorgio Armani or Donna Karan—but only up to a point.

DON'T HIDE

In every case, you should be proactive. Contact creditors before they contact you. Let them know in advance that a payment will be late or nonexistent. Tell them early on that the next six months are going to be pure financial hell for you, but that you want to work something out.

Once again, almost everything's negotiable. And your negotiating posture is strongest if *you* initiate contact—and if you have a clear idea of what you're willing to do.

AN ACTION PLAN

That willingness should depend upon what you *can* do. Before beginning negotiations, analyze your financial position as well as you can. Obviously, if you've been laid off, you can't know when you'll get another job, or what the job will pay, but you can certainly gauge how much cash you have on hand and how much borrowing power you have (if any). What does the immediate future look like? Can you pay everybody about 80 percent of what you owe? Fifty percent? Three cents on the dollar?

As you proceed, keep in mind that you have a variety of important goals:

- To get some breathing room.
- To remain as sane as possible so that the nonfinancial parts of your life don't fall apart.
- To protect your credit rating and your property to whatever extent possible.
- To handle the present crisis in a manner that least imperils your future.
- And, less significantly, to maintain decent relationships with your creditors. Follow a reasonable action plan, though, and that's quite likely to happen.

So, before initiating contact, sit down and get an idea of how bad things really are. Add up all the debts. Write down your expected income for the next few months. If the news is really bleak, it might be a good idea to call a nonprofit credit counselor (see box on page 264).

MAKING CONTACT

Want a good-news story? Creditors can be surprisingly accommodating. Norman Dawidowicz, a senior financial consultant with Personal Capital Management of New York City, recalls a client who went on a spending binge, then woke up one morning to discover she owed American Express $8,000. "She simply could not pay it off in one month," Dawidowicz says. "So we contacted them and worked out a schedule of four monthly payments—without interest." (When you agree to such a payment plan, your credit rating does take a moderate hit, but you stand a good chance of salvaging the relationship with the creditor. This woman still has an American Express card.)

Although my aim is not to teach you how to get interest-free loans from creditors, such a story is not unique. When you call and say you're in trouble, some creditors—Macy's, Spiegel, Citibank, Discover, National Westminster Bank, Banc One, Bank of New York, Chemical Bank, Bank of America, and Household Credit Services, among them—will shut off the interest-rate meter and stop charging late fees. You still owe what you owe, of course, but at least the amount won't grow. (A credit counselor negotiating on your behalf is more likely to get this sort of concession than you are acting alone.)

TIPS

• The more forthcoming you are, the better the deal you're likely to strike. If you've made mistakes, admit them.

• Make your initial contact with the creditor by phone. Ask for the credit-card manager at a bank or the credit manager at a retail store.

• If that person's response approximates a civilized version of what a loan shark might say—"I'm sorry, Mr. Feinberg, but our terms are not negotiable"—try moving up the pecking order until you find someone more sympathetic.

• When you do, consider asking for a 3- or 6-month moratorium on principal payments. You'll have to keep paying the interest—and, over time, you won't save any money—but this can take away some of the immediate pressure.

• If that doesn't work, make your best offer; say what you can really afford to pay and when.

• Don't, however, let yourself get talked into paying more than you can afford. This can only create additional problems. First, the creditor will be angry when it becomes clear your promise was hollow. Second, you'll drive yourself crazy, because instead of having created a new plan with payments you can make, you've set up an impossible situation. Now, you can only fail. Your self-esteem will suffer. Worse yet, you may start running up new debts, falling victim to the I'm-in-so-deep-already-how-much-more-could-it-hurt? syndrome.

• Whenever you succeed in negotiating lower monthly payments, ask the creditor to have the new payments recorded as timely on your credit report. (You won't always prevail.)

• Don't automatically accept a much higher interest rate for the privilege of stretching out your payments. Negotiate. (If a higher rate is the best you can do, plan to restructure the debt 6 or 12 months down the road.)

• If all your offers are rebuffed, consider this high-risk ploy. (It often works, but use it only if you're in real trouble.) If no one in the organization is willing to accept your terms, then unilaterally enforce them anyway. Regularly pay what you can afford. In his *How to Get Out of Debt, Stay Out of Debt & Live Prosperously*, Jerrold Mundis tells a great story about an actor named Glen who owed $3,500 on his Chemical Bank credit card and was supposed to pay $148 per month. All he could afford was $20 per week, so that's what he sent, even though the bank told him his obstinacy would lead to a lawsuit.

Every Monday at 9:00 A.M., Glen called the same bank officer who had threatened the lawsuit to tell him how his life was going financially. (You don't have to do this, but it is cute.) "Eventually," Mundis writes, "he developed a telephone relationship with the man that bordered on friendship. After several months, when Glen's situation had improved, he increased his payments to $30 a week."

Chemical never sued.

CAR PAYMENTS

Some lenders, such as the automobile finance companies, may be especially willing to work with you. If you're having a short-term problem, they can "refinance" your loan by extending the repayment period. If the matter is more serious, they may rewrite the entire loan. Another alternative: trading down to a less impressive vehicle with cheaper monthly payments.

THE IRS

A lot of people suspect they owe money to the IRS. They aren't sure. They'd have a better idea if they opened the letters the IRS has been sending them, but they're too afraid. *Don't ever do this.*

"When some people receive letters from the IRS, their initial reaction is pure fear," says Jerry Schneider, a Great Neck, New York, CPA.

When it is ignored, the IRS responds just like any other collection agency: it goes into pit-bull mode—except that it does it better than anyone else. The IRS, for instance, has special phones that will automatically redial your home number for months until someone answers. Agents will call you at work—relentlessly.

Imitating an ostrich is also foolish because IRS assessments are often wrong. You may not owe anything.

But what if you owe money and can't pay? Respond to the first letter in writing and request more time. An agent will then call you. Consider pleading hardship. Under its growing "offers to compromise" program, the IRS will occasionally accept a settlement for less than the full amount owed—if, that is, the agency is convinced this is the best deal it can cut. (Note: In most cases, filing for bankruptcy will not erase a debt to the IRS.)

If you can pay up eventually, you and your accountant can negotiate a repayment schedule with the agency. But watch out: this may be unpleasant. "You have to fill out a ton of forms and explain exactly why you spend X dollars for groceries," says Schneider. (If you owe less than $10,000, negotiating a plan won't affect your credit rating. But for payment plans involving $10,000 or more, the IRS must put a lien on your property—and this does hurt your credit status.)

Other accountants report that successfully completing a repayment plan offers no guarantee that the IRS will stop dunning you for money you *don't* owe. The agency's system is improving, but once it sinks its teeth into someone, it is loath to let go.

So if you can, it may be better to get a cash advance on a credit card to settle the claim. But what if some smart friend tells you it's cheaper to hold off paying the IRS, because the interest and the penalties together may come to less than 18 percent? Technically, this is true—but it could be a sucker's play if you try to get away with it for too long.

Still, if you've got the stomach for it, borrowing from the IRS can be significantly cheaper than using a credit card. As a short-term ploy, it may be a smart move. Here's an example:

It's April 14 and tomorrow Henry is supposed to send the IRS $20,000, which he does not have. He could tap his five credit cards for the money, but then he'd have to pay interest of 18 percent plus cash-advance fees.

So he files his return but doesn't send a check. From that moment on, he will be hit with interest of 7 percent a year, plus penalty interest of .5 percent a month. The cost of owing the IRS for three months would be $650. The cost of using credit cards instead would be $900, plus another $50 or more for the cash advances.

How long can Henry safely profit from this interest-rate spread? Not too long. Dunning letters will probably begin arriving in July. By November the IRS might slap a lien on his property or levy his bank accounts.

(Note: the most disastrous course would be not filing at all. Then Henry would be liable for an additional 5-percent, rather than .5 percent, penalty per month, up to a total of 25 percent of the amount owed.)

If, for any reason, the IRS *wrongly* says that you owe money, contact its Problem Resolution Program (PRP). This is one government office that can really help. Each IRS regional office has a PRP. Look in the government listings section of the phone book or call 202 566-6475 for information.

(Note: If you're being audited and you expect to pay more taxes and penalties, you can stop any additional interest from accruing on money you owe by making a deposit in the nature of a cash bond with the IRS. Ask your accountant for details or call the IRS.)

WHEN THE CREDITOR GETS TOUGH

If you're not making any payments to a creditor, or if the creditor decides it will no longer tolerate your individualistic repayment plan, you'll start getting rude letters. Some of these communications may have a surreal quality. A credit-card issuer may send you a notice stating it will soon turn your account over to a collection agency, while the same envelope contains fliers pitching new products for you to purchase.

Creditors determined to get ballistic have two options. They can sue you and win a judgment, or they can turn your account over to a collection agency. Both alternatives represent an acknowledgment of financial defeat, however. Lawsuits cost a lot of money. Collection agencies get to keep 30 to 50 percent of what they collect, which means a big loss for the creditor.

This helps explain why consumers are sometimes able to make a lump-sum payment to the creditor, equal to 70 percent to 80 percent of the debt, to settle the account right before either a legal or a collection action begins. Realize, though, that there are three problems associated with this approach:

1. It assumes you have the money for the lump-sum payment, which may not be true.
2. The creditor won't be thrilled about continuing its relationship with you.
3. The creditor may not tell credit bureaus the account has been "squared." It has the right to report any amount you did not pay as a bad debt or a charge-off. (Pursue the lump-sum payment plan only if the creditor agrees not to do this.)

COLLECTION AGENCIES

Bill collectors aren't as abusive as they used to be. Nonetheless, they can do a lot to make your life miserable—sometimes legally and sometimes not.

Before the Fair Debt Collection Practices Act was passed in 1977, collectors' main weapon was fear. Now they're far more likely to play on feelings of guilt or shame—to ask, for instance, whether your children or your neighbors know you're a "criminal," because you take things without paying for them.

You can shut them up. Many people don't know it, but there is a perfectly simple way to get a collector to break off virtually all contact. Send the agency a letter by certified mail requesting that it leave you alone.

That's it. Once you've done that, a collector may legally contact you only to announce that collection efforts have ended or that some legal action—usually a lawsuit—is being taken against you.

Even if you never request that the collector cease trying to contact you, there is a broad range of prohibited conduct for collectors. A collection agency may not:

• Contact any third parties except your lawyer, credit bureaus, and people who might help the agency locate you.

- Tell a third party that you owe money.
- Send you anything by mail that indicates on the envelope that it is trying to collect a debt.
- Call at an unusual time—before 8:00 A.M. or after 9:00 P.M.
- Call you at work if it knows that your employer prohibits such collection calls (feel free to say that your employer forbids them).
- Call you repeatedly.
- Use obscene language.
- Use or threaten violence.
- Make false claims (such as claiming you'll be imprisoned for non-payment, threatening to have welfare payments cut off, or sending a document that looks as if it's from a court or government agency).

If a bill collector violates any of these provisions, complain to the Federal Trade Commission (see Appendix A) or your state attorney general.

(Warning: Just because you're able to stop bill-collector harassment does not mean that collectors pose no serious threat. When they huff and puff about a lawsuit, they may mean exactly what they say. Collectors are allowed to sue you. Some won't because of the expense, but many will, after having gone through an appropriate risk-reward assessment.)

WHERE TO GET HELP

If you're feeling overwhelmed by debts and need either professional help or an emergency solution, consider seeking advice from a nonprofit counseling service. In 1991, over 500,000 people got low-cost or free advice from Consumer Credit Counseling Service offices. CCCS usually charges clients an average of $10 a month but will waive the fee when appropriate. Call 800 388-CCCS to locate the office nearest you.

If you live in a rural area, it might be easier to get help from Cooperative Extension, an educational network combining the resources of the federal government, universities, and nearly 3,150 county offices. Call your local county office or a land-grant university near you for details.

WHAT CREDIT COUNSELORS KNOW

When things get rough financially, women seek help faster (they see doctors faster, too). "When a man comes in to see us," says credit counselor Luther Gatling, "he's generally in deeper trouble."

Women are less likely to fool themselves about their financial situation. "They're more honest," says Tom Hufford of Consumer Credit Counseling of Northeastern Indiana. "They think in terms of net income. Men often think in terms of gross."

Clients sometimes become hysterical when they are told to cut up all their credit cards. "The cards are real symbols of maturity, independence, and freedom—like driver's licenses," says Fred Waddell of Auburn University. "Many men seem to feel emasculated when you take their cards away."

Credit counselors expect as many as half the people who make initial appointments not to show up. "There's a tremendous fear that if you acknowledge the problem, you'll be considered a failure," Gatling says.

25

HOW TO RE-ESTABLISH CREDIT

$ While the promise-you-anything ads in the supermarket tabloids and local newspapers may not help you reacquire the credit status you want, there are some magicians out there who can really help you bounce back from a serious credit problem. Some of them, believe it or not, are lawyers.

For a reasonable fee—usually several hundred dollars—lawyers who frequently deal with local financial institutions can assist you in getting a loan or a mortgage even when you have bad credit. They know exactly who might be willing to take a chance on you. They have a track record with these institutions. The institutions trust them. They realize that, over time, it's not in the lawyer's interest to parade a succession of deadbeats through their doors.

How do you find this kind of wizard? Accountants often know who they are. So do lenders. Your local bar association might also be helpful.

Occasionally, these lawyer-negotiators can find you a loan or a mortgage with standard terms; at other times, you may have to pay a premium for your prior sins. The more steps you've already taken to rehabilitate your credit, the better the deal your hired gun can strike.

STEPS IN THE RIGHT DIRECTION

What are some of those steps? Many have already been discussed in the previous chapter, but some apply specifically to people whose efforts to get credit are often being undermined by their past problems.

• First, if possible, pay off any liens or judgments against you. You eventually want to present a lender with something approximating a clean slate, so work at eliminating your overhanging obligations. It's especially important to take care of a tax lien as soon as you can, because it will remain on your credit record for seven years *after* you've paid it off.

• Next, attack debts you might owe to merchants and credit-card issuers. Before sending them a check for the full balance owed or setting up your own repayment plan (see chapter 24), use your leverage. Politely request that the creditor remove all negative information from your credit file in exchange for your taking care of the entire outstanding balance. Negotiate. Try gentle extortion, mentioning that you would like to remain a lifelong customer, but perhaps you'll have to take your business elsewhere. Although the creditor is under no obligation to agree, try anyway. Maybe you'll compromise, and the creditor will erase some of the black marks, if not all.

• If an issuer has repossessed your credit card, paying what you owe is usually the simplest way of getting it back. The more established your relationship was with the creditor before you hit the credit skids, the more the creditor will want you to remain a customer. Don't be offended, though, if you start with a very low credit limit.

• Consider getting credit from a merchant in unorthodox ways. A local furniture store, for instance, might let you buy on credit if you meet one or all of the following requirements:

1. Make a large down payment (perhaps 30 percent).
2. Pay a high interest rate (quite possibly several points above the national credit-card average of 18 percent).
3. Find someone to co-sign or guarantee the balance.

Whenever you fill out an application for credit, stretch your job title to very near the breaking point. Don't lie, but relentlessly give yourself the benefit of the doubt. Say you're an administrative assistant, for instance, not a secretary. Credit-scoring systems often respond to such distinctions. You might as well play the game.

26

SECURED CREDIT CARDS

$If you have bad credit or no credit—or if you're one of the 2 million people who had a credit card revoked last year—it is still easy to get plastic in America. In fact, it's now probably simpler and cheaper than it has been for two decades.

That's because secured credit cards, which require you to make a minimum deposit before obtaining a card, have become acceptable—perhaps almost respectable.

Ten years ago, the nation's biggest lenders shunned the business. Now, institutions such as Citibank and State Street Bank, eager to make money from the 40 million Americans who cannot get plastic via traditional means, have launched secured-card programs. The added competition has helped lead to better deals for you. Minimum deposits and processing fees should continue to drop for the next few years.

If you have a job, you can probably obtain a secured card—unless you've been convicted of credit-card fraud or are significantly behind on your payments on existing cards. When some secured-card issuers say "Bankruptcy No Problem," they actually mean it. Regardless of your financial circumstances, you may be able to get a secured credit card automatically when you complete a credit-counseling program (such as the one offered by Budget & Credit Counseling Services of New York).

WHAT TO AVOID

Don't try to get a secured card by responding to 900 numbers, ads in newspapers and supermarket tabloids, or TV commercials. Although a few of the offers are reasonable (I'm being very charitable here), most are not. Usually, one of several things is likely to happen:

- The up-front fees will be outrageous.
- You'll get a card that is good only for purchases from a particular catalogue.
- Your up-front fee will buy nothing more than a list of lenders who might or might not give you a card.
- The secured card you receive will be real and quite useful. Unfortunately, it will levy an extraordinarily high annual fee and sock you with a very high interest rate on outstanding balances.
- In exchange for your money, you'll be promised a card—but it will never arrive.

(See chapter 21 for more disgusting details.)

HOW TO DO IT RIGHT

Secured cards can be very expensive, particularly if you neglect to price-shop. The range of terms and fees is extraordinary—far broader than it is for standard cards. This means, unfortunately, that the people who can least afford it have a good chance of being taken to the cleaners if they're not careful. But if you don't expect to be gouged, you probably won't be.

These are the key variables to consider.

Conversion feature. Many secured cards have a conversion option, but not all do. When possible, find a lender who will tell you exactly when you might be able to convert to an unsecured card, assuming you've handled your secured card responsibly.

Deposits. Most issuers require minimum deposits (i.e., collateral) of $500 or $1,000. Some have minimums as high as $5,000, which doesn't make much sense, considering that a person needing a secured card isn't likely to have that much cash. Avoid anyone with a minimum this high. (The lowest minimum now available, $250, is offered by First Interstate Bank of South Dakota, N.A., but the issuer imposes high up-front fees.)

The interest paid on your deposit can vary from nothing to typical market rates. You don't have to settle for nothing. Generally, you'll earn slightly less than prevailing passbook-savings rates. Some institutions, though, will let you place your deposit in a CD or money-market account.

When can you reclaim your collateral? On rare occasions, you can get your deposit back in as little as 6 months, although you'll still technically have a secured credit card and be subject to the appropriate fees and restrictions. Most institutions don't move so fast. If you've made all your payments on time, many will return your security or let you graduate to a standard card in 12 to 24 months. When you shop for terms, be sure to ask each lender about its policies on deposits and upgrades.

(Note: When you do switch to a standard card, don't be annoyed if your deposit is frozen for about 45 days. This is standard procedure; it's not a rip-off. The lender wants to be sure it can cover any unreported charges you've made with the card.)

Credit lines. Typically, your credit limit will be somewhere between 50 percent and 100 percent of the amount you deposit. If you don't want to settle for the 50 percent limit, make an extra call or two, and you're likely to find an issuer that can beat it. If you ask, some lenders will raise your credit limit after 6 or 12 months.

Finance charges. Interest rates on outstanding balances range from 8 percent to 24 percent, with stops everywhere in between. The more you're willing or able to deposit, the lower the rate will be, and vice versa. Lenders with the lowest minimum deposits often charge some of the highest interest rates, so consider whether the trade-off makes sense for you. If your credit limit is only $400, you can charge the limit and pay 5 extra percentage points in interest, and the annual cost difference will only be $20. If $400 is all you can round up, the extra cost may be worth it to you. (Naturally, you can avoid the additional charges by paying your balance in full.)

Application fees, processing fees, annual fees, etc. The secured-card business is fee-crazy, so be careful. One card, marketed by United National and issued by First Interstate Bank of South Dakota, charges a $25 "Account Set-Up Fee" and a $35 "Program Fee" in addition to a $35 annual fee. For the first year alone, that's $95 in fees, which is ridiculous. (If you get this awful card, you won't earn any interest on your deposit, either.)

With fewer fees, the Bank of Hoven, which operates one of the biggest secured-card programs, extracts even more money from first-year cardholders. The bank has a $35 annual fee and a $65 application fee (which at least is refundable if you're turned down). That's $100 up front for the privilege of paying 21 percent interest on charges and 24 percent on cash advances. The card's low minimum deposit of $380 may entice many who could actually cut a much better deal elsewhere.

Some issuers' first-year fees can top $200. What's truly appalling about such price-gouging is that it's not as if the fees are going to be amortized over a long period of time, like points on a mortgage. Basically, everyone wants to get rid of their secured cards as quickly as possible and move on to the real thing. If you're a good customer, you may have the card for only one year, anyway. There's no reason for you to shell out $100 or $200 for what amounts to a single year's annual fee.

THE BEST DEALS

Here are some of the best secured-card offers, according to Bankcard Holders of America and RAM Research. (Note: It's likely that some of the terms cited below may have changed.)

American Pacific Bank, P.O. Box 19360, Portland, OR 97280-0360; 800 879-8745. Visa card is available nationally except in Vermont and Maine. $400 minimum deposit with a 100-percent credit line; deposit earns 5 percent; 18.9-percent variable finance charge; $30 annual fee; 30-day grace period.

Bank One, P.O. Box 450, Lafayette, IN 47902; 800 395-2555. $500 minimum deposit with a 80- to 100-percent credit line: deposit earns 3 percent; 19.8-percent finance charge; $35 annual fee; 25-day grace period.

Central National Bank of Mattoon, Secured Credit Card Program, Broadway and Charleston at 14th, Mattoon, IL 61938; 800 876-9119. $500 minimum for Illinois residents, $1,000 for everyone else; credit line up to 100 percent; savings account earns 5 percent, CD earns market rates; 8-percent finance charge if secured by savings, 12.5 percent if secured by CD; no annual fee; 25-day grace period.

Citibank, Citicorp Credit Services, P.O. Box 7001, Hagerstown, MD

21742; 800 743-1332. $300 minimum deposit with a 100-percent credit line; deposit earns 4.5 percent; 19.8-percent finance charge; $20 annual fee; 25-day grace period.

Community Bank of Parker, Spirit Visa Card Program, 19590 East Main Street, Parker, CO 80134; 800 779-8472 or 303 840-9945. $500 minimum deposit, which earns no interest, and a 100-percent credit line; 14.9-percent finance charge; $49.95 annual fee first year, $20 thereafter.

Dreyfus Thrift and Commerce Phase One MasterCard, P.O. Box 6003, Garden City, NY 11530-9841; 800 727-3348. $500 minimum deposit earns 3 percent; 100-percent credit line; 19.8-percent finance charge; $25 annual fee; 25-day grace period.

Signet Bank, P.O. Box 85547, Richmond, VA 23285-5547; 800 333-7116. $300 minimum deposit earns 5 percent; 100-percent credit line; 19.8-percent finance charge; $20 annual fee; 25-day grace period.

Pioneer Federal Savings Bank, Secured Visa Program, P.O. Box M, Lynwood, WA 98046; 206 771-2525. $1,000 minimum earning market rates; credit line 50 percent (70 percent over $2,000); 12-percent variable rate finance charge; no annual fee; 25-day grace period. (Only available to people from Washington.)

Texas Bank, N.A., 1845 Precinct Line Road, Hurst, TX 76054; 800 451-0273. $368 minimum deposit earning 4 percent (5 percent over $1,000); 90-percent credit line; 21-percent finance charge; $35 annual fee; $35 setup fee; 25- to 31-day grace period.

For a more complete and up-to-date list of the best secured-card offers, send $4 to Bankcard Holders of America or $10 to RAM Research (see Appendix A). You can get a much less comprehensive list for free by calling the consumer affairs office in your city or state, or by contacting the nearest Consumer Credit Counseling Service branch.

Some lenders don't like to deal with anyone from out-of-state, whereas others become picky if you have certain financial problems. So when you call, be sure to tell them where you live and give a quick description of your financial situation. You never want to apply for a credit product that you have no chance of getting.

WHAT YOU SHOULDN'T DO

Try not to get a secured card from an issuer that does not report to credit bureaus. Ask if the lender reports. All issuers listed above do report regularly. (If, however, you've done a lot of research and can't find an issuer that will report your account activity and whose fees you can afford, don't despair. Having a secured card can help you get a card from a local retailer. From there, you can follow the "trading-up" strategy described in chapter 7.)

Don't go to a credit-repair firm or credit clinic to get a secured card. Their markups on the cards are often astronomical.

If you're eager to graduate quickly from a secured to an unsecured card—and you should be—don't ever make a late payment. This will stall the conversion process. And it will cost you money in penalties, as well.

CONCLUSION

The rise of secured cards will continue to be a boon to the tens of millions of consumers who, for whatever reasons, have credit histories that most lenders find unacceptable. The trend is so clear, in fact, that secured-card holders who *don't* try to graduate to unsecured cards will find that after two years or so, they may begin to receive unsolicited mail offers for unsecured plastic.

If these lenders don't look down on holders of secured cards, there's no reason you should hesitate to become one.

AUTHOR'S NOTE

In the interest of full disclosure, I thought you might like to know that I have worked for the following companies in the financial-services industry, either directly or indirectly, and have been compensated accordingly: Citicorp, Continental Corporation, Fidelity Investments, John Hancock, Merrill Lynch, and J. P. Morgan.

I have tried not to allow prior associations to color my opinions or my reporting. If you feel I've failed in my attempt to be objective, please let me know.

Actually, I hope my experience with financial companies will be beneficial to you. My goal throughout the book has been to provide information—every possible kind of information, no matter how strange or unlikely the source—to help you tackle existing debt problems and save money every time you borrow.

When you really take control of your debt, the rewards aren't just financial. You get an extraordinary emotional payoff as well. You worry less and enjoy life more—a pretty nice combination, as far as I'm concerned. So if *Downsize Your Debt* saves you money, I'll be satisfied. And if it makes you feel better, then I couldn't be happier.

FURTHER
INFORMATION

$

APPENDIXES

APPENDIX A: RESOURCES

Bankcard Holders of America
560 Herndon Parkway
Herndon, VA 22070
800 327-7300; 703 481-1110

Consumer Credit Counseling Service
(call 800 388-CCCS for the office nearest you)

Debtors Anonymous
General Service Office
P.O. Box 20322
New York, NY 10025-9992
212 642-8220

Federal Trade Commission
Washington, D.C. 20580
202 326-2222

RAM Research
P.O. Box 1700
Frederick, MD 21702
800 344-7714

U.S. Public Interest Research Group
215 Pennsylvania Avenue, S.E.
Washington, D.C. 20003
202 546-9707

Local offices of the Better Business Bureau are listed in the White Pages.

Your state attorney general's number is in the State Government Offices section of the White Pages, sometimes under "Law Department."

APPENDIX B: MONTHLY PAYMENTS
AND TOTAL FINANCE CHARGES FOR A $1,000 LOAN

MONTHLY PAYMENTS AND TOTAL FINANCE CHARGES
$1,000 LOAN

INTEREST RATES

Years to Maturity	2.0%	2.5	3.0	3.5	4.0	4.5	5.0	5.5	6.0	6.5	7.0	7.5	8.0%
1	$84.24	84.47	84.69	84.92	85.15	85.38	85.61	85.84	86.07	86.30	86.53	86.76	$86.99
	$10.87	13.59	16.32	19.06	21.80	24.54	27.29	30.04	32.80	35.56	38.32	41.09	$43.86
2	42.54	42.76	42.98	43.20	43.42	43.65	43.87	44.10	44.32	44.55	44.77	45.00	45.23
	20.97	26.25	31.55	36.87	42.20	47.55	52.91	58.30	63.69	69.11	74.54	79.99	85.45
3	28.64	28.86	29.08	29.30	29.52	29.75	29.97	30.20	30.42	30.65	30.88	31.11	31.34
	31.13	39.01	46.92	54.87	62.86	70.89	78.95	87.05	95.19	103.36	111.58	119.82	128.11
4	21.70	21.91	22.13	22.36	22.58	22.80	23.03	23.26	23.49	23.71	23.95	24.18	24.41
	41.37	51.87	62.45	73.09	83.79	94.57	105.41	116.31	127.28	138.32	149.42	160.59	171.82
5	17.53	17.75	17.97	18.19	18.42	18.64	18.87	19.10	19.33	19.57	19.80	20.04	20.28
	51.67	64.84	78.12	91.50	104.99	118.58	132.27	146.07	159.97	173.97	188.07	202.28	216.58
6	14.75	14.97	15.19	15.42	15.65	15.87	16.10	16.34	16.57	16.81	17.05	17.29	17.53
	62.03	77.91	93.94	110.12	126.45	142.93	159.56	176.33	193.25	210.31	227.53	244.89	262.39
8	11.28	11.50	11.73	11.96	12.19	12.42	12.66	12.90	13.14	13.39	13.63	13.88	14.14
	82.96	104.37	126.04	147.97	170.17	192.63	215.35	238.33	261.58	285.08	308.84	332.85	357.12
10	9.20	9.43	9.66	9.89	10.12	10.36	10.61	10.85	11.10	11.35	11.61	11.87	12.13
	104.16	131.24	158.73	186.63	214.94	243.66	272.79	302.32	332.25	362.58	393.30	424.42	455.93
12	7.82	8.05	8.28	8.51	8.76	9.00	9.25	9.50	9.76	10.02	10.28	10.55	10.82
	125.62	158.52	192.01	226.09	260.76	296.01	331.84	368.25	405.22	442.77	480.87	519.53	558.73
15	6.44	6.67	6.91	7.15	7.40	7.65	7.91	8.17	8.44	8.71	8.99	9.27	9.56
	158.32	200.22	243.05	286.79	331.44	376.99	423.43	470.75	518.94	567.99	617.89	668.62	720.17

How to use the table: If you borrowed $5,000 at 10 percent for 5 years, what would your monthly payment and total finance charges be? Look under interest rates for the figure 10 percent and then to the left for the term of 5 years. They intersect at the numbers $21.25 and $274.82, which are the monthly payments and total finance charges for a $1,000 loan. Multiply each by 5 to get your answers. The monthly payment would be $106.25; the total interest cost would be approximately $1,374.10.

INTEREST RATES

	2.0%	2.5	3.0	3.5	4.0	4.5	5.0	5.5	6.0	6.5	7.0	7.5	8.0%
20	5.06	5.30	5.55	5.80	6.06	6.33	6.60	6.88	7.16	7.46	7.75	8.06	8.36
	214.12	271.77	331.03	391.90	454.35	518.36	583.89	650.93	719.43	789.38	860.72	933.42	1,007
25	4.24	4.49	4.74	5.01	5.28	5.56	5.85	6.14	6.44	6.75	7.07	7.39	7.72
	271.56	345.85	422.63	501.87	583.51	667.50	753.77	842.26	932.90	1,026	1,120	1,217	1,315
30	$3.70	3.95	4.22	4.49	4.77	5.07	5.37	5.68	6.00	6.32	6.65	6.99	$7.34
	$330.63	422.44	517.77	616.56	718.70	824.07	932.56	1,044	1,158	1,275	1,395	1,517	$1,642

INTEREST RATES

	8.5%	9.0	9.5	10.0	10.5	11.0	11.5	12.0	12.5	13.0	13.5	14.0	14.5%
1	$87.22	87.45	87.68	87.92	88.15	88.38	88.62	88.85	89.08	89.32	89.55	89.79	$90.02
	$46.64	49.42	52.20	54.99	57.78	60.58	63.38	66.19	68.99	71.81	74.62	77.45	$80.27
2	45.46	45.68	45.91	46.14	46.38	46.61	46.84	47.07	47.31	47.54	47.78	48.01	48.25
	90.94	96.43	101.95	107.48	113.02	118.59	124.17	129.76	135.38	141.00	146.65	152.31	157.99
3	31.57	31.80	32.03	32.27	32.50	32.74	32.98	33.21	33.45	33.69	33.94	34.18	34.42
	136.43	144.79	153.19	161.62	170.09	178.59	187.14	195.72	204.33	212.98	221.67	230.39	239.16
4	24.65	24.89	25.12	25.36	25.60	25.85	26.09	26.33	26.58	26.83	27.08	27.33	27.58
	183.12	194.48	205.91	217.40	228.96	240.59	252.27	264.02	275.84	287.72	299.66	311.67	323.74
5	20.52	20.76	21.00	21.25	21.49	21.74	21.99	22.24	22.50	22.75	23.01	23.27	23.53
	230.99	245.50	260.11	274.82	289.63	304.55	319.56	334.67	349.88	365.18	380.59	396.10	411.70
6	17.78	18.03	18.27	18.53	18.78	19.03	19.29	19.55	19.81	20.07	20.34	20.61	20.87
	280.04	297.84	315.78	333.86	352.09	370.45	388.96	407.61	426.40	445.34	464.41	483.61	502.96
8	14.39	14.65	14.91	15.17	15.44	15.71	15.98	16.25	16.53	16.81	17.09	17.37	17.66
	381.64	406.42	431.45	456.72	482.24	508.01	534.02	560.27	586.77	613.50	640.46	667.66	695.10
10	12.40	12.67	12.94	13.22	13.49	13.78	14.06	14.35	14.64	14.93	15.23	15.53	15.83
	487.83	520.11	552.77	585.81	619.22	653.00	687.15	721.65	756.51	791.73	827.29	863.20	899.44
12	11.10	11.38	11.66	11.95	12.24	12.54	12.83	13.13	13.44	13.75	14.06	14.37	14.69
	598.48	638.76	679.58	720.91	762.76	805.12	847.98	891.32	935.15	979.46	1,024	1,069	1,115
15	9.85	10.14	10.44	10.75	11.05	11.37	11.68	12.00	12.33	12.65	12.98	13.32	13.66
	772.53	825.68	879.60	934.29	989.72	1,046	1,103	1,160	1,219	1,277	1,337	1,397	1,458
20	8.68	9.00	9.32	9.65	9.98	10.32	10.66	11.01	11.36	11.72	12.07	12.44	12.80
	1,083	1,159	1,237	1,316	1,396	1,477	1,559	1,643	1,727	1,812	1,898	1,984	2,072
25	8.05	8.39	8.74	9.09	9.44	9.80	10.16	10.53	10.90	11.28	11.66	12.04	12.42
	1,416	1,518	1,621	1,726	1,833	1,940	2,049	2,160	2,271	2,384	2,497	2,611	2,726
30	$7.69	8.05	8.41	8.78	9.15	9.52	9.90	10.29	10.67	11.06	11.45	11.85	$12.25
	$1,768	1,897	2,027	2,159	2,293	2,428	2,565	2,703	2,842	2,982	3,123	3,266	$3,408

Years to Maturity

INTEREST RATES

	15.0%	15.5	16.0	16.5	17.0	17.5	18.0	18.5	19.0	19.5	20.0	20.5	21.0%
1	$90.26	90.49	90.73	90.97	91.20	91.44	91.68	91.92	92.16	92.40	92.63	92.87	$93.11
	$83.10	85.93	88.77	91.61	94.46	97.31	100.16	103.02	105.88	108.74	111.61	114.49	$117.3
2	48.49	48.72	48.96	49.20	49.44	49.68	49.92	50.17	50.41	50.65	50.90	51.14	51.39
	163.68	169.39	175.11	180.86	186.61	192.39	198.18	203.98	209.81	215.65	221.50	227.37	233.26
3	34.67	34.91	35.16	35.40	35.65	35.90	36.15	36.40	36.66	36.91	37.16	37.42	37.68
	247.95	256.78	265.65	274.56	283.50	292.47	301.49	310.53	319.62	328.74	337.89	347.08	356.30
4	27.83	28.08	28.34	28.60	28.86	29.11	29.37	29.64	29.90	30.16	30.43	30.70	30.97
	335.88	348.07	360.33	372.66	385.04	397.49	410.00	422.57	435.21	447.90	460.66	473.47	486.35
5	23.79	24.05	24.32	24.58	24.85	25.12	25.39	25.67	25.94	26.22	26.49	26.77	27.05
	427.40	443.19	459.08	475.07	491.15	507.33	523.61	539.97	556.43	572.99	589.63	606.37	623.20
6	21.15	21.42	21.69	21.97	22.25	22.53	22.81	23.09	23.38	23.66	23.95	24.24	24.54
	522.44	542.06	561.81	581.70	601.72	621.88	642.16	662.58	683.12	703.80	724.60	745.53	766.59
8	17.95	18.24	18.53	18.82	19.12	19.42	19.72	20.03	20.33	20.64	20.95	21.27	21.58
	722.76	750.65	778.76	807.10	835.66	864.44	893.43	922.63	952.05	981.68	1,012	1,042	1,072
10	16.13	16.44	16.75	17.06	17.38	17.70	18.02	18.34	18.67	19.00	19.33	19.66	19.99
	936.02	972.93	1,010	1,048	1,086	1,124	1,162	1,201	1,240	1,279	1,319	1,359	1,399
12	15.01	15.33	15.66	15.99	16.32	16.65	16.99	17.33	17.67	18.02	18.37	18.72	19.07
	1,161	1,208	1,255	1,302	1,350	1,398	1,447	1,496	1,545	1,595	1,645	1,695	1,746
15	14.00	14.34	14.69	15.04	15.39	15.75	16.10	16.47	16.83	17.19	17.56	17.93	18.31
	1,519	1,581	1,644	1,707	1,770	1,834	1,899	1,964	2,029	2,095	2,161	2,228	2,295
20	13.17	13.54	13.91	14.29	14.67	15.05	15.43	15.82	16.21	16.60	16.99	17.38	17.78
	2,160	2,249	2,339	2,429	2,520	2,612	2,704	2,797	2,890	2,983	3,077	3,172	3,266
25	12.81	13.20	13.59	13.98	14.38	14.78	15.17	15.57	15.98	16.38	16.78	17.19	17.60
	2,842	2,959	3,077	3,195	3,313	3,433	3,552	3,672	3,793	3,914	4,035	4,157	4,279
30	$12.64	13.05	13.45	13.85	14.26	14.66	15.07	15.48	15.89	16.30	16.71	17.12	$17.53
	$3,552	3,696	3,841	3,987	4,132	4,279	4,426	4,573	4,720	4,868	5,016	5,164	$5,312

NOTE: Amounts greater than $999.99 are rounded off to the whole dollar.

APPENDIX C: CALCULATING THE TRUE INTEREST RATE

Bar bet stuff: What's the real annual cost of a 10-percent loan? That is, what's the annual effective rate when the nominal interest rate is 10 percent? It's 10.47 percent—and I'll show you how to get there.

First, we're assuming the monthly compounding of interest, which is the standard way to calculate mortgage payments. Then, divide the nominal interest rate, which is .1 (10 percent) by the number of monthly payments. (If compounding were done daily, you'd divide by 360.)

.1 divided by 12 = .0083333333333.

Then add 1, which gives 1.00833333333333.

Raise that figure to the twelfth power (if compounding occurred daily, you'd raise it to the 360th power, which is why there are computers). The result is 1.1047.

Then subtract 1 and you have .1047—the annual effective interest rate.

You can try this at parties when you think it's time for everyone to go home. And if you want to depress people even more, tell them the effective interest rate for a credit card with a 19.8 percent APR is 21.69 percent.

(Note: for most institutions, the banking year has 360 days.)

GLOSSARY

Adjustable-rate loan (variable-rate loan). The interest rate fluctuates, adjusting periodically to the moves of a key rate, such as the prime rate or one-year Treasury bills.

APR (annual percentage rate). The actual rate consumers pay on a loan, expressed as simple interest. Many, but not necessarily all, up-front fees are factored into APR. The APR can sometimes be misleading, however, because it is based on the often-false assumption that the loan will be held to maturity.

ARM (adjustable-rate mortgage). See above.

Basis point. One basis point equals .01 percent. If the average mortgage rate rises 10 basis points, that would translate into a jump from 8 percent to 8.1 percent.

Biweekly mortgage. Another form of prepayment. Fine in theory, though often a scam in practice. If you make mortgage payments every two weeks—or the equivalent of 13 payments a year, rather than 12—you can reduce the term of a 30-year mortgage by 8 to 12 years. Middlemen who set up such programs at great expense don't always forward payments as promised.

Collateral. Assets or property (car, home, boat, CD) offered as security to encourage a lender to make a loan.

Credit insurance. Insurance that pays off all or part of a loan if the borrower dies or becomes disabled or unemployed.

Credit scoring. A point system lenders use to assess your creditworthiness. Almost invariably computerized these days.

Loan-to-value ratio (LTV). The ratio of the amount borrowed to the value of the property. If a home costs $100,000 and you put down $20,000, the LTV is 80 percent. More liberal lenders permit higher LTVs.

Points. An up-front fee charged by a lender which, in effect, lowers the nominal interest rate on the loan. A point equals 1 percent of the total loan amount.

Prime rate. The interest rate banks charge their most creditworthy customers.

Prime plus two. A rate of 2 percentage points, or 200 basis points, over the prime rate. As we went to press, the prime rate was 6 percent, so prime plus 2 would equal 8 percent.

Principal. The amount owed, not counting interest.

Private mortgage insurance (PMI). The insurance homebuyers must maintain until their equity in the property reaches at least 20 percent.

Secured loan. A loan guaranteed by collateral.

Teaser rate. Something to beware of. Common with adjustable-rate mortgages and some home-equity loans, this is a rate that tells you things seem better than they really are. The teaser is almost guaranteed to rise whenever its term expires—and that could be after as little as one month.

Unsecured loan. A loan not guaranteed by the pledge of any collateral.

INDEX

FOR THE BEST IN PAPERBACKS, LOOK FOR THE

In every corner of the world, on every subject under the sun, Penguin represents quality and variety—the very best in publishing today.

For complete information about books available from Penguin—including Pelicans, Puffins, Peregrines, and Penguin Classics—and how to order them, write to us at the appropriate address below. Please note that for copyright reasons the selection of books varies from country to country.

In the United Kingdom: For a complete list of books available from Penguin in the U.K., please write to *Dept E.P., Penguin Books Ltd, Harmondsworth, Middlesex, UB7 0DA.*

In the United States: For a complete list of books available from Penguin in the U.S., please write to *Dept BA, Penguin*, Box 120, Bergenfield, New Jersey 07621-0120.

In Canada: For a complete list of books available from Penguin in Canada, please write to *Penguin Books Canada Ltd, 10 Alcorn Avenue, Suite 300, Toronto, Ontario, Canada M4V 3B2.*

In Australia: For a complete list of books available from Penguin in Australia, please write to the *Marketing Department, Penguin Books Ltd, P.O. Box 257, Ringwood, Victoria 3134.*

In New Zealand: For a complete list of books available from Penguin in New Zealand, please write to the *Marketing Department, Penguin Books (NZ) Ltd, Private Bag, Takapuna, Auckland 9.*

In India: For a complete list of books available from Penguin, please write to *Penguin Overseas Ltd, 706 Eros Apartments, 56 Nehru Place, New Delhi, 110019.*

In Holland: For a complete list of books available from Penguin in Holland, please write to *Penguin Books Nederland B.V., Postbus 195, NL-1380AD Weesp, Netherlands.*

In Germany: For a complete list of books available from Penguin, please write to *Penguin Books Ltd, Friedrichstrasse 10-12, D-6000 Frankfurt Main 1, Federal Republic of Germany.*

In Spain: For a complete list of books available from Penguin in Spain, please write to *Longman, Penguin España, Calle San Nicolas 15, E-28013 Madrid, Spain.*

In Japan: For a complete list of books available from Penguin in Japan, please write to *Longman Penguin Japan Co Ltd, Yamaguchi Building, 2-12-9 Kanda Jimbocho, Chiyoda-Ku, Tokyo 101, Japan.*